Praise for *Gator C*

A *New York Times* Edit

Best Nonfiction of 202

Best Reviewed Nonfiction Books of No

Best Nonfiction of 2023, Amazon

Best Books of 2023, *Christian Science Monitor*

Best Books of 2023, *Tampa Bay Times*

Must-Read Nonfiction of 2023, Chicago Public Library

Best Florida Books of 2023, *Creative Loafing Tampa Bay*

"Renner's debut is self-assured and full of poetry, and it will change Florida in the eyes of everyone who reads it." —NPR

"This nail-biter account . . . has the intensity of the best true crime. . . . A high-def tale that ensnares you from the start."

—*People* (Book of the Week)

"Renner gives the remarkable nature of South Florida, as well as the often hardscrabble folk whose families have lived there for generations, the love and respect they deserve. . . . Every species, and every person who fights for its continued existence, deserves a book like this—a book that explores the complexity of the nexus between humans and animals and the exploitation of the wild and considers the ambiguities of our fractured relationship to nature, morality, and history."

—*The New York Times*

"Captivating . . . What lifts Renner's work out of the true-crime muck is her devotion to presenting the natural world in all its glory—and humanity in all its frequent opposite of that. She never lets the thrill of the sting take away from the poverty-driven reality that poaching is usually a crime of sustenance. . . . [An] exceptional work."

—*The Washington Post*

"*Gator Country* is a book for anyone looking for the juicy mess of reality in pages so suspenseful they read like fiction. In the end, Renner writes about the blurry morality of the law, friendships, betrayal, loyalty, and family, all while expertly building toward the crescendo of the true villain's reveal, all of which gives way to an incredible ride and a riveting read." —*The Florida Review*

"Renner weaves together the often thrilling true-crime story of the undercover operation with her own investigation of Peg Brown. *Gator Country* is also, in parts, a memoir and a loving natural history of the irreplaceable Everglades." —*Tampa Bay Times*

"Renner is a natural storyteller, and she does service to wild Florida, igniting an answering passion in the reader." —*Orlando Weekly*

"I dare you to stop reading!" —*The Coastal Star*

"The fast-paced narrative is imbued with the atmosphere of tension that shapes any good mystery story. . . . [Renner] sketches a vivid portrait of the scraggly splendor of the land and its tenacious hold on life in a world that often fails to see its beauty." —*BookPage* (starred review)

"Come for the you'll-never-believe facts and an exploration of man vs. myth. Stay for the history and dive into communities." —*Book Riot*

"Part true-crime story, part memoir, part hymn to 'nature's savage beauty,' *Gator Country* makes for a rewarding reading experience."

—*Christian Science Monitor*

"Readers of this book are in for an adventure. It reads like a true-crime caper. . . . Audiences of all types will appreciate this easy-to-read narrative as well as Renner's knowledge of the area, her academic ability, her candor, and her insights into human nature."

—Steve Dixon, *Library Journal*

"Fascinating . . . Renner teases out the moral ambiguities with a grace and rigor reminiscent of Susan Orlean's *The Orchid Thief*. Beautifully evoking the 'sawgrass plains and wild strands of jungle' of its author's home state, this tale of power, politics, and tradition is a triumph."

—*Publishers Weekly* (starred review)

"Combining her skills for investigative reporting, nature writing, and personal anecdotes, Renner explores local folklore and legends, shares her personal experiences and observations. . . . Renner's passion for her home state, compassion for those less fortunate, and gift of storytelling make this book difficult to put down. Enlightening and full of suspense."

—*Kirkus Reviews* (starred review)

"This smart, nimble page-turner will leave you more thoughtful about why we mythicize alligators, eat their flesh, wear their hide, and protect their population. It will leave you reexamining the complicated nature of both the species and those who illegally hunt it. Most of all, it will leave you wanting more from Rebecca Renner."

—Jack E. Davis, Pulitzer Prize–winning author of *The Gulf* and *The Bald Eagle*

"Renner has a dandy story and a great, mythic figure to hang it on: a poaching legend named Peg Brown, who hunted illegally in the late twentieth century but whose poaching may have helped the environment. Renner also helps us understand that alligators are animals that can inspire fear but ultimately deserve our thanks and care."

—Chris Hewitt, *Star Tribune*

"In this fascinating blend of true crime and science reporting, Rebecca Renner's *Gator Country* tracks Jeff Babauta, an unassuming undercover conservation agent who risks it all to infiltrate an alligator poaching operation in the treacherous Florida wetlands. Told with fierce loyalty to nature and compassion for humans, Renner's *Gator Country* delivers all the suspense and subterfuge of a le Carré novel. It'll even make you love alligators."

—Erika Krouse, award-winning author of *Tell Me Everything*

"*Gator Country* brims with energy, confidence, and all the hallmarks of a true-life thriller, but Rebecca Renner's unique talent is her keen skill at bringing her characters to life and giving their motivations full color and context. The result is poignant and wonderful. *Gator Country* isn't just a thrill for thrill's sake, but a generous, thoughtful exploration of what it means for all of us to live in a habitat of predators. Rebecca Renner is a true talent."

—Adam Chandler, author of *Drive-Thru Dreams*

"A gorgeously rendered ode to the wild characters—both human and animal—of Renner's native Florida, *Gator Country* takes a deep dive into the fascinatingly blurry line that can exist between poachers and conservationists operating in our own backyards."

—Rachel Nuwer, author of *Poached*

"In *Gator Country*, Rebecca Renner takes us deep into the Florida swamps, where an undercover agent chases a ring of alligator poachers. From dimly lit backcountry bars where outlaws spin wild yarns to the reptile farm where the agent feeds fish guts to alligators, Renner shows us a hidden Florida that's changing quickly."

—Murray Carpenter, author of *Caffeinated*

"This astonishing book moves as fast as a hungry gator slicing through the water! Rebecca Renner spins an incredible only-in-Florida true-crime tale that's a must-read for anyone who cares about protecting our environment."

—Craig Pittman, author of *Oh, Florida!*

GATOR COUNTRY

DECEPTION, DANGER, AND ALLIGATORS IN THE EVERGLADES

REBECCA RENNER

FLATIRON
BOOKS
NEW YORK

The names and identifying details of some persons and entities described in this book have been changed.

www.flatironbooks.com

All photographs courtesy of the author unless otherwise noted

Map courtesy of Rhys Davies

Designed by Susan Walsh

The Library of Congress has cataloged the hardcover edition as follows:

Names: Renner, Rebecca, author.
Title: Gator country : deception, danger, and alligators in the Everglades / Rebecca Renner.
Description: First edition. | New York : Flatiron Books, 2023.
Identifiers: LCCN 2023018604 | ISBN 9781250842572 (hardcover) | ISBN 9781250842589 (ebook)
Subjects: LCSH: Poaching—Florida—Everglades. | Alligators—Effect of poaching on—Florida—Everglades. | Undercover wildlife agents—Florida—Everglades.
Classification: LCC HV6412.U6 R46 2023 | DDC 364.16/285979840975939—dc23/eng/20230817
LC record available at https://lccn.loc.gov/2023018604

ISBN 978-1-250-84259-6 (trade paperback)

Our books may be purchased in bulk for promotional, educational, or business use. Please contact your local bookseller or the Macmillan Corporate and Premium Sales Department at 1-800-221-7945, extension 5442, or by email at MacmillanSpecialMarkets@macmillan.com.

First Flatiron Books Paperback Edition: 2024

10 9 8 7 6 5 4 3 2 1

For my dad,
who taught me how to tell a story.
Ken Renner
(1958–2014)

CONTENTS

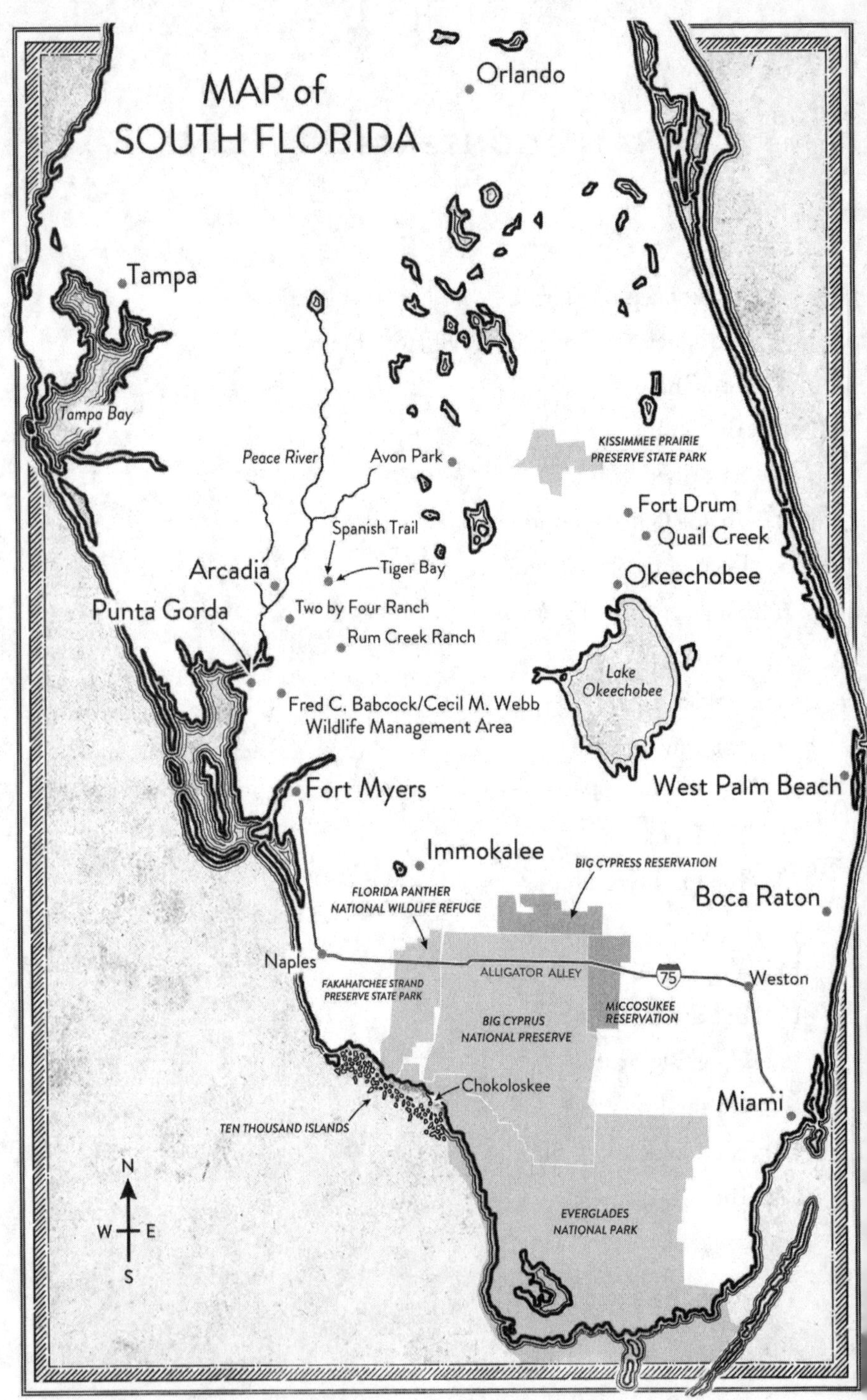
MAP of
SOUTH FLORIDA
Orlando
Tampa
Tampa Bay
Peace River
Avon Park
KISSIMMEE PRAIRIE
PRESERVE STATE PARK
Fort Drum
Quail Creek
Spanish Trail
Tiger Bay
Arcadia
Okeechobee
Punta Gorda
Two by Four Ranch
Rum Creek Ranch
Lake
Okeechobee
Fred C. Babcock/Cecil M. Webb
Wildlife Management Area
Fort Myers
West Palm Beach
Immokalee
BIG CYPRESS RESERVATION
FLORIDA PANTHER
NATIONAL WILDLIFE REFUGE
Boca Raton
Naples
ALLIGATOR ALLEY
75
Weston
FAKAHATCHEE STRAND
PRESERVE STATE PARK
MICCOSUKEE
RESERVATION
BIG CYPRUS
NATIONAL PRESERVE
Chokoloskee
Miami
TEN THOUSAND ISLANDS
N
W
E
S
EVERGLADES
NATIONAL PARK

INTRODUCTION

OPERATION ALLIGATOR THIEF

The first time I saw an alligator up close in the wild, I was seven years old. Before I ventured into the swamp by our house, my dad made sure I was prepared.

"The sun rises in the . . . ?" he asked.

"East," I said.

"And it sets in the . . . ?"

"West," I answered.

His call-and-response questioning ran me through the features of the wild country right outside our back door. That area of Central Florida, from the Mosquito Lagoon south by Cape Canaveral, north to the mouth of the St. Johns River in Jacksonville, and west out to Orlando, is one of the most biodiverse places in the country. It's home to temperate forests, savannas, grasslands, marshes and swamps, pineland scrub and hardwood hammocks, estuaries, rivers, beaches, and springs. My home is a place where you're just as likely to see cacti as two-hundred-year-old water oaks dripping with moss, where you're just as likely to get stuck behind a tractor on the back roads as a fanboat towed on a trailer.

"And when it starts getting dark, you . . . ?"

"Come home," I said.

"Atta girl," he said. "Be back in time for dinner."

I set out into the swamp with an empty jam jar, looking to catch something. The twin pair of sinkhole ponds at the edge of the woods teemed with tadpoles. I plunged my jar into the muddy water up to my elbow and brought it up to the light to see two or three tadpoles thrashing among the swirls of duckweed. A pitiful catch. Maybe, I thought, I would do better in the creek.

To get there, I had to hike down through the scrub into a gully where I would find the deepest part of the swamp.

At seven, I was beginning to understand the richness of my world.

I had petted baby alligators on display, their jaws taped shut, at the entrance of the new Walmart that had been built on swampland. I had swum with manatees and dolphins, watched in the tide as skates darted away from my feet in a plume of sand. Still, I hadn't quite grasped the majesty and the danger of the natural world that surrounded me. Down at Spruce Creek, I crossed a muddy stream on a fallen palm log. A foot below me, the water was black, dyed like tea by oak leaves. I was set on reaching a sandy peninsula, half hidden by saw palms, that jutted out into the creek proper. Stepping down at the end of the log, I slipped. When I tried to catch my balance, my other foot landed in the water, and I sank up to my thigh. Was this that ubiquitous childhood danger, quicksand? Would I sink deeper if I struggled?

Then a reflection, like a ray of light on the polished gems I collected, drew my eye to the peninsula. Now in full view, I saw that the small stretch of sandy beach was already occupied by a half-ton alligator. The creature had a hide like an old tire and eyes like fossilized amber. He blinked lazily, sunning himself, and I imagined him sighing at the interruption I had brought. I scrambled up onto the log, mud clinging to my legs. Scared, but also curious and eager for a better look, I scampered up the bank, leaving the jam jar, and when I peered down, I could see a sliver of the gator's glossy snout in the sunlight. Of course, he hadn't moved. He was far less interested in me than I was in him. You don't live to be that big by making unnecessary trouble with humans, even small, loud ones.

This encounter would prove to be the beginning of a lifelong fascination with reptiles, especially alligators. At every chance I got, I would troll the creek for them, hoping to find the same magnificent gator that first lit up my imagination. But gators didn't only pop up in the backyard ponds of my childhood. They took up residence everywhere in popular culture. In cartoons such as *All Dogs Go to Heaven*, fat and zany alligators provided comic relief. Although alligators can be dangerous, there is something in the way they move about the world, and especially in the way we react to them, that is inclined toward the slapstick. Explorers once thought of them as living dragons. They represented the wild, untamable swamps of the so-called New World. Now these extraordinary beasts have been reduced to toothy jesters. Alligators' association with the more recent Florida Man meme takes their inherent humor over the top. It doesn't help that all young Floridians are taught to run in zigzags to escape gators, leading to many a humorous scene where a panicked swamp visitor runs wildly from a stationary and unamused reptile.

But for me, and for many others who grew up in the swampy Deep South, gators are just a part of life, no more extraordinary than a raccoon pilfering seed from your bird feeder. Yet they have appeared in my life when I least expect them. My friend quit the high school swim team to take an after-school job as an alligator wrestler. On visiting my family in New Orleans, Louisiana, I glimpsed alligator heads and claws used as talismans. Sometimes I'll stop at a backwoods outfitter for some boiled peanuts only to be greeted by a head-high specimen, stuffed by a taxidermist to stand like a man and hold a tray of bagged pork rinds. I can't help but think, *You must be so embarrassed, friend.* I wonder what it's like to be such a regal predator, reduced in the afterlife to a junk-food display.

To my northern acquaintances, my relationship to alligators is often unusual. I grew up eating gator meat, a fact that elicits shock and disgust. But gator is fantastic breaded in cornmeal and immersed in peanut oil to fry. (And it's much more sustainable than chicken, even with the alligator industry's minimal regulations.) My family has been eating gator since before much of the South was part of the United States. On the Florida side, I come from a long line of Crackers, the local name for Florida cattlemen, and Floridanos, descendants of the first Spanish colonists to arrive in St. Augustine in 1565. These Floridanos may have been the ones who gave the alligator its name, begat by the term for lizard, *el lagarto*. Later in another southern swamp, my French Acadian forebears took up residence on the vast bayou at the mouth of the Mississippi River. It's been a long time since my family has lived out on that swamp: My great-grandmother, a Gibson Girl, was a famed debutante in the Big Easy. Generations of my family lived in the Garden District. Every once in a while, I visit and confuse my friends by slipping into French conversation with locals in the Quarter. The swamp is in my blood, just as alligators and primordial bayous, hoary with moss and alive with shadows, are a part of the mythos that is America.

So it was no surprise that a line about "Operation Alligator Thief" casually dropped by one of my twelfth-grade students caught my attention. It was 2017, and I was still working as a high school teacher and living in an apartment-size house wedged between the swamp and a railyard. Teaching in the place where I grew up meant that I was privy to my kids' struggles even when they hadn't told me the exact details of their stories. I had lived a version of them, and they knew that. Even as an English teacher, I understood that my students might not be able to afford books, and that the time they might have spent reading was instead focused on more dire needs: helping raise siblings, working afterschool jobs to pitch in for rent, sleeping on friends' couches during family quarrels, trying to kick drug habits, or starting families of their own, accidentally or otherwise. These kids—sixteen, seventeen, eighteen years old—already knew that sometimes you have to do questionable things in order to survive. It's easy to speak in terms of black and white, but most of us live in the gray. They knew, too, that like them, I had big dreams for my life even though I was still stuck in that little town. I wanted to be a writer, and I was just getting my first publications. I was surprised that they encouraged me like I encouraged them, but I shouldn't have been, because in viewing my future with hope, they maintained hope for themselves just as I had when I was their age.

The first time I heard one of my students talk about poaching, I was walking by the desk of a young man, eighteen, who came to school clad from head to toe in camouflage in the winter because those were the only warm clothes that he owned. He loved the woods, and all of his writing journal assignments were nature stories. Of course I stopped, because the conversation sounded interesting but also illegal. I was intrigued and concerned. He looked at me sideways and asked straight-out, "Would you narc if I told you somebody who isn't me is picking palmetto berries and selling them to a guy from a drug company for $60 a bag?"

"Well, Somebody-Who-Isn't-You better hope I won't," I said, "with that detailed hypothetical you just gave me." But of course, I reassured him. My dad didn't raise a snitch. "And don't write about that stuff, either," I said, pointing to his paper. "You never know who's going to find something."

He looked down at his paper, which he had already laboriously filled with chicken scratch, and then he looked up at me. "What if I call it fiction?" he said.

"Sure," I said with a laugh. "Looks like a good start to a short story."

Ours was also a storytelling culture down in Florida, and soon I would discover that this was doubly true for the ones among us who were poachers.

For those of you who imagine all poachers to be rich big-game hunters, the idea that high schoolers are out there poaching may come as a surprise. The fact is that the typical poacher has very little to do with glamour or the elephant-gun-toting villains we might imagine. By its simplest definition, poaching is the act of illegally taking flora or fauna from the wild. This is a broad umbrella, meaning the term encompasses everything from criminal syndicates hunting critically endangered rhinos to freegans foraging on public land where taking natural products is against local statutes. The definition gets even muddier from there, particularly when discussing legality, as I would see when I delved further into the tangled and confusing web of wildlife law. Sometimes the laws that govern these practices are difficult to understand, even by some of the people enforcing them. But the truth is that the vast majority of poaching is not perpetrated by high-profile hunters or even by criminal syndicates targeting charismatic megafauna. Those are just the ones you hear about. No, most illegal fishing and illegal wildlife hunting are done for subsistence. These poachers are usually living under the poverty line and hunting, fishing, or foraging to survive. You may not have realized it, but you've talked to poachers before. You may even be one yourself.

But that isn't the narrative the poachers I've known have spun around themselves. According to them, they're taking what should already be theirs. They believe nature is a resource that we all share, and the lawmakers and the officers cordoning off the wild for use by a select few are the ones in the wrong. These poachers see themselves as Robin Hoods. They are protesting the imbalances of power that have left them on the bottom. And interestingly enough, the poachers in my life would balk at the idea that they're hurting nature. They love nature. The wild belongs to all of us, they say. They take no benefit from destroying their world. Instead, they are often the ones with the closest view to witness our wildlands' destruction. All the best poaching stories share an intimate knowledge of nature.

Knowing then that he had an interested listener, my student wove a yarn—a veritable poacher tradition—about the lengths he went to while collecting palmetto berries. He went poking through the scrub with a big stick to whack the berries free inside a trash bag. Oh, the snakes he encountered, the spiders, the hogs, the bears. He even knew where the berries were going: Drug manufacturers turn them into men's health supplements. His berry buyer, according to him, was a researcher investigating the use of palmetto berry extract as a treatment for prostate cancer. To my student, this pricked at the tangled nature of morality. "I'm breaking the law," he mused to me, "but it could end up saving people's lives. How weird is that?"

"Pretty weird," I said, and again trying to redirect him to the assignment at hand: "You should write about it."

"Naw, you should," he responded.

Should I have reported my student? I don't know. There are people who would say yes. But I was far more interested in keeping his ass in class so he could learn to read and write well enough to graduate. My silence over a few palmetto berries seemed an infinitesimally small price to pay for that.

From that day on, anytime he had a good poaching tale, he practiced it on me. There weren't too many. Both of us saw our world as a bit mundane. Then one day, he said, "Miss Renner, you'll never believe what I heard.

"You know how I've told you about the berries and fish and ferns and stuff," he continued, talking animatedly with his hands. "This one is about *alligators*." He had heard from a friend of a friend who had just been arrested that the Florida Fish and Wildlife Conservation Commission, more commonly called FWC, was putting people so deep undercover that they were practically shapeshifters. You'd never know who they were until it was too late.

"There was this FWC guy down south that made this whole big fake alligator farm, but it was a trap. They had the whole place bugged like they were spies, and they arrested a whole bunch of people—like forty people—for catching alligators. My friend's friend was one of them. They hauled him off to county [jail], and he's over here like, 'For what?' He didn't think he was doing anything illegal." He was talking, of course, about Operation Alligator Thief, a multiyear undercover sting that led to the arrests of eleven alleged alligator poachers in one day alone, one of the biggest operations in the agency's history.

"Who knows how many others there are." Fake farms, he meant. Fake businesses. Fake people. Maybe even the researcher buying palmetto berries from him. There could be a face behind that face. Nothing was as it seemed.

"Don't worry, Miss Renner," he reassured me. "I'm not doing that stuff anymore. It's not worth it." He had gotten a job washing dishes at a steak house instead. "It's just—" he said, as I turned to walk away. "What if it was me? It doesn't seem right, what FWC did. Nobody's doing this because they want to. It doesn't seem fair."

As all good stories do, this yarn stuck with me. It stuck with him, too. We both did some research, and we updated each other as we learned more. I told him I would try to write about it, but when I pitched the story to magazines—me with my scant publications and nonexistent reputation as a writer at the time—I didn't get very far. After stories came out about Operation Alligator Thief a few months later, I read them, and in all but one, the writer treated Florida like an exotic backdrop. I couldn't help but feel that something major was missing, but I didn't have the time or the money to figure it out.

Yet the story came back to me again and again. I became obsessed. I needed to dig deeper. I couldn't let it go. So many people had insinuated that FWC broke the law, but details on that were minimal. What had they done? And no one, it seemed, knew anything about the men who ran the operation, not even their real names. Who were these shadowy figures, these puppet masters who had bent reality to work their scheme? I hustled and learned and grew, entering the world of journalism. In a matter of three years, I went from churning out clickbait for content mills to writing for *National Geographic* and *The New York Times*. I wrote about invasive species, pollution, imagination, neuroscience, and dreams. I had all but given up on Operation Alligator Thief, but every so often, it would return to me. I would daydream about it, but then I would refuse its call. Even when I pursued the story, obstacles leapt into my way. Chief among them was having to pay my bills. I was scraping by on tenacity.

When I requested information on Operation Alligator Thief, the state had only a few files to share. Thinking they were holding out on me, I got on the phone with the public information officer and tried to charm more out of her. I wanted recordings, pictures, logs. I knew they must exist. They had to. I wanted to see what happened. I wanted to be there. Had FWC really set up a fake alligator farm? Was it just a trap, an empty set, or was it real? Who was this officer, the main man in the sting, whose fake name had been Curtis Blackledge?

"I'd give it to you if I had it," the PIO said. "The undercover officer with the sting is the only one who has what you're asking for."

I had already looked for the officer. Using the scant information I'd gleaned from asking around—Blackledge, appropriately, had black hair; he had been a canine officer; he was perhaps Asian or a Pacific Islander—I combed through old social media posts by FWC until I found pictures of an officer who matched that description. There was only one. His name was Jeff Babauta. I dug up phone numbers that matched the name. I called each one, becoming more and more sure it was him as every line I reached came up disconnected. But a feeling, no matter how strong, is nothing without solid evidence. I couldn't find an address or any social media profiles. No voter records. Nothing.

Whoever this guy was, he had done his job well. He'd vanished before the sting even started. And he was still gone.

I wanted to talk to him more than ever.

"Can you put me in contact with him?" I asked the PIO.

"Sorry," she said. "He's retired. Even I don't have his contact information."

"Can you tell me his name at least?" I needed her to confirm it. I had to know. If I had gotten that far, maybe I could actually find him.

"Sure," she said. "His name is Jeff Babauta." She said this with a laugh, not so much at my expense as at the futility of this exercise. "Good luck."

In January 2020, I drove down from Orlando to the easternmost edge of the Everglades and booked a room in the neon-dazzled Miccosukee Casino & Resort, a hotel in the no-man's-land between the glitz of Miami and the seemingly endless wilderness of the glades. That night, I looked out of my window on the casino's tenth floor, drinking in the surreal feeling of the trip. I had come there on *Outside* magazine's dime to write a story about python hunters.

Out on the glades with the hunters, I quickly realized they weren't who I expected, some caricature of rugged, bloodthirsty hunters. They were intelligent, compassionate conservationists. They were funny, too, with a humor that was equal parts dark and zany, just like my own. I found kindred spirits in them.

After spending the entire day with the hunters, trawling the levees for invasive snakes, we stopped where the levees forked and took a break as the last breaths of light drained from the expansive sky. Before that day, I had always thought of the Everglades as a massive wilderness, untamed and inhospitable. In my mind, the glades had been home to alligators, pythons, a bounty of mosquitoes, and not much else. Yet as fireflies drifted like motes over the sawgrass, a sense of wonder gripped my heart.

"When you really know the Everglades—and not many people do—that's when you fall in love," one of the hunters said. As we gazed out over the black water, a companionable silence fell between us, and we stood in mutual reverence at the altar of nature's savage beauty.

I've seen so many things and people here maligned and misunderstood. You could explore the Everglades for years and never see it all. To bastardize a Gertrude Stein quote, there is so much *there* there. But if you're looking for something else, you might miss it. Just as many writers miss the majesty of the Everglades while they're determined to find something else, writers miss the people of the Everglades, too. They get one concept in their minds—Florida Man, say—or they're too busy playing adventurer, and they manage to walk by the truly extraordinary without a second glance. They fail to be open to the real adventure, to the truth about the place, and to the real lives of the people who call it home; and they end up writing their stereotypical preconceptions.

This motivates me to be a better writer. Even when I'm not writing about Florida, I know I have to challenge my preconceptions, or I might just miss the truth as it goes flying so close to my face that it almost hits me. People make the story. Understanding them, not just why they do the things they do, but the complex and nuanced heart of who they are, is my writing raison d'être.

Of course, this brought me back to Operation Alligator Thief. It was a story of people like me, like these python hunters I sat with out in the glades—not outlandish characters, but folks who could have been my neighbors. So too did it seem a story in life's gray areas. Was what happened to the poachers caught in Operation Alligator Thief's trap fair? Was it legal? I wanted to understand what it was like to be a poacher in the glades. I wanted to live the lives of rangers and wildlife officers, too. I wanted to tell a story of people. No heroes, no villains, just the desperate choices that make us who we are.

When I reached the end of my clues, I knew that if I wanted to keep going there was only one thing I could do. I had to find Jeff Babauta.

As many a strange experience does, the next phase of my search began on Twitter. Completely by accident—after a misunderstanding turned argument turned thoughtful discussion on the social platform—I befriended Will, a former army intelligence agent, who volunteered to help me track Jeff down. We both hunted for Jeff's information and then compared notes. He found the same disconnected phone numbers that I had, and we used those as a touchstone to find an address. By then, the pandemic had hit, and I was locked down in Orlando. Will said he would check the address out for me. No one was home, so Will left a handwritten note. Jeff didn't respond. Not being one to give up, Will wrote another note with his name and phone number, and he stuck this one in Jeff's door handle. Then we waited.

Just when I had all but given up on this particular strategy, my phone rang. It was Will—with Jeff's phone number.

"He sounded a bit iffy about us, but he said to call him," Will said.

So I did. He answered on the second ring.

"Hi, this is Rebecca Renner," I said as brightly as possible, a smile in my voice.

"How are you?" he said, his voice gruff, wary, and—perhaps—curious.

Unbeknownst to us, Will's note had dislodged from the door handle and fluttered against Jeff's leg as he did yardwork. Reading the sender's name, Jeff had thrown down his rake and scuttled inside, locking the door behind him. He peered out of the blinds, wondering how one of the poachers' relatives had gotten his home address. Will, it turned out, shared a surname with someone nabbed in Operation Alligator Thief. However, they were not in fact related.

Jeff read the note again. It said that Will wanted to talk to him. That sounded ominous to Jeff, he would tell me later. But his curiosity won out, and he called the number nonetheless. Instead of a poacher-turned-stalker, Jeff found himself talking to an army-vet-turned-journalist. Will explained his mission and gave Jeff my phone number.

"Thank you for agreeing to talk to me," I said. His silence scrutinized me. "Um, I've been looking into your case, into Operation Alligator Thief. And I'm hoping to write a book about it."

"Is this a personal book you're writing, or is this for *National Geographic*?" he asked.

I usually wrote for *Nat Geo*, and I assumed that's why Jeff agreed to talk.

Jeff was suspicious of me at first. It wasn't in what he said but how he said it, making me feel I could only venture so far into his world as we chatted.

I knew as well as anyone how writers tend to swoop into Florida, get the titillating details of what they think is the story, and then retreat to New York as fast as they can—missing important facts in the process. But as we spoke, the drawl slowly melted back into my voice, and Jeff knew I was of this place just as much as he was. We talked about our love of nature and of Florida books. When he mentioned *A Land Remembered*, the quintessential Florida pioneer novel, I felt the possibility for a connection deep enough that he might really welcome me into his story.

Later, he invited me into his home and showed me his collections, collages of memorabilia in his sunroom from each of his big cases. He had kept his business card and newspaper clippings from Sunshine Alligator Farm. He had photos of the gators and one of him in his full undercover getup. He had also kept every document and recording, boxes of the stuff, and he said he would go through it and determine what he might let me see.

We sat on the couch for another interview, and his hundred-plus-pound yellow Lab, Ruger, wedged himself between my legs, laid his head on my knee, and insisted on being petted. I obliged enthusiastically. Jeff offered to shoo Ruger away, but I said it was fine. We carried on the interview like that, the dog slobbering on my left leg as I scribbled on the notepad perched on my right.

When Ruger suddenly growled, Jeff said, "I'm sorry. He's never like this."

"No, I'm sorry," I said. "It's because I stopped petting him." I started again, and Ruger recommenced his full-body wag. That made Jeff smile, and we talked about our dogs. I had a black Lab–hound mix named Daisy, then thirteen, the same age as Ruger. "You gotta love old dogs," I said. I had tried so hard to win Jeff over, and I had only gotten so far. When I stopped trying and started being myself, the kind of person who's never met a dog she didn't want to befriend, who thinks all creatures—whether fluffy or scaly, feathered or slimy—are cute, who tends to talk to wild birds and otters the same way she talks to her cat, that is when I felt something click into place. I had to be open first for him to be open.

When he showed me a video of dozens of baby gators in a kiddie pool, my heart melted at the sound of their squeaks. Jeff was more somber. He wished he could have done more for them. He felt like he had failed the gators, because they ended up at the tannery anyway. Part of him was confident that the sting had been the crowning achievement of his career. Another part clearly wondered if his efforts had been in vain. Even some of his fellow officers had said, "Alligators? What's the point?"

"Well, what did you say to them?" I asked. We had been poring over documents on his family computer, tucked into a nook of bookshelves.

"I said, 'What's the point?'"—his tone remembering his anger. "'Sure, they aren't endangered, but they have been before. We don't want them to go back there again. You don't wait around for an emergency before you prepare for it. You try to stop these things before they happen in the first place. *That's* the point. More than just the gators go if gators disappear. Everything falls apart.'"

It's hard to spend time in Florida's wilderness without seeing the environmental impact of humanity. Even in my hometown near Daytona Beach, it's there. Just south, the Indian River Lagoon is embroiled in a decades-long fight to clean up Florida's waterways. Once one of the most biodiverse estuaries in the Northern Hemisphere, boasting as many as forty-three hundred species of plants and animals, the lagoon is now dying. Nutrients from runoff have twisted the water composition. Algae took over, sparking a chain reaction that led to the most brutal manatee mortality event on record. More manatees died in the first three months of 2021 than in any other full year. Our love affair with lawns and golf courses is to blame. I was just as much part of the problem as any of my neighbors. It's so easy to forget that our actions, no matter how small they seem, have environmental consequences. We defy nature, bending it to our will. That impulse is so prevalent in Western civilization that most of us have stopped noticing it at all. Nowhere is that animosity so clear as in the Everglades. For centuries, settlers have ripped up, paved, and drained the glades, and now we wonder why those ecosystems seem so irreparably broken that they're poisoning us as we have done to them. The same is happening in coastal wetlands around the world. Just like in the Indian River Lagoon, many wetlands are dying, falling prey to developers, suffering from pollution, or transforming into ghost forests with the pressure of sea-level rise. With so many enemies threatening them from all fronts, wetlands' days are numbered, as are those of the wildlife that call them home, if humans continue our banal and careless destruction.

Jeff saw something similar in alligators. Their security as a species rises and falls with humanity's view of wetlands. When people pave swamps—and when floods, fires, and hurricanes devastate the Deep South—alligator populations take a downturn; and without alligators, a keystone species and apex predator, a ripple effect sends changes throughout the food web, back to the land, and back to us.

Caught between his love of animals and his care for people, Jeff grappled with difficult decisions throughout the sting. Some meant the difference between life and death. Others came from stickier ethical questions: How far do you go to catch a criminal? Is it right to commit a crime yourself if you're bringing the "bad guys" down? At times, that's what Jeff called them, defending his choices, saying that punishing the poachers to the fullest extent of the law was the only way to protect the wild. Other times, he wondered if he could have done more for the poachers themselves. Surely, there must have been a way to stop them without destroying their lives.

Since Operation Alligator Thief first made headlines, the sting had come under question. The agency's head quit, and a great upheaval followed. Some detractors said that what Jeff and FWC did was illegal, that they should have been the ones punished and not the poachers themselves. What happened that was so terrible?

Months passed, and I interviewed Jeff again and again. Jeff himself got into the habit of calling me to check in. Just when I felt too stuck to write anymore, as if by magic, my phone would ring. The screen would read, JEFF BABAUTA CALLING.

I had known him for about half a year when he trusted me enough to hand his case documents over, all of them, every game cam photo, every recording, everything I could have possibly wanted.

The deeper I went into the investigation, the further I realized there was to go. What I found is that it's easy to cast judgments from the sidelines. No one is the character we think they are. The truth confronts us only after we challenge our expectations.

One truth I came across on the way is this: To be at odds with nature is to be at odds with ourselves. We, as a species, stand at a crossroads. We can choose to live with nature or against it. Our centuries of war with the swamp have shown that when we attack nature, nature will fight back, and both humans and nature will lose. However, powers that serve to lose monetarily have presented us with a false dichotomy: that choosing to save nature is a choice for animals, against people. It's not. The equally false idea that humans are an invasive species is the other side of that coin. We're not. We're animals, too, but unlike other animals, we're greedy, and we know, deep down, that when we take too much, it's wrong. What do these two sides have in common? Storytelling. Stories bind us. Stories tell us who we are. They'll rally us. Then we'll have the power to strive and survive.

My hope is that by the end of this book—the story of Operation Alligator Thief—you will come to understand that a gator is not just a gator, and a poacher is never just a poacher.

While I was researching for this book—after interviewing Seminoles and gladesmen, rangers and poachers, digging through the national park archives, driving to every outpost in the glades big and small, and doing a lot of exploring by car and boat and on foot—I ended up below Everglades City, past the edge of nowhere in Chokoloskee, in pursuit of the legend of a man named Peg Brown. If the stories I had heard were true—and by that point, I'd heard dozens—Peg had been the most deadly and prolific alligator poacher who ever lived. The stories about him seemed impossible. He had killed thousands of gators, they said. He had bamboozled rangers, played tricks on them in the swamps, and he always got away. Peg had been a real person, but he had died in the 1980s, so I went searching for his next of kin in hopes of getting to know the man behind the legend and, through him, understanding the poachers of the Everglades. Their stories brought new depth to Jeff's, and so while I dive into the story of Operation Alligator Thief, I will also detail the days I spent pursuing the truth behind the legend of Peg Brown.

During this quest, I went on an adventure with two old gladesmen to see the former hunting grounds where they once, allegedly, poached alligators. To them, that wide and wild expanse of glades was a part of them as much as it belonged to them. As we ducked under vines in wild sanctuaries made of ruins held together by strangler figs, we talked about birds and how some were disappearing. Zipping on a motorboat among the Ten Thousand Islands, they told me about how trees could migrate, a slow escape along those distant latitudes so that the whole landscape had changed without any intervention. They told me about the hurricane that obliterated the town and caused fish to fall from the sky like manna in the desert. It struck me how down there the tallest tales were the truest ones, because no one has taken the time to sand down their edges and make them abide by the laws of what we're willing to accept as true. I saw so much of myself and my family in them, too. It was clear we shared a culture, one of storytelling and a deep connection to our own fragile estuaries. So as I witnessed the beauty of their world, I realized that I had grown numb to the magic and wonder of my own. After my adventure ended, I would need to return home and see it with new eyes.

That is what this book became—the tale of a wildlife officer who disguised himself as a poacher to protect the swamp and the American alligator, true, but also a study in awe. Writing a book is itself an adventure. No matter how much you plan, you must be open to the unexpected, the outlandish, because that is where the story lives. Along the way, it occurred to me just how many orchids I had stepped over without a second glance. So hell-bent was I on forward motion that I became numb to the quiet splendor of the wild world at my feet.

Without that revelation, I might not have seen these gladesmen or the people in Jeff's story for who and what they really were, people who are greater than the sums of their parts—because everyone is. In that, this book became more than a study of crime and character. The instability following on the heels of climate change has put us all in a crucible. Some of us are already making difficult decisions in order to survive. What we do when we're faced with these impossible choices reveals who we really are. Jeff would come to such a crossroads, a choice between saving alligators and saving poachers. The deeper I went into the story and into the Everglades, the more I realized that this is not such an easy choice at all.

When I was with the gladesmen, we went to a local museum, an old trading post where famed Wild West–style murders had taken place. It all seemed to have a sepia hue to it, but maybe that was because they were saving on lighting and had left the windows open to the breeze and the mangroves and the salty afternoon sky with its forever horizon on the gulf.

While they showed me around the museum, they stumbled upon an artifact it seemed they had forgotten: an alligator scute, one of the bony plates that grow under the skin of an alligator's back, forming an armor-like protection beneath the hide.

It was about the size of a quarter, squarish, and raised in the middle to a ridge. I had seen the things all my life, sitting on my great-grandfather's windowsill down by the canal, heaped like potpourris in a bowl in my grandmother's sunroom, and after I became a journalist, adorning the porch railings of the Old Florida types I went to interview, finding their homes full of cast-off treasures, coral and harpoons and dolphin skulls. One of the gladesmen told me that these scutes were shrinking just like their gladeland home. He put this on my list of things to discover, and placed that small bony plate in my palm. I can't explain why, but it felt imbued with magic. I would learn later that some cultures, including the one I'd left back home, use them in folk magic practices as talismans. Sure, I'm a science journalist, but there will always be a bit of gator country in me.

I carried the scute in the pocket of my jeans for the rest of my interviews and placed it on my desk back home, hoping for good luck. The more I thought about it, the more I realized why it meant so much to me. When the gladesman pressed it into my hand, that porous white bone warmed from his own, he was entrusting me with the unknown, with the fears of that land in transition, with its life, its loss, its hope, its despair. That small gift was a symbol. It said: *This is our story. We give it to you. Our story is your story, too.*

There is powerful magic in that.

1

THE CHASE

It was nighttime in the orange grove, and the sound of helicopter blades beat overhead. Otherwise, it was dark, and the dark was quiet. No frogs chirped. No crickets sang. Not even a mosquito whined through the open windows of Jeff's patrol truck. He blamed the smell for the quiet. The grove exuded the sickly-sweet scent of acetone. Pesticide. Of course it was quiet here. When the *chak-chak-chak* of the helicopter blades faded, it left only the hum of his idling engine and the sigh of his K-9 in the back seat.

Jeff's CB radio crackled. He sat up straight, and so did his dog, a Goldador named Mack, dressed in his working vest and looking very official. They were ready to track down the poachers whose flashlights the chopper spotted from the air. But it was too soon, the crackle just radio chatter. Mack rested his chin on his paws.

This wasn't Jeff's first time on a detail, where a group of Florida Fish and Wildlife officers like himself would spread out on the edge of the Everglades and wait. When the time came, an alert would snap over the airwaves, and the trucks would come to life all over the county and close in around the suspect. Sometimes it was a small-time hunter bagging deer out of season. Other times, they were something more, endangered fern thieves, turtle smugglers. Jeff never knew what they were going to flush out of the swamp until it came.

But first he had to wait.

Jeff was fifty-three years old and coming to the end of his long career as a wildlife protector, so he knew there was no such thing as a usual day on the job. A lifetime ago, his family had moved from Guam to Colorado then down to the Everglades, replacing one kind of big sky for another. There in Homestead, the southernmost town before US-1 hops the southern glades and Blackwater Sound to become the Overseas Highway, he became a short-order cook and fell in love with the waitress who would become his wife. He fell in love, too, with the glades and the swamps, with the untamable backcountry that most people who don't know any better revile, mistaking the grasses and tangles of cypress domes for wastelands when in reality they are the most abundant tracts on Earth, paradise within paradise. It called out to him. Soon he joined the Florida Game and Freshwater Fish Commission as a fisheries technician. His career evolved from there into game warden then patrol officer. For nearly thirty years, Jeff ventured out into that rough land determined to protect every scraggly inch, from the most charismatic flora and fauna—your orchids and your panthers, your sugar gliders and your black bears—to the crawling things and the slithering things, the fearsome, the slippery, the bug-eyed, the things it seemed no one loved except for him. He saw the beauty in them. He often wondered, *Why can't everyone else?*

No matter how much he loved the wild, he was glad that his time as an officer was coming to a close. His black crew cut was beginning to salt. Smile lines touched the corners of his eyes. He had kept in shape, his five-foot-eight frame maintaining a martial boxiness. He ran, lifted weights, practiced tae kwon do and karate. Yet the aches of age had come all the same. He was anxious, too, for a chance to enjoy the wilderness he had fought so long to protect. Still, he knew he might have to move. As the only Pacific Islander on the force, he was recognizable, though no one could ever exactly place him. *Hawaiian?* they would guess. *Māori?* Never Guam, but that was okay by him. The better for his anonymity. Unless they had been in the military, most people whom Jeff talked to had never met anybody from Guam before. He worried that the men he had put in jail would come back to take their revenge. Retirement, and the choice to move or stay, was three years away. There were days when it couldn't come soon enough.

Jeff sat with his thermos full of coffee, windows down, glad for the humid chill in the air and the lack of mosquitoes, even though he found the void of sound and the reason for it unsettling. While he waited, he contemplated the future, perhaps a cabin in the mountains, time to spend with his wife and son and his dogs, a stream where they might fish, the wild duck that would be their dinner, the trails they would hike, winding up through the oaks and hemlocks to a rocky edge overlooking the misty uplifts of the Blue Ridge and the valley below where the setting sun hit reservoirs and rivulets, turning them into molten gold.

But what did leaving mean, really? Sometimes it felt like escape, other times, like abandonment. The Everglades and the swamps around them were more than a place to Jeff. They were part of him. Sometimes it seemed he knew them better than he knew himself. He could identify every type of grass in a glade, every species of tree, every paw print in the mud, every plaintive hoot punctuating the usual music of the night. He saw himself as doing good for the people, too. He was quick to let folks off with a warning. He preferred educating them to slapping them with fines or worse. As much as he felt a strong connection to his job at FWC, Jeff knew not everyone at the agency felt the same way. When he left, they might replace him with someone who held the law in higher regard than he held humanity. That kind of thinking didn't help anybody, and it certainly didn't stop wildlife crime.

Could he leave that life? Even if he did, would it ever leave him? For that matter, did he want it to?

Though outwardly gregarious, Jeff was a big reader and a contemplative man. Waiting for the call from dispatch, he sank into thought, brooding about the fate of this wilderness, or what remained of it, after he left. This grove was wild no more. The rows of orange trees, taller than his truck and heavy with round, ripe fruit, were so long and straight—controlled—that they shrank into the distance, met the horizon, and kept going on into the dark. The cities surrounding Tampa Bay gave a faint, sallow glow to the lower edge of the sky. Jeff listened, hoping to hear a lonesome croak or yowl.

Nothing.

There had once been a time, twenty years ago when Jeff was a game warden, when more panthers prowled up to this latitude rather than remaining in their paltry preserve just north of the Fakahatchee Strand. While on patrol, he could cruise for miles without seeing any hint of human presence except the highway, his only company the ephemeral flash of orbs on the roadside, the spooked eyes of white-tailed deer raising their timid heads before they fled past the tree line, or, if Jeff was lucky, the lumbering boulder of a black bear or a glimpse of a tawny Florida panther tail as it slunk into the scrub. Such sightings were brief and rare, even then, like the glimmer of a comet seen through a telescope, there and gone. When Jeff looked into his rearview mirror, these atavistic figures would invariably have vanished, leaving him to wonder if he had seen the creatures at all or if they had been will-o'-the-wisps, tricks that swamp gas had played on his tired eyes.

Such was the state of this disappearing wilderness, even more so now than it was then: Sightings of some animals were becoming so scant that they had risen to the level of the supernatural, the extraordinary. Jeff knew there was a time before, when the swamps and humanity had lived with each other, before *swamp* had become a cursed word, before developers and vacationers and miners and factory farmers pushed the things that had crawled and dug and swum and flown there since time immemorial to the margins so they could take larger bites of a place they said they loved and would ultimately destroy. But Jeff hadn't seen that time. No one alive had, not really. Only the oaks and cypresses had been there that long, and their numbers had shriveled, too.

Yet still, within his own memory, the night had once writhed with wildness, with songs and chirps and croaks and growls. That was why Jeff could recognize a bull gator's guttural bellow. He knew, too, that a panther's roar sounded almost human, close to a scream but more sharp-toothed and primal. These days, folks thought the woods were haunted if they heard such a fiendish noise out there in the dark. They had all become interlopers there, hiding along the coasts, disconnected from the shrinking wilderness just beyond their backyards, its dwindling night music fading to an echo of a vanishing chthonic past. Jeff admitted he had become one of them, living in a safe world of manicured yards and trappers capturing the wild things to keep them where they supposedly belonged.

The radio squawked once more, rousing Jeff from his ruminations. The chopper had spotted lights in the brush not far away, outside the little town of Wauchula. When the closest officer checked in on the man and his accomplice, they sprinted to their pickup truck, jumped in, and fled. That officer was in pursuit already, but the suspect refused to pull over. They had a car chase on their hands. Dispatch summoned all nearby units to join the pursuit. Sheriff's deputies were on their way as well. So much for that quiet night.

"Let's go to work!" Jeff exclaimed to Mack, and the dog perked up.

Jeff snapped his seat belt and flicked on his lights and sirens. They wailed into the silence of the grove, now lit a swimming blue. He peeled out and sped through the back roads, heading for where he predicted the chase would go. He swerved onto the county road, and there, ahead of him, a single set of blue lights was shrinking rapidly into the distance. Jeff floored it.

Speeding off in pursuit always got Jeff's blood up. He felt alive, excited. He was doing something to protect that wild country instead of just thinking about it. But also, he admitted, he liked to go fast, to get out on a clean stretch of road, so straight that he could see the wink of oncoming headlights from miles away, and really open up his engine. He raced between the pines and cypresses, zipping around a semi-truck like a streak of light beneath the tufts of palm heads standing on their spindly trunks below a limitless sky and its splash of stars.

The blue lights in front of him grew until he was right behind them. He and the first officer had a quick exchange over the radio. The officer was pulling information on the license plate, but Jeff already knew who it was. He recognized the truck, a green Dodge with a topper. It belonged to a man named Clyde, a habitual poacher. The last time Jeff saw Clyde was when he sent the man to prison. That was several years ago. In the intervening time, Jeff had worked in the Florida panhandle. Even while he was away, landowners in Manatee County, his old jurisdiction south of Tampa Bay, called him up to shoot the breeze and tell him about any nefarious goings-on down there in the swampland. One had said Clyde had gotten out of prison and was back at it again, not only poaching but frequenting local bars and hangouts and bragging about how many deer he'd killed. Jeff was nothing if not meticulous. He wrote himself a note—he kept notes for everything—to check in on Clyde and others if he ever worked in Manatee again.

So when Jeff transferred back a few weeks prior, he began to investigate the leads from his notes. He asked around about Clyde but didn't find anything. Now here he was, racing through the swamp with a growing herd of black-and-whites on his tail.

Clyde wouldn't let up. The chase zagged from Hardee County down into DeSoto, deep river country beneath enormous live oak trees heavy with Spanish moss, before swinging into gladeland, back roads, sawgrass, and open sky. By two thirty in the morning, they had careened across three different counties, twenty-one miles. Their attempts to cut Clyde off or reroute him had failed. They reached speeds over a hundred miles per hour, going so fast that Jeff could smell his transmission burning. Now the Dodge veered onto a levee, lit from above by the helicopter's spotlight.

He's going for the canal, Jeff thought. If they got to it, the suspects could steal a boat—or perhaps hop into one that was waiting for them—and abscond into the alligators' kingdom like many a fugitive before them, never to be found.

They had left the domain of so-called civilization behind and had entered the swamp. There, the primordial past still reigned, stubborn and unconquerable, rebuffing all the future's attempts to push its way in. The swamp has swallowed whole planned subdivisions. A Space Race–era rocket facility sits abandoned in the southern glades, its warehouses and missile silos the prey of wet air, graffiti, and nature as the land takes itself back. Shot-up planes downed in cypress domes tell the story of cocaine cowboys and a lawlessness that lives on just out of sight. Skeletons of 1940s automobiles nestle in the saw palm fronds. People have dumped just about everything in the glades: cigarette machines, backhoes, pet snakes, dead bodies. In that country, it is easy to disappear. It's almost hard not to.

Jeff couldn't let them get that far. He sped up. The other officers followed suit.

Clyde's passenger flung something out the window. Possibly a gun. Jeff only had a split second to note the location of where whatever it was flew into the scrub. The chase kept going. By then it had started to rain. They had drifted back into farm country. On a slick stretch of road, Clyde lost control of his vehicle. He hydroplaned, and no sooner had Jeff blinked than the Dodge had run off the side of the road. It hurtled past the ditch and crashed through a fence, sending posts flying into the air like Popsicle sticks. They rained down. Some stuck into the soft ground, standing straight up. The Dodge kept going through barbed wire. It finally stopped in a sod field, wheels spinning, stuck and flinging mud. The rain was really coming down by then. A witching-hour mist hovered over the grassland, and the air seemed colder than it should have been. It was a wet kind of cold that sticks in your bones and makes your jaw ache. In the swamp, the wet had a way of amplifying everything. It sharpened the cold, inflamed the heat, enveloped you, and made you aware of your skin and the heaviness of your body, that you were a corporeal thing, animal and fragile, and at risk in that wild country.

Clyde fumbled out into the slop and tried to run. He bent double, close to the ground, as if he could escape detection in the sawgrass. His passenger ran in the other direction. Like a snap, the officers ran after both. Jeff made for Clyde. He slogged over the wet earth, picking his knees up high with each step, but Clyde was almost to the tree line. Jeff drew his firearm and used the flashlight on its top to cut through the downpour. Seeing a suspect ready to wriggle out of his grasp, another officer might have shot. But Jeff had made it through his entire career without firing his weapon outside of training. He wasn't about to start now. He kept the safety on. This wasn't cops and robbers. Their pistols weren't toys or props, despite how some yahoos treated them. Jeff wasn't the kind to go out and act like a cowboy.

Instead he dug down deep in himself and found a burst of speed. He closed the gap between himself and Clyde, grabbed the man by the arm, and wrestled him to the ground, where they both got a mouthful of mud. Other officers closed in around them. As they read Clyde his rights and cuffed him, he looked over his shoulder and spotted Jeff.

"Buta, you're back!" Clyde exclaimed, using a nickname that only Jeff's intimates knew. After stalking this fellow through the woods for fifteen-some-odd years, Jeff supposed that made them familiar enough to be friendly even while on different sides of the law.

"Yep, I'm back," Jeff said. "Now, where's your gun?"

Jeff had first met Clyde some years ago, back when he was a new game warden in Manatee County. Jeff worked weekends and odd hours then, but on Sunday mornings, he took his son to catechism and followed along with Mass. In the pews next to him sat the same landowners who would call in tips about strange lights they saw in their woods at night. Next to these ranchers, unbeknownst to them, sat some of the same poachers whose spotlights had glinted among their trees.

On Sunday evenings, Jeff worked through the list of tips he kept in his black leatherette-bound notebook, some leads from conversations he'd had, others thoughts he'd jotted down. Jeff knew how to work a source. His greatest asset, he believed, was his mouth. Other bullet points were from the tip hotline. One tip referred to a man named Clyde, a convicted felon well known in those parts for getting drunk at local bars and boasting about his crimes to anyone who would listen, a veritable poacher tradition. Jeff followed the tip to an approximate location in the scrub. Soon he spotted lights bobbing among the trees. He chased the poachers down, but they made it to their truck before Jeff could nab them. A short chase ensued. While they sped through the backwoods, Jeff watched Clyde pass his rifle through the truck's back window and lay it in the bed.

That was what Jeff had been there to arrest him for. Not only for poaching but for possessing a firearm while on probation for a felony. Clyde knew it, too. After ridding himself of the offending rifle, he banged on the roof, clearly telling the driver, his girlfriend, to pull over.

While Jeff was talking to them, the landowner rolled in and listened for a bit and then said, "Come to think of it, I did give old Clyde permission to hunt back here."

The landowner and Clyde shared a look.

That night would have to be a catch and release.

It would take more work to bring Clyde in that first time, including some sleuthing to track down how he had come into possession of a rifle. After finding surveillance footage of Clyde's girlfriend buying the gun for him, Jeff informed Clyde's probation officer, who told him to put a warrant out for Clyde's arrest.

That was how their odd sort of relationship started. They were adversaries. That was true. But they weren't enemies.

By the night that long car chase had ensued, Jeff had already arrested Clyde twice and sent him to prison both times. Each time, on their way to the jail, Clyde sitting cuffed in the patrol truck, Jeff would give him what he called his come-to-Jesus talk.

"Why are you doing this to your mom and dad?" Jeff said the second time. "You need to grow the fuck up."

Clyde nodded his head and said, "Buta, you're right."

Despite this seeming sincerity, Jeff's talks never really stuck. Still, Clyde wasn't a bad fellow, Jeff thought. He clung to the idea that even the worst criminals still had a grain of good in them. Most folks who crossed his path in the woods were one-time offenders. He'd try to educate them, make them understand what they had done, that it was more than breaking the law: Out in nature, even a small crime can affect an entire ecosystem. Jeff had decided long ago that he would rather do this and never see that person again than hike up his arrest numbers. Those didn't matter. The people and the animals did.

When Jeff found a man out poaching to feed his family, he remembered what it was like to be poor. He had grown up on Guam in a large family who struggled to make ends meet. What a lot of people don't realize is that in paradise, everything is expensive. What you had then were beautiful views and hard work. Jeff had never poached himself, but he could imagine the line of thought that brought a man to that place. It was one not of evil but of cold necessity. He felt for the people brought to that kind of need. Fines or court dates would just add more weight to their load.

Instead, he'd tell them to pack up, dump their catch, and go. "Just get out of here, man," he would say. "Don't do this again."

To Jeff, helping his fellow man was the moral thing to do. So what if it let them slip through the cracks of the law. Doing the right thing was far more important, and maybe, he thought, doing that one right thing would make them do the right thing later: They would get the opportunity to poach again, but perhaps they would remember Jeff and how he'd let them go, and they would let their quarry go, too.

Then there were times when they didn't. Like with Clyde. People were still people, imperfect. You could still be friendly with a man even if he remained on the wrong side of the law.

Trying to help, even rehabilitate, people like Clyde complicated Jeff's relationship with poaching even more than that of the typical wildlife officer.

While I was writing this book, an article about a very different kind of wildlife officer appeared in my Reddit feed. Titled "Kaziranga: The Park That Shoots People to Protect Rhinos," the BBC article boasted that park rangers in India shot poachers on sight in the name of conservation. I cycled through a plethora of emotions—joy at the thought of saving rhinos, horror at the denial of human rights like the right to justice in a court of law and the right to life, disgust at the commenters cheering on that violence. The next time Jeff called me out of the blue, I asked him what he'd do.

"I'd probably shoot 'em," he said. "It's easy to say whatever from the sidelines, but when you're right there, in the heat of the moment, and you're the only thing standing between that rhino and extinction, you'd do it, too."

I was shocked. But he was right. I probably would.

"But what about the poachers?" I said.

Half a lifetime of wildlife law enforcement had brought both nuance and conflict to Jeff's view of poachers. He cared about those folks who crossed his path in the woods. They had a lot in common, sometimes histories of poverty, definitely a love of the wild, and a little bit of that hardscrabble cunning that defines those who make their lives on the land.

"In this job, sometimes you have to make tough choices," Jeff said.

At one time, the popular imagination viewed poachers as lovable rogues. One such poacher has come to represent the archetypal heroic rebel, a gentleman thief. He robs from the rich to give to the poor. Sound familiar? The character of Robin Hood, the green-clad archer and trickster who uses his cunning and charisma to best his foes, was already popular in pre-Renaissance Britain before the printing press arrived to spread his tales. Robin Hood represented the class struggle of the late Middle Ages, especially conflicts over landownership and use. But he was also a classic anti-hero, and one of the world's most well-known tricksters.

The trickster has been one of the most popular archetypes to occupy narratives for as long as humans have been telling stories. From the Coyote spirit in Indigenous myths of the American West, to the spider Anansi in West African folktales, to the Norse god Loki (and the continued popularity of his Marvel character), it seems that every corner of the world has their beloved tricksters. Over the centuries, the trickster archetype has remained much the same, with the character playing both hero and villain, but always with a complicated ethos and a great deal of panache. Many modern tricksters are thieves, like Arsène Lupin, the gentleman thief and master of disguise in his eponymous novels by Maurice Leblanc; the crew in the Ocean's movies; and scores of others.

While thieves have seemingly risen in popularity along with culture's ongoing love affair with anti-heroes, poachers have not enjoyed the same forgiveness from the zeitgeist. Poachers were once folk heroes, but they have now become acceptable targets. If a beloved character happens to be a poacher, readers tend to push that fact under the rug rather than explore it.

Poaching is complicated because it's theft of a living thing, a theft that sometimes leads to its death or, using more loaded language, its murder. That is true in the case of alligator poaching, where the point is often to obtain the hide, which eventually becomes leather goods, often soaring in price along the way. That means alligator poaching, in some ways, has multiple victims. Unlicensed alligator hunting doesn't only take a resource from the public, if done on public land such as national parks like the Everglades, but also takes freedom and life away from the alligator itself. The matter becomes even more complicated from there. Unlicensed hunting on the small scale typically has little effect ecologically or monetarily against the greater good. But when unlicensed hunting tips into larger scales, it can do lasting damage to the environment, not just to the species in question but to the landscape, too, and everything and everyone that depends on it.

"You try not to get to that point, where it's life and death," Jeff had said while we were talking about the article. "It's better for everyone, humans and animals included, when things don't get that far." That's what they'd been trying to do with Operation Alligator Thief, to stop us from ever living in a world where alligators became so rare that rangers could shoot alligator poachers on sight. That almost happened once already.

In the early twentieth century, alligator populations began to take a downturn. By the 1950s, biologists estimated that fewer than one hundred thousand gators remained in the swath of land across the southeastern US that I call gator country. Alligator populations are sensitive. Since alligators depend on precise temperatures and water levels to ensure viable clutches of eggs, even small fluctuations in weather can take their toll, leaving them especially sensitive to habitat destruction, flooding from hurricanes, and sea-level rise. Such inhospitable conditions can ruin nesting seasons, killing tens of thousands of eggs and creating a gap that could become the first domino in the row toward steep population decline. Alligators aren't a traditional sentinel species, but perhaps they should be. They would be if we paid close enough attention. It takes more than legislation to save a species. So, what was truly at fault for the species' peril? And how did alligator numbers rise again?

Raising the alarm, environmentalists sought to protect the remaining fragile enclaves of gators from further decline. Those same states listed the alligator as an endangered species in 1967. With Everglades National Park already extant from 1947, the newly minted self-proclaimed environmentalists who had come to live in all that former swampland in the Sunshine State felt they had taken care of the problem of habitat destruction—not that they had anything to do with that in the first place. Whether it was obliviousness or selfishness (or a fun combination of the two), all the people who had suddenly moved down to the coastal redoubts that ate away at the edges of the glades didn't seem to see the toll taken by all their new houses, subdivisions, condominiums, and roads that stanched the Everglades' natural southward flow. Coming to live in the paradise they'd fallen in love with in *River of Grass* and *The*

Yearling may have done more to change it irreparably than any poacher ever could.

Nonetheless, armed with their prejudices, South Florida's newcomers demanded action. They hounded the park service into one escalation after another. Even as alligators were making a comeback—by 1970, their numbers were already double the low they'd hit two decades before—the park service was buying more planes and staying out all night to watch for poachers.

Were the rangers justified in their escalation? I'm not so sure. Going after the latter-day robber barons building condominiums would have done more good. They were the ones who took more than they needed in the first place, who snatched the land and made hunters into poachers. The more they built, and the more people came, the more expensive life became in the Everglades. It was no longer a remote place of quiet wonder, where the immortal flow breathed life into the water that in turn gave life to everything around, man and beast and flower. The glades and the islands and the coastal cities that bound them became a playground for the rich. Movie stars came down to the Rod & Gun Club, a hotel in Everglades City, to live like Hemingway. The newcomers held the keys to the kingdom. They were the law. They pointed metaphoric guns stronger than any real firepower. They said it was the poachers' fault, and so we blamed the poachers. The poachers, in their way, fought back. Not by taking more than they needed, never that, but by telling stories. And so the poacher as folk hero was reborn in the Everglades.

The most legendary among them, the one whom the rangers would never catch, was Peg Brown, whose real story, I would learn, was even more fantastic than his legends.

More land down there would become protected over the years, and alligator populations would skyrocket into the millions. "But the old ways die hard," as John Rothchild wrote in his story "Poacher" for *Tropic*, the now defunct magazine insert in the *Miami Herald*, "and there is probably no such thing as a truly retired poacher."

That sentiment seemed to ring true with Clyde. Jeff, on the other hand, was ready to get going. Just a few more years and he was out. The agency had other plans.

2

THE CALL

Driving up into the panhandle, the landscape on the roadside gradually shifted from prairie and palm scrub to oak hammock and upland hardwood forest. It was spring, so the air was cooler. As Jeff drove, he approached the thriving center of the North American Coastal Plain, an area that incorporates much of the southeastern United States and is one of the planet's most vital biodiversity hot spots. This majestic coastal plain is also home to the American alligator. Though not endangered, *Alligator mississippiensis* is no stranger to threat after the species' brush with extinction in the 1950s.

Recently, alligators in Louisiana had faced another challenge. Storms and floods, along with the already looming threat of sea-level rise, had nearly wiped out an entire bayou nesting season. Alligator farms rely on wild-harvested eggs to replenish their yearly stocks, as alligators almost always refuse to breed in captivity. Faced with a dearth of eggs in their home state, many Louisiana farmers turned to Florida, where the harvest was still plentiful and local farmers with egg-collecting permits were more than happy to sell their bounty for 1,000 percent of its usual price or more. Whenever the price of a wildlife commodity skyrockets like this, poaching skyrockets along with it. Poachers, if nothing else, are opportunists. They go where the money is. So poachers across the state of Florida became alligator thieves, stealing from both farms and the wild, and selling their take for as much as they could get. Unbeknownst to Jeff, FWC took notice, and they started building a sting operation to curtail the onslaught of alligator poaching before Florida lost another nesting season, too. But their sting had already run into trouble, and they needed a new agent to step in. This was a sensitive case. That agent had to be the right person, someone who knew the wilderness like the back of his hand.

With his encyclopedic knowledge of the woods, Jeff could identify every tree and shrub, the poetry of their names as thick as the overstory that shaded the road. There were loblolly pines and laurel oaks, white ash, American sweetgum, hickory, and beech. There was hophornbeam and devil's walkingstick, winged elm, magnolia, gum bully, flowering dogwood, and cherry. Perhaps somewhere among them grew the critically endangered Florida nutmeg, considered by some botanists to be the rarest conifer in North America, or more elusive still the spindly Florida yew, one of the rarest trees in the world.

Tangles of greenbriar and trumpet creeper vines, with their red-orange flowers, a favorite of fast-flitting ruby-throated hummingbirds this time of year, languidly strung themselves among the lower branches. Summersweet flowers and cinnamon ferns, carnivorous pitcher plants and fly-eating sundews, visited the limestone-cragged understory and speckled the swampland below.

Even though he was driving too fast to see all of these things, the delicate birds and their flowers danced in Jeff's imagination. He knew the trees down to the splay of veins on the undersides of their leaves, the birds by their calls and the gloss of their wings. He conjured, too, less charismatic creatures, the things, it seemed, few people loved except for him: Cave walls came alive with the fuzzy chittering of threatened gray Myotis bats; an eastern indigo snake curved like living obsidian through the brush; reticulated flatwoods salamanders wriggled their slick speckled bodies back beneath a hoisted log. Jeff had spent most of his life mentally cataloging the natural world, especially the things that many people would see but never care to know about, as though if he did not hold them in his thoughts at least once they might be forgotten completely.

Among these natural wonders hidden in plain sight seemed to him an apt place for the agency to hold undercover training for wildlife officers, and that was what brought him to the panhandle that spring morning. About ten miles from the Florida-Georgia line, Jeff found the law enforcement academy campus. It was hidden in the forest back from the main road, the same sort of building floor plan used and reused for schools and prisons alike. After signing in, Jeff reported to the barracks that would be his home for the next week. About twenty other wildlife officers, his classmates, trickled in to claim their beds. Some came from as far away as Montana and Alaska. Some still looked turned out and spit-shined, with pristine grooming and crisply ironed clothes that would peg them as cops to anyone with even an ounce of savvy. Jeff and a few others knew better. Their instructions said to show up in plain clothes and pack the kinds of everyday outfits that would allow them to blend in with civilians. The agency would furnish unmarked units. Jeff arrived dressed, in his mind, like a "dirtbag." He tied a bandanna around his head to hide his crew cut. He had cut the sleeves off a T-shirt so the armholes practically hung to his waist. The groomed fellows in the dorm eyed him with suspicion. But that just told him he'd hit the mark.

The officers didn't spend much time in the classroom. Most of their days happened in the field, running through scenarios that mimicked real-life undercover missions, something Jeff never planned to encounter. Even though he did a little bit of his own covert surveillance while running down leads for poachers—chatting folks up in bars, listening in on a conversation serendipitously heard through a display at the hardware store—Jeff saw the training as merely the opportunity to learn something new and have a little fun so close to the end of his career. He had signed up out of curiosity, chose the course from the lineup because it seemed interesting. Even though he never planned on going undercover, he liked a challenge.

The first scenario his group received mirrored a real-life tip-line report. In the parking lot of a local Walmart, a suspect had been seen exchanging money for fish from his coolers' stock.

Jeff and his team set out to investigate. They were dressed down, most of them in flip-flops, unusual footwear for Jeff. He considered that someone used to dressing like that would have a flip-flop tan. His feet, pale compared with the rest of him, would give him away. He chided himself for not thinking about that. He was always so meticulous.

His team drove in separate unmarked cars to the Walmart. They split far apart. They took notes, describing the man, the scene, what he was dealing—it looked like fish. Jeff held his phone up like he was sending a text message and snapped a photo. His team reported in to one another. Some changed positions or went inside to buy something so they could walk past. Jeff was used to this part of the job, the watching and waiting. He settled back into it so quickly that for a while, he forgot that this wasn't reality. Every time a buyer walked up to the poacher and his coolers, Jeff noted his features, his clothes, his approximate height and weight, the time of their exchange, and what it looked like was changing hands—catch for cash. All the while, the officers in charge of the training were watching them, grading. At the times Jeff remembered this was just a training exercise, the whole thing felt surreal: The officers in charge were watching them watch others. He was pretending to pretend to be someone else. The suspect left the parking lot. They tailed him. Jeff kept several car lengths' distance so as not to arouse suspicion.

Jeff followed the suspect for about half an hour, staying just out of his sight in traffic, all the while talking on the radio with his team, trying to determine the suspect's destination. Finally, the suspect stopped at a dollar store.

Jeff didn't turn in to follow him. That could have been too suspicious. Instead, he informed his partner in the car behind him, and she took over the tail. Jeff circled the block while she parked, grabbed a shopping cart, and went inside. By the time she arrived at their meeting place, it was well past dark. Jeff wasn't tired. The electric thrill of excitement was keeping him awake.

"They were buying a bunch of fishing gear," his partner said, informing him of her observations. "I think they're gonna do this thing tonight."

It all felt so real.

Except when it didn't.

When the trainees arrived at a bar the next day, their instructor gave them the scenario: Your partner has been compromised. Create a distraction that allows them to escape the scene and reach safety without being compromised yourself.

Act normal, Jeff told himself. Yet he was all too self-conscious.

The man whose turn it was got down on one knee in front of one of the female officers and proposed. Of course, everyone around them looked and cheered when she said yes. The officer who was supposed to slip away stood up from his table. He walked toward the restroom and disappeared down the hall.

At the next bar, the trainee went up to the house band's microphone and gave his eloquent proposal as the band accompanied him with a love song. Too many of the female trainees suffered these public professions of love. The next morning in the classroom, one of the officers in charge stood in front of them and said, "No more." The sudden rash of amorous proclamations was becoming suspicious.

When Jeff's turn came, he roughed himself up and stuck wads of bags in his pockets. He went into the fried chicken restaurant where his partner was in trouble and proceeded to dig through the trash looking for something to eat. He swallowed his pride and thought only about the task as his character would have, searching in desperation for something to eat while not meeting anyone's eye. He found a bone and started gnawing on it. That was when a man approached him and gently offered to buy him some bread. By then, his partner had vanished.

Jeff had no idea that more people than just the instructors were watching him.

Back down in Manatee County, Jeff settled into his normal life, to early-morning runs and dark evenings of peering into the overgrowth in search of spotlights, of weekends with his family. He tinkered on his truck, grilled, and gardened. He took pride in the look of his yard like he took pride in his grooming. There was seldom a blade of grass out of place. Early one Saturday morning, Jeff pushed his lawn mower along the edge of his driveway, stray shoots of turf snowing the concrete and sticking to his blue jeans and the dew-slick sides of his sneakers. He reveled in the herbaceous smell of the freshly mown grass. It was the smell of youth, of summer, of running through sprinklers in the heat of July. It was aimless and easy, two things his life had never been but would be soon when retirement finally arrived. There awaited ten thousand days like this one.

His cell phone rang. Reaching to answer it, Jeff saw the name on the caller ID and said aloud, "I'm in trouble."

It was Lieutenant George Wilson, someone Jeff had known *of* since the 1980s. He didn't know much about the lieutenant at all actually. He outranked Jeff. He was in a different section of FWC, but Jeff had no idea what the lieutenant did. Maybe in-house investigations or internal affairs, the branch that investigated accusations of misconduct within the agency. Jeff wondered what he could have done.

Then another thing struck Jeff as odd. *How did I get his phone number?*

He answered quickly, worried about letting the call go to voicemail.

The lieutenant wasn't much for pleasantries. After a brief exchange, he launched straight into his business. "Have you thought about doing any undercover work?"

"No," Jeff answered, aware of his lawn mower engine chopping in the background.

The hurricanes. That was how Jeff had this spook's phone number. Back in 2014, they had been assigned to the same recovery area. The lieutenant had been Jeff's supervisor for the deployment. But they hadn't traded more than a few words.

"We've got a crime we're investigating," the lieutenant went on.

When Jeff pressed for details, he wouldn't say. Jeff shook his head. *Why am I even asking? It doesn't matter what this thing is. I'm not doing it.*

"Hell, no," Jeff said, only barely letting the lieutenant finish. "Sir," he added.

Jeff was too close to being retired. In less than five years. If he got hurt—or worse—he could say goodbye to his ten thousand days of summer. No job was worth that. He knew his wife would likely agree.

Now he had to get the lieutenant off the phone before he agreed to anything he didn't want to do.

"Nice to hear from you, Lieutenant," Jeff said. "You take care of yourself."

They hung up, and Jeff hoped that was the end of it. But it wasn't. Of course it wasn't. Investigators are nothing if not persistent. Another officer, Rett Boyd, called Jeff while he was hunting in North Carolina. A third called when he got back home. Wilson called several more times in the following months.

Jeff thought back to the first time they had met. It was 1988. Jeff was working as a lab technician in Osceola County, where he helped manage Three Lakes Wildlife Management Area, a sixty-two-thousand-acre plot of land about seventy miles southeast of Disney World comprising major portions of the Kissimmee Prairie, the second-largest dry prairie in the United States.

Connected by an interlocking chain of lakes with the headwaters of the Everglades, that expanse of grassland transformed with each season of renewing fire and life-giving flood. A stunning multitude of birds abounded there. Red-cockaded woodpeckers tapped out an insistent tempo in the pine savannas' lonely heights. The orange-and-white-beaked crested caracara swooped down through an oak dome, a dense patch of tree cover over a watery gash in the limestone bedrock. Endangered grasshopper sparrows nested hopefully in the wire grass under a seemingly boundless sky.

These quiet ecosystems once covered about ninety million acres of the peninsula, but due to urbanization, farming, settlement, and the disruption of natural fire cycles, longleaf pine forests and savannas now measure less than three million acres, according to the Florida Forest Service. It's the same story for their neighboring grassland prairies. Such habitat loss has played a major role in the endangerment of some species and the extinction of others, such as the dusky seaside sparrow, a small bird with black-and-white mottled feathers that once nested in the salt marshes of nearby Merritt Island. The United States Fish and Wildlife Service declared the sparrow extinct in 1990.

Though they were already exceedingly rare in Jeff's time, he may have been lucky enough to see one. In those days, his management area was largely devoid of human activity, save for the odd hunter or birder. The nearby Kissimmee Prairie Preserve State Park would earn a designation as an International Dark Sky Park in 2016. Before that, darkness was just darkness. Due to the area's isolation, there is no light pollution to dim the brilliance of the stars.

The great splash of the Milky Way enveloped the prairie's tremendous sky the night a hunter went missing inside the wildlife management area. Jeff went to meet with the law enforcement personnel in charge of the search, and he told them about seeing spent shell casings on the ground. Wilson was the canine officer whose dog would nose around the palm hammocks in the hope of turning up a trail.

Each time Wilson called him again, they spoke longer. Jeff remembered the wild country where they first met and his motivation for becoming a wildlife officer in the first place: It was all well and good to catalog nature. But he had wanted to do more, to defend it, to be the champion of the wild things he loved so much instead of just watching as the tamed and greedy part of the world continued to swallow them. Why mourn for something when you can fight to save it instead?

"How would you like to go out with a bang?" Wilson asked.

He liked the idea: one big mission to finish his career. It would be something to look back on and know he'd really done something, that the world had been a better place for his being there. The lack of details about the mission only served to whet his curiosity and his excitement.

"All right," Jeff said. "You've got me. I'm interested to hear more." Jeff agreed to meet with the investigation's leaders.

They told him to come in plain clothes and borrow another officer's unmarked vehicle. His curiosity reaching a crescendo, Jeff drove to Tampa to meet them. He pulled into the restaurant's palm-shaded parking lot and looked around, as if someone might be watching him.

Inside, he found a table with Boyd and Wilson. They both stood to shake his hand. After they sat, Jeff leaned in and whispered, "So what's this all about?"

"The agency needs someone to go undercover to finish a job," said Boyd.

"You already told me that, sir," said Jeff. "What am I going to be doing? What's involved?"

"We can't tell you just yet," said Wilson. "We need a commitment first. The operation's already underway. We can't risk it by giving away details to anyone who isn't involved in an official capacity."

"Well, tell me this, then—" Jeff said, leaning back to scrutinize both of them. "Why me? Why send some old guy into the field when you have so many young bucks who'd jump at a chance like this?"

Wilson stayed stone-faced, but Boyd smiled. "We don't need somebody out here trying to make a name for himself," said Boyd. "We need someone seasoned, someone with experience." They also needed someone smart, someone who could learn.

"It's because of how well you did at undercover training," said Wilson, all business. "You're a natural. Plus you have the background for this."

A spark went off in Jeff's mind. *That was a clue*, he thought. He'd been at this for around thirty years by then, doing everything from counting birds and testing water to chasing down poachers. His career had started in fisheries. Could this job have something to do with aquaculture? Or some fish poachers running amok, maybe?

Jeff looked at Wilson hopefully, as if he would say more, but he didn't. Jeff wanted to say yes. He felt compelled to at this point. They had pursued him.

They told him all the right things. They said he could make a difference. They seemed to need not just someone like him but him in particular. Ridiculous as it sounded, he was the one. Nonetheless, he lived in reality. He needed to know how this would affect his life. "What's the commitment?" Jeff asked. "How long will I be at this? Can you tell me that? I need something to tell my wife."

Sandy, his wife, hadn't wanted him to go into law enforcement. She dreaded "that call," she said, the one that comes in the middle of the night to tell you your loved one will never come home again. She had been against the undercover mission, too. "You're almost done," she'd said. "Why would you take such a big risk?"

"For the challenge," Jeff had answered.

She studied him with both unhappiness and—was that understanding in her eyes? She was a blond woman with a large, opinionated personality that shouldn't have fit into her small frame. They had been married nearly thirty years at that point. No one in the world understood him better than she did.

"You're going to do it, aren't you?" she said.

"Not if it makes you this unhappy."

"I'll manage," she said, her arms crossed, her expression hard.

He shook his head.

"You should," she said. "You'll regret it if you don't."

"At least a year," Wilson said at their meeting, across from him at the table.

"Does that mean you're in?" Boyd asked.

"I suppose it does," Jeff said. "I'm in. I'll do it."

3

SOFT SHELL

The secrecy continued even as Lieutenant Wilson began to outfit him for the job. *A job* was more like it. He still knew nothing when Lieutenant Wilson arrived at his house in plain clothes, driving an unmarked vehicle, and told Jeff to get in. Jeff already knew not to ask where they were going. Lieutenant Wilson demanded absolute trust. He would see Jeff through. From this point forward, secrecy would be a usual part of his life.

They drove to a parking lot near the airport. "I know the guy who owns this place," Lieutenant Wilson said. As the lieutenant in charge of undercover operations, Lieutenant Wilson kept all the gadgets for his officers. Likely not there, Jeff realized. This was a middle ground. He probably kept them somewhere else, a warehouse, maybe a storage unit, some nondescript box secretly full of handguns, Tasers, discreet security cameras and listening devices, and keys to any vehicle they might need—ATVs, trucks, airboats.

They stopped and got out beside a white Ford F-150.

"This is your unmarked," Lieutenant Wilson said.

They started it up to make sure it worked. The needle on the gas gauge dipped down toward empty.

"Damn," Jeff said.

"Could have sworn I just put gas in this thing," Lieutenant Wilson said. "Looks like you'll need to fill the tank. That's your next stop."

Lieutenant Wilson had Jeff's gun, too, a Smith & Wesson .38 revolver. It didn't look like a cop gun. It looked like the kind of gun fellas buy as an accessory to look like a 1930s gangster. *That'll do*, Jeff thought. He didn't have an undercover character in his mind yet. He didn't want to have to improvise. But without knowing the scenario, what could he do? Trust that he'd know when it was time, that's what.

"I'll have more for you later," Lieutenant Wilson said. Jeff hoped he meant information, not gear. Jeff could only have so much faith before he started to get antsy.

A few blocks away, Jeff mused about his daring new undercover life while pumping gas.

"Hey!" someone shouted. "Hey! Hey, buddy!" When the man finally got Jeff's attention, he said, "Something's pouring out from under your car!"

Jeff stopped the pump and contorted to see underneath. Liquid was gushing all over the concrete. It was coming from his—gas tank? Jeff swore under his breath.

He called Lieutenant Wilson and a tow truck. The truck got there first. With an irritated frown, he watched it winch his brand-new unmarked onto its bed.

Off to a great start, he thought.

In his now fully functional truck, Jeff and Lieutenant Wilson drove out to Lake Placid, a small town about thirty miles northwest of Lake Okeechobee. Along the way, Lieutenant Wilson filled Jeff in on the work ahead.

The species at the center of this investigation was *Apalone ferox*, the Florida softshell turtle. Measuring between the size of a dinner plate and that of a hubcap, this dark-brown amphibious reptile resembles a large mud pie with a piglike snout. While not the most fetching creature in the swamp, the Florida softshell turtle has other strong points that make it a target.

Though not a species of concern to the International Union for Conservation of Nature (IUCN), softshell turtles play an important role in their habitats, feeding on snails and fish, which keeps the population of those organisms in check. (Larger softshells, however, have been known to snack on prey as large as ducks and herons.) A sharp dip in their numbers could distort populations in other parts of an ecosystem, and when an ecosystem's balance goes awry, its most vulnerable inhabitants, especially the protected ones, are the first to suffer. So FWC was looking out for the state's less photogenic fauna as well as its charmers.

Because of their lack of protected status, catching softshell turtles wasn't illegal, but smuggling them out of the country was. While the difference between poaching and hunting isn't as clear-cut as it seems, the definition of wildlife trafficking is much more straightforward. At the most basic level, poaching is taking organisms from the wild without appropriate licensure. This "illegal take" comes in many forms, most of which aren't nearly so obvious as the act of a big-game hunter shooting a rhinoceros. Poaching can be as small as catching a fish that isn't the right size and not throwing it back. Hunting certain animals outside their designated season is poaching. Harvesting plants from public land can be poaching. Sometimes, taking anything at all from the wild on public land without the appropriate permits is poaching, too. Laws governing humanity's rights to the natural world get more complicated from there. This poses the question: If the law is incomprehensible—not just to the average person, but even to the educated one—can carrying it out be justice?

Wildlife trafficking, however, is a more obvious crime. If you don't have a permit, you can't take that turtle anywhere.

National and international law enforcement agencies were tracking the trafficked softshell turtles across the world. On the ground in the Sunshine State, FWC had investigations underway to locate the poachers snatching turtles from the wild and selling them to the traffickers.

"There's big demand for them in the Asian markets," Lieutenant Wilson said. Softshell turtles are a favorite addition to traditional Chinese dishes like hot pot and congee. It's so popular, in fact, that in recent years wild populations of Chinese softshell turtles (*Pelodiscus sinensis*) and related species have suffered a decline. The Chinese softshell is now listed as vulnerable by the IUCN.

The agency already had a list of suspects lined up, Lieutenant Wilson explained, and he needed Jeff to go undercover and investigate one of them with him.

Is this the big mission I've been waiting for? Jeff wondered. His gut told him it wasn't. His gut was right. This short operation turned out to be field training for Jeff, and it gave Lieutenant Wilson the opportunity for one last evaluation before the agency took the final risk on Jeff and divulged its secrets.

Lieutenant Wilson's first lesson for Jeff would be on improvisation. They parked at a house near the suspect's that looked run-down and abandoned. Lieutenant Wilson brought out a measuring tape.

"People will get suspicious if they think we're here for no reason," Lieutenant Wilson said, nodding toward the house. "So today we're real estate agents checking out this house while we're really watching them over there."

"It's a real fixer-upper," Jeff said.

This was Jeff's next lesson: Use what you already have to craft a backstory. The fewer lies you have to tell, the better.

They watched the house for several days, noting comings and goings. As the day when they would finally make contact with the suspect loomed closer, they began preparing their backstories and accumulating the props that would set the stage. This would be Jeff's first time playing a character undercover. Lieutenant Wilson scrutinized him as they prepared.

"You backed into that spot," Lieutenant Wilson noted the next morning upon Jeff's arrival. They'd met in a parking lot, as poachers often did. "Why'd you do that?"

"I don't know," Jeff answered. "Force of habit, I guess."

"You see anybody else here who backed in?" Lieutenant Wilson asked. "Not many. It's a law enforcement habit, one you have to break if you don't want to get burned."

Burned, meaning discovered, his cover blown.

"Ten–four," Jeff said, catching himself before the code for *yes* slipped all the way out of his mouth.

Wilson smiled knowingly. "That, too. The cop lingo? You have to break all of those habits."

So much of who he was, Jeff began to realize, came down to muscle memory. He had to practice being a civilian, on a deadline, too. The closer they came to the day, the more pressure piled on his shoulders. But he was also excited. This was new, exhilarating. He hadn't switched up his routines in so long.

Before they set out, they rigged a hidden camera setup, hollowing out the locking mechanism on a toolbox and tucking in a camera smaller than a nickel. Jeff pressed the button to turn the camera on and tucked the box into the front end of his truck bed.

The morning they planned to make contact, Jeff faced off with his mirror again, practicing. He slouched and turned to look at his reflection. *Should I stand like this?* Jeff straightened up, shoulders back, chest out the way he normally stood. He pulsed with nerves and excitement. Even if the suspect didn't know why, the way Jeff held his body might telegraph that something was off. His posture made him look like someone with too much respect for authority. He stood like an officer of the law. *Have to unlearn that*, he thought. He raised and lowered his shoulders, watching them move in the mirror. He shook out his arms. He imagined being the kind of person whom no one had ever called to attention. He had saluted no man. Still, he had respect for himself. Jeff eased into a comfortable stance, straight but loose.

"I'm Jeff," he said, offering the mirror a handshake. They didn't have fake names yet. First names only would have to do for now. *Do normal people stand like this?* Jeff thought, turning to the side.

He started over again, introducing himself to the poacher he imagined standing beyond the mirror. "Who's buying these turtles?" he asked. He made a sweeping gesture. It looked weird, stiff, like he was trying to sell a used car or get a part in a Shakespeare play. He shook out his shoulders again. Besides, that question was too straightforward. *Got to be more subtle.* He glanced at his watch, *shit*, it was time to leave. He pulled on a camouflage shirt, a dirt-cheap one he'd picked up at Walmart. He roughed up his scruff of a goatee, situated a camo baseball cap on his scraggly hair, and slipped on a pair of rounded glasses. He frowned at himself. "Ready or not, it's time to go."

Jeff and Lieutenant Wilson had loaded up his unmarked truck with landscaping supplies. Fake real estate agents no longer, they were partners in a landscaping business. That let them go pretty much anywhere. Few people give lawn guys a second thought. Today these props included a new addition, a hundred-quart cooler with a softshell turtle inside.

Their target lived out in the backwoods, several miles from the main drag of that little town. Lieutenant Wilson had already driven by and had a plan for how to make an introduction without raising suspicion.

He shared that plan with Jeff before they set out. They needed to make a connection with the turtle seller, preferably a business one. The goal was to get him to buy turtles from them. The rest they'd play by ear.

They pulled into a small clearing of mossy oaks and drove down a sandy semblance of a driveway. The house was concrete block, painted an egg-yolk yellow and backed up by a series of sheds. Kids shouted and laughed somewhere in the back, accompanied by the sound of dogs barking.

They parked beside a pickup truck with a dog box, a mobile kennel used to transport hunting dogs, in the bed.

"Follow my lead," Lieutenant Wilson said as they got out. They slammed their doors. Dogs bayed at the sound. Jeff's adrenaline soared.

While they were walking up, a middle-aged man with brown hair and a mustache emerged from the house. He appraised them as he approached. "Can I help you guys?" he drawled.

"We own a nursery up around the Tampa area," Lieutenant Wilson said. "And we noticed your dog box here. You wouldn't happen to be catching hogs, would you?"

"That's all I do," he answered. "I love catching hogs."

"Do you have any hog meat we can buy?" Lieutenant Wilson asked. "Preferably a whole hog. We're feeding a lot of people." He went on to explain that they owned a landscaping company, and they were throwing a barbecue for their employees and their families. It would be a big crowd, so a pig roast would surely take care of them and be something to remember.

"Yeah, let me get your name and number," the hunter answered. "My name is Alonso, by the way."

Jeff felt awkward, like his nerves were getting the best of him. He wanted to be the best, to show Lieutenant Wilson he was ready for the big show, but here he was, not doing anything.

As if on cue, the turtle scrabbled loudly in their truck bed. "What was that?" Alonso asked.

"I'll show you," Lieutenant Wilson said. He lifted the lid of the cooler to reveal the softshell turtle inside.

"Where'd you get this?" Alonso asked.

"I caught this at our nursery," Jeff said.

"There's a canal out back, and we see these things all the time," Lieutenant Wilson said.

Reading the interest on Alonso's face, Jeff added, "You want this thing?"

"Hell, yeah, I want it," Alonso answered.

"What are you gonna do with it?" Jeff asked, playing dumb, a valuable tool in his investigative arsenal, as he would learn. It seemed like a realistic enough question. *What the hell do people want with these things anyway?*

"I've got some Chinese guys who are interested in buying some turtle meat." Alonso pulled out his phone and showed Jeff and Lieutenant Wilson pictures of large softshell turtles and a huge snapping turtle. Men posed around them, showing off their prehistoric size. *These are the buyers!* Jeff realized. Their recognizable blue van was parked in the background.

It can't be this easy, Jeff thought, amazed but wary. *Don't stop now*, he told himself. *Keep going.*

"Man, if you show me how to really catch these things, will you buy them from me?" Jeff asked. "I'm always trying to make extra money myself. I mean, cutting lawns gets old after a while."

"Sure!" Alonso said. "Follow me into my backyard."

While they talked, Jeff glanced around. *This guy wouldn't be keeping turtles back here, would he?* Outside the shed, there were several tubs covered in palm fronds. "What's in here?" he asked.

"Come see," said Alonso. He crossed to the closest tub, lifted up its makeshift lid, and nodded for them to come over.

Jeff and Lieutenant Wilson peered over the edge. And there it was. The guy had shown them right to it. An enormous softshell turtle, so big it took up the whole width of the tub. Its claws scrabbled against the bottom as it tried to get away from the light.

Next, Alonso showed them the large hooks he used to catch them. He went on to explain the types of fishing line they needed.

Jeff already knew how to catch turtles. *Just play the game*, he told himself. *Make him comfortable. Make him like you.*

"For bait, you can use chicken or gizzards or whatever," Alonso continued. As Alonso spoke, his voice tightened. *Why?* Jeff wondered.

Jeff considered himself a perceptive person. He could read people. It seemed to him that Alonso knew what he was doing was illegal. Jeff needed to ease that tension so they could strike up a partnership and he could figure out where all of these turtles were going. Usually, Jeff would cut tense moments by cracking jokes, but this didn't seem like the right time for a zinger.

He nodded along and acted excited, hoping his high spirits would affect Alonso. Gradually, Alonso loosened up and began to smile, too. They agreed on a price for Jeff's future turtles and shook hands. Then Jeff and Lieutenant Wilson got going. They'd hardly made it out of the driveway when a blue van turned the corner and headed toward Alonso's house. *Too easy*, Jeff thought. He whipped out his phone and snapped a picture of the license plate.

Now how the hell am I going to get all these turtles?" Jeff said as they drove through the woods back toward Tampa.

"I know a guy," Lieutenant Wilson answered.

That guy, a fellow named Mike, was a commercial fisherman who'd found Jesus and turned his life around. Now he was eager to Bible-thump and, luckily for FWC, eager to give back and make amends for his own past transgressions. For three months, Jeff got up before dawn about once a week and drove to Auburndale—a little town between Orlando and Tampa that was made more of lakes than it was dry land. Jeff and Mike baited hooks, sometimes as many as eight hundred, strung their lines clear across lakes, and caught the turtles he would later give to Alonso.

In those quiet hours just this side of daybreak, the morning light seemed awash with memories. As they worked baiting hooks, their hands slick with juices from the gizzards, Mike looked up at the fading sunrise, a somber expression on his face. "In my day, we would be able to catch sixty or seventy turtles with one line like this," he said. "Now I'm lucky if we catch four. Nobody was thinking about the future."

Jeff hadn't expected Mike to say something like that. It floored him. Mike knew that he was a plainclothes officer, vaguely understood his purpose there. Still, he kept up a neutral friendliness toward Jeff that acted like a wall. He hadn't trusted Jeff. Their shared moment over the quiet morning water had broken that. Mike's words had given Jeff a glimpse into the fisherman's hidden depths. Mike regretted so much. Most of all, it seemed, he regretted the greed he'd been caught up in. It had been so ubiquitous, they hadn't recognized it for what it was.

Usually talkative, Jeff just nodded and listened. The truth was that somehow he'd seen this epiphany through Mike's eyes. He already knew humans exploited nature to its breaking point. Understanding that was his job. But to have this fisherman suddenly give voice to his part in the careless destruction of his own livelihood and home opened Jeff's eyes again and reminded him of his purpose, of why he was wading into the unknown, bearing all that secrecy, to go undercover in the first place: to protect the wild from threats most people would never see.

Each morning before he made a delivery, Jeff would go through his routine, practicing what he would say in the mirror. He couldn't seem like he knew too much. In this scenario, he was just some fella who cut grass for a living, but that didn't mean he didn't have an inner life. If Jeff the landscaper didn't know too much, perhaps he wanted to know more. Jeff mused that his character was a curious fellow, asking questions not to lead to any particular place, but because he had recently realized that he had lived too long without a sense of wonder, and now he wanted answers to all of life's small mysteries. He just wanted to know how things ticked. Jeff made the last delivery to Alonso alone. Before he set off, he situated the hidden camera in the back of his truck so it would pick up everything Alonso said as they unloaded. He drove around back, and Alonso sauntered out of his screen door to meet him. The dogs bayed.

The landscapers hadn't seen as many of the turtles this month. That was Jeff's excuse for his delivery being smaller.

"Can you use this?" he said, opening a burlap sack to show Alonso the turtle. It was about the size of a dinner plate, a small one at that.

"I'd have to ask him," Alonso said, meaning his buyer, the one with the blue van from the pictures Jeff had seen before. Other agents could track that van to see where it was going. Jeff needed to gather intel that would keep them on its trail.

Don't be too forward, he thought. You had to meander toward your questioning, just chewing the fat like a regular person. He mentioned the cold front they'd been having. "Maybe that's why there are so few," Jeff said. "I think it's because they like hot weather, right?" It was right. Jeff knew that. But his character shouldn't, he scolded himself, watching nervously for a reaction from Alonso. Knowing too much might arouse suspicion.

"Yeah, they're more active in the sun," said Alonso.

They kept talking casually while they unpacked the turtles, carefully removing them from their sacks. Once they had freed a turtle from its pouch, Alonso placed it in a laundry basket that hung from a nearby tree limb by a spring scale. All the while, his dogs created a ruckus, barking and shouting and whining. Alonso stuck two fingers into his mouth and let out a loud whistle. "Quit!" he yelled at the dogs, and their chaos momentarily dwindled. He called out to his kids in softer-toned Spanish, and Jeff switched the conversation to hog hunting, slowly meandering his way toward the information he wanted to know. He was a hunter himself. He knew how to walk softly in the forest. This was much the same but with words.

While they chatted, Jeff opened a cooler on his truck bed and offered Alonso a beer. He took one himself, popped the cap, and put it to his lips as if taking a swig. The beer only touched his lips and the tip of his tongue. This was another set piece, another layer of disguise to make him seem believable. Even though Alonso seemed like a friendly enough guy, Jeff needed to stay sharp just in case all these layers of cover fell away and he found himself exposed. If he got "burned," as Lieutenant Wilson said, he would blow this case and lose the chance at the bigger one. Getting burned would put his life in danger, too. Alonso *probably* wouldn't pull a gun on him. Probably, not definitely. If he did, he wouldn't be the first.

Alonso called out to his wife inside and asked for a saltshaker. She brought one out to him. "I like salt with my beer," he said.

Weird, Jeff thought. So weird that it signaled Alonso had grown comfortable enough for Jeff to push forward.

"I still have a whole 'nother line of these fellas to take in," Jeff lied, acting like he'd been catching the turtles on his own instead of enlisting help.

Alonso seemed alarmed that Jeff had left turtles out on a line. It had rained earlier that day, and Alonso said hurriedly that they could have drowned. Money down the drain. Then he slowed down. "As long as they can surface for air, they should be fine."

Jeff stopped himself from clarifying the lie. He'd just been making chitchat. No point in digging himself in further. Jeff let the conversation settle, and let his nerves settle, too, and then he asked Alonso how much he was going to pay for this batch of turtles.

"I can't give you nothing right now, 'cause I don't know what he's gonna give me," Alonso said, referring to his buyer again. "Or if he'll take 'em. Some of 'em are real small."

They were edging close to something—information Jeff could use. He couldn't push too hard on this. Alonso was perceptive. But if he knew where the turtles were going—and what the buyers were doing with them—that was the difference between a deliberate crime and an accidental one, *and* he had the information Jeff needed.

"Oh, they like the big ones?" Jeff asked. "I figured they'd clean it and eat it. You know, get the meat off."

"I'll try to get him here so he can look at 'em and tell me." Alonso was starting to sound annoyed, like he didn't give a damn what they did with it as long as they paid him.

"Well, what are they doing with it, just selling it at a market?" Jeff asked. He was pushing it, but they were right there. If only he could push a little harder without getting caught, Alonso might tell him something.

"They pick 'em up and take 'em. I don't know," Alonso said sharply. "I don't know more than I want to know. The less you know, the better."

Jeff felt like he was running up close to the edge. One more push. "What are you sayin'?" Jeff asked, a conspiratorial note to his voice. He leaned in slightly. "I better not get caught with these? This illegal or something?"

Alonso paused for a moment. Sometimes people say more with their silences than they do with their words.

"I don't know," Alonso said. He sounded grim, as if he had once been inquisitive, too, and he had asked too many of the right questions, and they had led him down a rabbit hole to a place that he couldn't unsee.

The other side of the investigation saw that place. At 3 AM, another set of officers placed a tracker in with the turtles. They followed the turtles on their long journey, one set of officers passing the surveillance detail off to the next, out into the Everglades to a farm where the smugglers collected and fattened up their catch. Another tracking device and a fresh set of officers tailed the shipment of turtles up from Florida all the way to New York State, where a crew smuggled them hidden in false bottoms of shipments leaving the port. Eventually, they sold for $65 per pound, up from the $0.75 to $1 per pound that the buyer was paying the poachers.

Other FWC officers made the arrests for that takedown. Alonso only ended up paying fines. His Chinese buyers, on the other hand, had bigger trouble to contend with. By then, Jeff had completely faded out of his uniform, and putting it back on would risk blowing his cover. Nearly three months had passed, and the agency still hadn't told Jeff what the big undercover operation would be. He had put complete faith in Lieutenant Wilson. Yet he still wondered how much the two jobs had in common.

The turtle operation gave him some clues, though. For one, it had much higher stakes than was first apparent, and Jeff guessed that what lay ahead did, too, if not more so. While softshell turtles aren't endangered, their loss would cause a domino effect through the food web, affecting organisms both lower and higher, including plants and their habitat itself. Rather than waiting for such horrific effects to take place, FWC hoped to avert them entirely by rooting out the problem of softshell turtle poaching before it took hold. To Jeff, this was the best way to do conservation: Solve problems before they get out of control. And, you know, solve problems while it's still within the budget to do so. Poaching, and the trafficking of animals, had to be the subject of this upcoming case; he was sure of it. Hopefully, Jeff was getting there before the situation had gotten out of hand.

High-profile poaching cases, of endangered species especially, have come to our attention because they are already out of control. The stakes are dire. The combatants are armed. Violence escalates. Poachers kill game wardens. Game wardens kill poachers. Like cutting the head off the Hydra of Homeric myth, another poacher comes back in his place, this time more heavily armed. The cycle goes on, escalating into the sky, and no one is winning. Taking the long view, in protecting the smallest and most unlikely creatures, FWC was preventing such an eventuality from ever happening. As Jeff has said, if you have to pull your weapon, you've already lost.

The case that awaited Jeff existed a few steps further down the line from the turtles toward that danger. The animal in question was worth more, in the monetary scheme of things, at least. He would find that the animal itself was more dangerous, too. And closer to being in danger. It had once nearly gone extinct, and in the wake of its near disappearance, changes rippled through the swamp. Saving this animal was saving the swamp itself, and with the swamp, that fertile and maligned paradise of nature's wild splendor, humanity's hopes to bring our world back from the brink of disaster. That animal, of course, was the American alligator. The risks Jeff would take to save it would defy his worldview and change his life. He would soon find that even he did not truly know the swamp.

A few days after the takedown of the turtle poachers, Jeff received a set of keys and an address. The agency instructed him to report there immediately. That was where his real undercover mission would begin.

4

THIS IS GATOR COUNTRY

Driving down toward the Everglades, I soon passed from the thick of river country into an unlimited landscape of marsh grass and sabal palms, and when the trees finally parted, glades seemed to stretch on in all directions. My GPS location dot had gotten stuck in place several miles back. Good thing it was a clear day so I could navigate by the angle of the sun. Not that I really needed to in a place where I could see everything for miles and all the roads were straight; but people get lost there nonetheless. The deeper I drove, the more my cell signal dwindled, and soon I was out of contact with the rest of the world, with no one to answer to except the wilderness, no source of help except myself.

I was driving down there to pursue the legend of Peg Brown, the infamous poacher who had become an Everglades folk hero, partially due to the sheer number of gators he'd allegedly killed, which reached into mythic proportions, and partially due to the storytelling itself, which had elevated him from mere mortal into the rarified ranks of legends. I wanted to understand the man behind that legend, who he really was and what that said about the glades. Peg himself had died before I was born, but he'd left behind numerous kin. I was about to meet up with some of them for the first time. First, I had to get there. Not such a daring feat, normally, but my car had one wheel in the junkyard and was quickly becoming what my father would have called a Willit, as in, *Will it start?*

My dad and his jokes and stories were on my mind a lot, so much so that they had become a part of me. He was the one who taught me how to tell a story. That journey started on my grandmother's dock on the St. Johns River, an anomaly itself as, unlike most rivers, it flows north like the Nile. The kids would sit on the planks at the feet of the grown-ups and listen to them tell stories about the way things used to be. They did not see the past through a rosy sheen as it seems many people do. No, these were stories of hard times, always, of felling palm trees down by the bay for swamp cabbage, of my great-grandfather poling down the creek in his skiff on the hunt for whatever might feed them, of wading out into the river to cast a net for shrimp, of baking biscuits and handing them out hot in handkerchiefs to the migrants who rode the rails and hopped off at their little town because that place was as good as any. Each story had a moral. Many of them were the same: You are never too poor to help your fellow man. Keep yourself honest, even when you think no one is watching. Grit and storytelling are the keys to survival, and when those fail, the swamp will provide.

As I got older, I started telling stories myself, and when I was fifteen, I decided I wanted to be a writer, a declaration that many families meet with scorn. I grew up in a house full of books, in a culture immersed in stories. It's no surprise how my family answered.

"You can do anything you set your mind to, kiddo," my dad said.

"If you want to be good, you have to work hard," my grandmother said, her voice the rasp of a lifelong chain-smoker. "You're not good yet."

"Mom," my dad scolded.

"She'll never amount to anything if you coddle her like that," she said.

"No, she's right," I said. "I'm already working. I'll keep working."

"Good," she said, smiling.

She would die four years later of lung cancer, and my dad would die five years after that, colon cancer, leaving me with a house full of books, a head full of stories, and a broken heart. Every story worth telling orbits around a core of grief. Because what are stories if not memories made into myths? This one, I suppose, is no different. My dad and his storytelling shaped how I understand the world. The yarns he spun showed me that every person, from the most educated to the least, holds a story close to their heart that tells them, and others, who they are. Places, especially ones as alive as the Everglades, are the same. If you listen closely, you can hear them.

Above all, that was my mission there: to go into the Everglades and listen.

If there was an untold story at the heart of the Everglades, it was the story of Peg Brown. Nobody from outside seemed to have ever heard of him. Such local fame piqued my interest. There was something mysterious about it. Who was this Peg Brown person, really? And why had his legend lived on for so long unnoticed by the outside world? I believed that if I could find the truth behind the tall tales, it would illuminate the Everglades for me and would help me understand the underworld Jeff took on as he disguised himself as a poacher. So far, I had only gotten small tastes of tales secondhand.

One that stuck with me had a pang of familiarity. It was something I could imagine my family doing. When Everglades National Park came in, the rangers hired locals to help them map and memorize the area. One of these locals was Clarence Brown, a fishing guide whom everyone except the rangers knew as Peg. He arrived on the rangers' dock with the rest of that motley guide crew, including his ever-talkative brother Loren "Totch" Brown. When the ranger made note of their names, he asked, "Y'all related to this Peg Brown I keep hearing about?" Peg had only recently returned from the war, but already his reputation preceded him.

"Peg?" Totch said. "Never heard of him. What kind of name is that?"

"Beats me," said the ranger. "You keep an eye out for him. He's been up to no good."

"Doing what?" Totch said with a straight face.

"We've had reports he's poaching alligators out in the park," the ranger answered.

"Oh no, we can't have that," Totch said. He looked at his brother, whose smile betrayed nothing. "We'll keep our eyes peeled, won't we, Clarence?"

"Of course we will, Loren. Like it's our job."

Still, they set about showing the rangers around. Each took one or two out on his flat-bottomed skiff, a small boat that they called a pitpan in those parts. They wove through cuts between the islands and shady hammocks in the sloughs, telling the names of those places and their stories, too. They made sure that the rangers knew the shallows where their boats might run aground, the places where these outsiders could get stuck or hurt, because they didn't want that. Even if the Browns saw the rangers as their adversaries, they knew full well that if these fellows got lost, they'd be the ones to run in and find them: Nobody gained if these dopes died in the glades. Still, the tales they wove on their way made all those islands and marshes seem properly dangerous. It was best to scare the rangers and keep them in their little huts, safe and out of the way.

If that failed, there was always misdirection. Before they had met on the dock, the guides had convened at a bar and laid out all the places that—as far as the park service was concerned—would not exist. The trees where Peg strung up his hammock at night vanished. The lakes where the most gators gathered were gone. For every main waterway, a separate and invisible cut zagged through the vegetation, a ready getaway for a poacher who needed to disappear.

Only a few nights after the tour of the swamp, the rangers put Peg to the test. They bore down on Peg, the might of their motor against his. When he glanced over his shoulder, he had to squint against their spotlight. He could have shot it out, of course. But what was the point in that? It would scare those goons and leave them stranded in the dark. Or maybe it would make them want to shoot back. Who knew? Not everyone had had their fill of that in the war. No, he left his rifle under the seat and turned his rudder for a bend between the islands. He gunned the motor, the nose of his boat lifting over the water, skipping like a stone the faster he flew. With one hand, he extinguished his lantern. With the other, he cut the power to his engine. Silently, he glided toward the shore and between the trees into a creek, one not on the rangers' maps. He slowed among the cypress knees. Just beyond that stand of trees, the rangers' engine grew louder as they approached. Their spotlight swiveled in Peg's direction. Peg lay down in his boat. The light passed over him. He watched it make the cypress shadows dance.

"Are you sure he came this way?" one ranger called.

"I guess not," said the other. "Maybe he took the other fork. Let's double back."

Peg waited for their engine to leave earshot, and then he waited longer, counting the stars that winked through gaps in the canopy. The rangers might have been making a play to lure him out. They weren't that smart, but he had to be sure. When the only noises came from the mouths of frogs and owls, he rose and poled his boat in silence toward the hunt.

Did it all really happen that way? I don't know. Through my interviews, I heard several variations of the story, each subtly different from the last, except the most harrowing parts. Those always remained the same. The legend of Peg Brown seemed to reside somewhere in that murky space between folktale and history. But where did one end and the other begin? Now I was going to where his stories allegedly took place so I could disentangle the facts from the fantasy, and through both sides, the storytellers and the story, the truth and the myth, come to understand the heart of the Everglades.

Alongside the highway where I drove, a creek writhed, the blue-black reflection of that limitless sky practically tying itself in knots within the canebrake. A little powerboat zipped along with it, to and fro, each angle sending a cascade from its propeller. I passed a tackle shack, a concrete-block building painted a utilitarian white. Its sign touted both lunch plates and live bait, a Florida special. It sounds like a bad idea, buying lunch at the same place where you get bait. But honestly, the best food in Florida is at the dives, your greasy griddles, *lechoneras*, truck stops, and tackle shacks. I smiled as I passed the sign. Even if I was out of cell service, I was very much still connected to the rest of the world, the real world. The deeper I went into the glades, the more the haves and the have-nots stood in contrast. Beefy 4x4 pickups, gleaming with chrome, hauled pricey motorboats. Others carefully dipped theirs into the river down at the ramps. I felt a little jealous of them as I whizzed by in my Honda Civic. But I wasn't venturing down into the glades to vacation.

I was there on a mission. I also wanted to really get to know the Everglades and its people. I already knew quite a bit, but I had to make sure that didn't stifle my curiosity and prevent me from learning. Instead, it had to be a starting point. I was tired of reading stories that treated the glades, and all of Florida, really, as a wild and wacky backdrop where characters and tall tales abounded, where "normal" folks vacationed but where real people didn't live. While some folks treated the glades as their playground, thousands of others made their lives in little hamlets, some the poorest places in the country, inundated with smoke from sugarcane burning or toxins from algal blooms, and try as they might to fight it, they found too frequently that other people's money always shouted louder.

That was the story all across gator country, that large swath of the Deep South stretching from Florida Bay at the outflow of the Everglades, up the entire state of Florida, along the Low Country wetlands of Georgia and the Carolinas to touch Virginia; and to the west, from the Florida panhandle, across Alabama, Mississippi and its river delta, Louisiana, and the Gulf Coast of Texas down toward the Mexican lagoons. It is roughly analogous to the biodiversity hot spot that is the North American Coastal Plain and a nearly perfect overlay of the impoverished Deep South. This is the kingdom of the American alligator, where marshes, swamps, and bayous harbor hundreds of endemic species of flora and fauna, many of which occur nowhere else in the world. Over the centuries, gator country has drawn the roughest of settlers. Before the invention of air-conditioning, only the hardiest survived there, and only the most stubborn bothered.

Before the railroads came, each small town was like an island in a sea of wilderness. Venture past the tree line, and you were—metaphorically, and quite literally—on your own. Since then, more and more people came to live against the land instead of with it, creating an adversary of gator country itself. Destroyed and maligned, the swamp has fought back. This wild country itself is as stubborn as the American alligator.

As I drove, the levees around Lake Okeechobee rose above the grasslands and the narrowing highway in the distance. Up ahead, the Caloosahatchee River met the lake. Folks from outside the state, and even from clear across the world, know about Lake O, because it's the largest landlocked body of water in Florida, so big that it showed up on early satellite photography. These days, satellites are recording something there other than wonder. The green plague on the lake, as it's called, is a toxic algal bloom, thick with cyanobacteria that contain the neurotoxin BMAA. That's beta-Methylamino-L-alanine, exposure to which has been linked to neurodegenerative disorders such as Alzheimer's, Parkinson's, and amyotrophic lateral sclerosis, more commonly known as Lou Gehrig's disease. Research on the link is ongoing but strong.

Bodies of water are never closed systems, even when they're technically landlocked. This is especially true of Lake Okeechobee. When colonists first arrived in South Florida, the flow of the Everglades covered nearly half the state, with the headwaters springing from Shingle Creek, a small waterway about ten miles east of Disney World, and about two hundred miles north of the uppermost boundary of Everglades National Park. Besides the theme parks, in that area, you'll find the sprawl of suburbia, and within every decorative retention pond, as if by law, there is at least one alligator. Leave the Orlando sprawl in any direction and you'll quickly find yourself in river country, the alternating patches of pasture, of cows languidly chomping grass under a hill's sentinel tree, of sandhill cranes; of creeks and pine scrub, of red-bellied woodpeckers ra-ta-tatting out the forest rhythm through the flaking bark of a longleaf pine, of scrub-jays who quirk their heads at the hikers who've ventured onto their dune island that has risen above the savanna—this, too, is gator country.

Going east from the headwaters, you'll find thick oak groves and cypress standing heavy with Spanish moss. A single fanboat might buzz by. Along the banks of the Halifax River, shrimp boats float past paddle wheels and hurricane-weathered docks slump into the sallow estuary over the oyster beds, one flood away from driftwood. Dolphins play in the wake and manatees drift like weightless stones just below the surface, bronzed in rippled light by the brackish water.

South along the coast, the Indian River Lagoon system stretches behind barrier islands. The lagoon once flourished, but now abuse of the state's water—especially the dumping of pollutants, such as phosphate runoff from agriculture—has caused other toxic algal blooms, which in turn spur die-offs in the seagrass beds, leaving gentle manatees with nothing to eat and causing them to die by the hundreds. Across the river, past arching water oaks and a thicket of sea grapes, white sand beaches stretch north and south, so far in each direction that they disappear into the distance.

Inland once again, in a bog, the many-colored heads of rare carnivorous flowers wait arrayed in sticky spindles or heavy cups, shooting up among the reeds and the unctuous muck. Sundews open up like land-bound anemones, each stalk capped with a pearl of mucilage like a dewdrop in the morning, a beautiful and deadly trap to lure its prey. Butterworts hang their hooded purple heads, and bladderworts peek above the water's surface like daffodils with a dark secret. The air hangs heavy with petrichor from the sweet, wet decomposition that keeps the understory alive. Within the bog itself, the muck scarcely remembers that, when dinosaurs walked the Earth, it was once plant matter. Its constituent parts have congealed beyond recognition, becoming something new, a fertile mire that is in turn both disgusting and wonderful. Beneath this muck lies concealed the truth about Florida's history. Researchers at the Windover Archaeological Site near Titusville, Florida, have uncovered the remains of 168 people who lived in the area during the Stone Age. Even though carbon dating estimates indicate the "bog bodies" could be as much as eight thousand years old, the unique composition of the bog's muck has kept them remarkably whole. And who knows what else lurks beneath that primordial ooze.

Death and life are the same in the swamp. After the spark leaves, life goes on, becoming muck that scintillates with microscopic organisms, the muck itself a living thing that continues, not by volition but by perpetual motion, forever keeping itself alive with itself, a snake eating its tail. Outsiders only see the death, the decay, the unruly rawness of this wild country, without seeing the beauty in it, much to our harm and the detriment of this world.

For millennia, the Everglades dominated the Floridian peninsula. Back in the early 1800s, when that wild country only seemed to call out to the most rugged, the most desperate, and those wanting to disappear—and of course, those who were already there—the Everglades began at the headwaters, flowed south through unmarred grassland, and collected in Lake Okeechobee before proceeding down through swamp, then sawgrass prairie, over the porous limestone shelf that encases the Floridan aquifer, through a strip ridged like the whorl of a fingerprint with sloughs of clear, flowing water, ridges of sawgrass, and tree islands of cypress and palm rising above the rest. To the west, pine flatwoods and Big Cypress Swamp guarded the flow's border. The verdant scent of life rested amid the grass. Cypress stands and the Atlantic Coastal Ridge swooped down from the east to guide the flow south into marl marshes, then to squeeze into the Shark River Slough, which released through the Ten Thousand Islands, a variegated scatter of mangrove-clawed cays, of keyholes in that spiny vegetation, and of flows like Lostmans River, so named because it was easy to wind up there and disappear. That was outlaw country then. It may well still be, though to some extent defanged like the rest. Past that still, the Everglades breathed out into the gulf through Florida Bay. Tiny outposts dot the coast, some largely unchanged since settlers got there, others consumed by tourism as a lure is by a hungry goliath grouper. The last sentry between there and the map's edge is a flat bean of grass ringed with mangroves, called Little Rabbit Key. After that, it's open water.

Settlers already had the great body of the glades in their sights by the 1840s. Like much of North America that has been called frontier, no matter what was there before they arrived, settlers saw it as future farmland. They saw swampland as waste in both senses of the word: one as soil not put to the plough and therefore not living up to its full potential; in the other as an uninhabited wasteland, terra incognita. Beyond here be dragons. So, these settlers petitioned the federal government for help laying claim on this land against itself. This is man versus nature, only nature is not the assailant here. It seldom is.

However, the land got a reprieve as the Civil War came, and then it became embattled once more as the United States went to war against the Seminole Tribe for the third time that century. The US fought for this land that they sought to wring out like a sponge. Perhaps it wasn't so much for the land itself as it was to go against the Seminoles, who allied with that impassable landscape. Though the US forced many Seminoles out, several hundred remained in the Everglades, fortified and defended by the depths of Big Cypress Swamp, a land their assailants reviled and feared and did not understand. And so, to this day, some Seminoles call themselves, their tribe, the Unconquered; and others still consider themselves at war with the United States, because they never lost, and they never gave in.

By the time Theodore Roosevelt and his Rough Riders galloped through in 1898 on their way to Cuba to fight the Spanish-American War, those who wanted to carve some civilization into the glades had won out, and the Army Corps of Engineers was already laying out their plans to dynamite and divert the incredible River of Grass into oblivion. Over the next few decades, their canals and dikes manhandled the Everglades' southward flow into submission, diverting it east and west to create hundreds of thousands of acres of farmland, and intractable plots destined for waterlogged homesteads, some sold for as little as five bucks a pop—and worth even less.

The growing wealth of the roaring twenties gave rise to a new middle class to dupe. Con artists and pyramid schemers sold any land they could get their hands on, and some they could not. They peddled plots sight unseen to working-class folks looking for a slice of paradise, and they could have it, they found, if they were willing to suffer the mosquitoes and wade into their new property, which was inaccessible except by flat-bottomed boat. This, the Florida land boom, ushered more than a quarter of a million new residents to the state between 1920 and 1925. It also gave a foothold to Florida's time-honored tradition of the grift and the phrase, "And if you believe that, I've got some swampland in Florida to sell you."

One of the dupes who moved to this fractured paradise was landscape architect Ernest Coe, who witnessed the casual poaching of orchids and wildlife with horror. Even worse was the developers' quest to gobble up the land, regardless of the flora or fauna hidden in its foliage. Intent on saving the glades, Coe spearheaded the move to consolidate Everglades National Park. But by the time his dream came to fruition in 1947, the result paled in comparison with what he had envisioned.

It also gets more complicated than that. When the national park came in, they kicked longtime residents out, people whose families had been living there more than a century—or in the cases of many of the

Seminoles, since time immemorial. The story of the Everglades isn't just one of environmental strife and a need for redemption, it's one of class struggle, too: All environmental stories are if only you dig past the topsoil.

As I drove deep into the Everglades, the roadside came alive with the stories of Florida's past. Just as Jeff could name every creature and sprig that he saw, every part of the landscape launched a story into my head. I saw visions of war with Seminoles crouching in sawgrass, smugglers' planes going down in the mangroves, poachers stalking through the sloughs. The main one who came to mind, of course, was Peg Brown.

He was the logical continuation of the story of the Everglades, which went from paradise to paved, free and unbound to owned, partitioned, captive, and, most importantly, taken away from the people, both Native and settler, who had once called it home.

The federal government said the national park would protect the Everglades, but it did so at the expense of the people who lived there, so has it really protected the Everglades at all? Don't get me wrong. National parks are wonderful. I love visiting them just as much as anybody else. But many of them began as theft. If we want to do better by the wild and by our fellow human beings, we have to learn from these past mistakes, so it's far from environmentally sacrilegious to admit them. It's necessary. The advent of Everglades National Park pushed whole communities into crime. It pitted environmentalists against hunters, against the working-class people who lived there, the people who were already stewards of the environment in the first place. In removing the glades' keepers, and removing their livelihood as well, the park struck a false wedge between the gladesmen, the Natives, and the wild.

Some folks down in Chokoloskee said that the park came in and separated them from what was rightfully theirs and had been theirs for generations. The park represented the government, the powers that be, coming to oppress the little man. Of course, in their minds, anyone who broke the new laws was standing up for the downtrodden. That's where the stories of Peg Brown came in, and that's what I was hoping to understand in going to Chokoloskee, a place whose name had become nearly synonymous with poaching.

I had driven through the entirety of the glades to get there, passing from the marshes and savannas below the headwaters, through wide tracts of open space; past the phosphate mines of Bone Valley; past farms of every variety—orange groves, strawberry fields, cornfields, cow pastures; through little palm-studded towns with only one stoplight, where smoke from sugarcane burns drifted over makeshift migrant trailer-villes and the collective life expectancy had dipped below that of decades before; past rodeo arenas and fishing villages, abandoned gas stations, RV resorts spangled with a battalion of American flags whipping in the wake of passing cars; past Presbyterian churches with steeples reaching into that limitless blue sky; past Native American casinos; past luxury subdivisions with rolling golf course greens; then miles and miles of wide-open country, until the grasslands gave way to hardwood slough. Cypresses towered before me, casting cool shadows over the road. I had entered the Big Cypress Basin, a wetland watershed where the rare Florida panther still prowled, and ghost orchids bloomed in the night.

Past the crossroads at Alligator Alley, a stretch of highway that links Naples on the west coast and Fort Lauderdale in the east, obstructing the flow of the river of grass in the process, another fifteen miles of the most sparsely inhabited swampland put me in Carnestown, a mere intersection punctuated by a gas station and a monolithic radio tower. By then, the vegetation along the roadside had turned to mangroves, the once solid ground beneath to a clear stream, giving the feeling that the road itself was on an island hovering over the water. I rolled down my windows, turned off my air-conditioning. Truth be told, it wasn't working that well anyway. I had driven my little Civic to death, and it was on its last legs. The AC only puffed out hot air. I didn't have money to fix it. The breeze, though, would always be free.

The wind that whipped at my hair was alive with the verdant smell of flowing water. For those who have never been to the Everglades, it may be easy to imagine that wide expanse as a turgid mire of foul water, dangerous creatures, humidity, and mosquitoes. There are definitely mosquitoes, but the real glades are neither turgid nor foul. The Everglades is a living thing. It filters our drinking water. Before it sinks back into the aquifer, the water flows over the lime rock, watering the plants, carrying their pods and polyps; a symphony of microorganisms connects one living thing to another, and the result is what seems to me like the glades exhaling. Anyone who has ever been to the glades and stopped for a moment to just take in their surroundings and *breathe* knows that they are surrounded by a vibrant cosmos of life. The Everglades isn't a foul backwater or a hostile wasteland. Most of it isn't even a swamp. It is part of the lungs of our planet.

Although the Amazon rain forest garners more fanfare as an ecological sentry against climate change, wetlands such as Florida's coastal estuaries and swamps account for a larger percentage of the globe's carbon sink biomass. Wetlands cover nearly four million square miles of the Earth's surface, or about 7 percent of the world. By comparison, even the magnificent Amazon covers about 4 percent. Destruction of the Amazon is met with outrage. Destruction of swamps should be, too. The Everglades are one of the largest wetland ecosystems in the world. Deriding and destroying the glades puts us in a perilous position, one that threatens the water we drink and the air we breathe.

What do the gladesmen think of that? I wondered. As I drove on to Everglades City and then the long bridge over Chokoloskee Bay, I had a feeling I knew the answer.

They saw themselves as part of that maligned swamp, didn't they? Even as the outside world destroyed their home, pushed them out, told them who they were and who they should have been instead, and what they would have to do to save the glades—as if they hadn't been doing those things already—they rebelled against those powers, and they immortalized that rebellion in story.

I parked beside a long, rocky shore, the only car in the lot without a boat trailer. I turned around and took in the bay on every side. Whenever I'm in nature, I find myself consumed with such simple joy that sometimes I have to go where my whims take me. After that long drive down the state, the salt air beckoned me across the road to the sand, where I slipped out of my flip-flops and dipped my feet into the water.

Bright silvery leatherjackets, tiny herring, minnows, and little needle-nosed ballyhoo shimmered along the shoals. I wondered if I might chance a glimpse of an endangered smalltooth sawfish, a sharklike ray with a gnarly chain-saw-shaped snout. As few as two hundred of them may still exist in the wild, and most of those in Florida. If I was going to see one, it would be there. The sadness of that struck me. I hated the idea that I was excited to perhaps see an animal before it disappeared. I don't want to live in a world of disappearances when there is so much beauty to preserve.

I could admire the fish later. Right then, I had work to do. It was time to chase the legend of Peg Brown.

5

BECOMING BLACKLEDGE

We've given you a false identity, the letter said. The envelope, from FWC headquarters, had arrived in Jeff's mailbox like any other. Yet it contained an entire life, an alternate reality where a man who looked remarkably like him had lived out an existence totally unlike his own. The details were few—a name, identifying information, an address. He would have to come up with the rest. It was January already, a new year, and Lieutenant Wilson still hadn't given him the particulars on his undercover assignment. *Secrecy with this kind of thing is normal*, Jeff reassured himself again and again. He hadn't expected both his anxiety and excitement to build so much as the final revelation of those secrets loomed. Now Jeff would have to begin sloughing off all the things that made him who he was, a life and sense of self that he had built up for more than forty years, and transform himself into someone who, as a wildlife officer, would have been his antagonist. What kind of life had he lived? What was his story? What compelled him to get up every morning and do the things that he did? What did he hope for? What did he fear?

His name was Curtis Blackledge, and Jeff would have to search within himself to find him.

The physical transformation into Blackledge began while Jeff was still in uniform. Every morning after washing his face, he would look up into the mirror and see a different person. He found it somewhat unsettling. By January, his once neatly buzzed black hair had grown into a shag, his clean shave replaced by a disreputable-looking goatee. He dyed his salt-and-pepper hair an inky black. He looked fifteen years younger and a quarter as wise.

"I don't recognize you, man," he said to his reflection.

His mother seemed to feel the same way. As his undercover work took on a new life around him, the increasingly few times that he had seen his mother, he had watched a gradual expression of grief sweep across her face. She and Jeff had always been close. He would proudly call himself a mama's boy. Every time he got the chance, he would visit her and help her with anything she needed, building, fixing, you name it, or just spending time with her, soaking up the comfort of her constancy. She was a matriarch, a pillar, her love for Jeff and all of them as steadfast as the sun coaxing flowers into bloom.

Yet now that secrecy had consumed his life, he could no longer come to visit. She missed him when he was away and missed him in person, too. Despite her unchanging love, Jeff himself was changing before her eyes. He imagined the pain that caused her. He wanted to remedy it, to hug her, to reassure her that he was still Jeff inside, that the disrepair he'd fallen into was a costume. Watching the heartbreak in her eyes hurt him all the more, because he couldn't tell her a thing, not even that he was undercover. So every time he saw her, he looked forward to his mission's end. That mission had hardly started. He was still crafting the person who Blackledge would be. As he looked at himself in the mirror, thinking of the life he was leaving behind, he came upon the biggest difference between Blackledge and himself: his mother. Now Jeff had to imagine who he would have been without her.

He liked to think of himself as the kind of person who would always do the right thing, even when it hurt. Jeff worked hard. He came up from nothing, made a life for himself, found a slice of the American dream. Yet he made a conscious effort not to think less of the folks who couldn't do that. It went beyond putting himself into another person's shoes. He wanted to believe that everyone deserved a little grace, a second chance. The world didn't work so well without that.

But the things that had shaped Jeff's life hadn't happened to Blackledge. So it was hard to see Blackledge feeling the same way. Jeff imagined a person who had experienced some of the same hardships, perhaps, but he hadn't made a conscious effort to look beyond himself. He hadn't striven for the life Jeff had, either. He wasn't married, didn't have any kids. Perhaps he liked to party a little too much, Jeff considered. Maybe the pleasures of life had called to him more loudly than family and career. If it ever came up, Jeff decided he would say Blackledge had once been addicted to crack cocaine, but "I'm not about that life anymore." Other undercover officers had found themselves in situations where they'd been offered drugs. Jeff needed a way to turn them down without blowing his cover. Sobriety added a level of believability. The detail from his past made a story people would remember. In their minds, he would become a real person, a flawed one with a history. But maybe when it came down to it, Blackledge wanted to work hard. He'd make that clear, too. He wanted a chance at something bigger than himself. Didn't everyone?

After the first letter, a second letter had come, this one from the Department of Highway Safety and Motor Vehicles. It summoned Blackledge to a secure location to have his photograph taken for a new ID. He stood in front of the white backdrop, trying to think of how he should hold his face for the picture when the camera flashed. The print came back like the typical ID mug shot. The ID looked real. It *was* real. Only the man inside it was not. But back at home, he started receiving credit cards in Blackledge's name. Little by little, all the paper trail of a typical life built up around him.

Soon after that, Jeff received the envelope that contained the address and the keys. From then on, Lieutenant Wilson would start fading back, too. More and more of their contact would come in envelopes.

Following these latest instructions, the ones that appeared along with a key, Jeff drove out to Arcadia, a small frontier town about sixty miles due west of Lake Okeechobee and a little less than a hundred miles north of Everglades City. One hundred years ago, a lawlessness that rivaled the Wild West reigned there. Truly, the place had made the West look tame, because at least in the West, you could see where you were going. In that junglelike growth where river country oak hammocks and seedy uplands met the shadowland of the swamp, outlaws could disappear just past the tree line, and only those who knew the way—or those that brave or that foolish—could follow. The fact was that not much had changed since then.

That Arcadia came to be in a time of poets, Romantics and transcendentalists, who sought to leave the squalor of city life behind and immerse themselves in nature in search of the sublime. Some centuries before them, the pastoral poets used "Arcadia" to represent utopia, a place in perfect harmony with itself. In Greek mythology, that Arcadia was an untamed wilderness, an idyllic glade where the spirits of nature resided apart from the vulgar realities of civilization. Thus, the poets reimagined it, a world apart from their own, unspoiled by human endeavors. Their Arcadia remained wild and therefore pure, noble.

The original mythic Arcadia was a kind of paradise, and home to Pan, god of the wild. Pan was the archetypal trickster. Often depicted as a satyr playing a syrinx, better known as a pan flute, this Pan became associated with many things, among them mischief and chaos. At times he was playful. At others, frightening. The word *panic* is derived from his name, from the feeling he inspired in the nearby folk when he let out a terrible shout upon an unceremonious arousal from his afternoon nap.

This real place, Arcadia, Florida, had once been on the edge of Jeff's patrol territory. He had spent many days cruising along the Peace River in an airboat, on the lookout for poachers. He knew the place, knew it to be untamable, a last bastion of the ever-shrinking wild, and so, too, a mysterious borderland between the safe, known world and the edge of the map.

The address the agency had given him was no different. Kudzu hung like land-bound clouds over the fences. Grass sprang up like the place itself was a glade, though it seemed to have once been a lawn. A strange concrete dome rose among the blades like an immense tortoise. Farther back in the clearing there was a dilapidated mobile home. Beside it, a new-looking camper gleamed white in the fading daylight.

My God, Jeff thought. *Look at this dump. It's a damn jungle.*

Jeff had talked to other officers who had done short-term undercover work in the past. They told him how the agency had put them up in swanky apartments or rented fully stocked suburban houses with pools. Didn't look like that was going to happen for Jeff.

He entered the combo and unlocked the gate, then drove into the thick of it, following a barely recognizable path, two lines of grass-blades slicked over to form faint tire tracks. Inside, the trailer didn't look much better. The smell of mildew hung heavily on the air. Wallpaper peeled and shed like longleaf pine bark. Trash littered the floor, and craters remained where appliances had been ripped from walls.

Is this where I'm supposed to live? Jeff thought. He enjoyed camping and do-it-yourself projects, but this was ridiculous.

He found the camper in less of a state. It gave off the hopeful smell of new upholstery instead of moldering decrepitation. Still, as he poked around, he held on to a hope that he wouldn't have to live here, even temporarily. He thought of his wife and his dogs, his carefully kept lawn, the bougainvillea dripping from their pergola, hummingbirds dipping their beaks into the spring hibiscus, and he found a pang of regret. He had kept his life meticulously curated. *I'm leaving all of that for this?*

His adult son, Chris, had made a surprise visit before Jeff left. When Jeff told him about going undercover, Chris's face fell. He might as well have said, *I can't believe you're doing this, Dad.* This visit went on longer than he'd planned. Chris had inherited both worry and steadfastness from their family, so he made the decision to move home to be there for his mother while Jeff was not.

Despite the sometimes-treacherous adventures Jeff fought through to track down wildlife crime, his was a safe life, tame. More than that, his family—his wife and son, his mother, his siblings and their big, involved clan—they were everything to him. What did he want with going out with a bang?

You must've lost your damn mind, Jeff, he thought.

But there was no going back now. The reality of it settled heavily over him as he explored deeper into the property. It was more of the same, about nine or ten acres of increasingly dense growth. Jeff had seen enough. He hopped in his truck and headed for home, about an hour's drive north. On the way, he called Lieutenant Wilson.

"Did you go by your place?" Lieutenant Wilson asked.

"Yeah," Jeff said. "It's not exactly what I was expecting. What's this all about?"

"We've been having some issues with alligators," Lieutenant Wilson said. He went on to explain—finally—that reports of some nefarious dealings among alligator farmers had made their way to the agency.

Preliminary evidence pointed to laundering: Farmers were concealing the origin of their eggs, possibly to pass off illegally harvested eggs as ones obtained fairly. Lieutenant Wilson believed that rampant poaching was going on, particularly during nesting season, which was coming up. "We need you to pose as one of them." They wanted him to start an alligator farm, a real one, and stock it with full-size gators. Then he would infiltrate their numbers and find the poachers from the inside.

To make his task even more difficult, it came with a built-in ticking clock. As soon as Jeff witnessed a violation of the law, that clock would start counting down the days until the statute of limitations ran out, and the state could no longer prosecute. For felonies like alligator poaching, the state could take three years to gather a case. Longer than Jeff wanted to be out there, sure, but it gave him plenty of breathing room. Misdemeanors, on the other hand, such as the violation of alligator egg collection permits, had a statute of limitations of one measly year. If the state filed charges while Jeff was in the field, they risked blowing his cover—and the case as a whole. So as soon as Jeff saw an infraction, the case would go into overdrive, and he and his handlers would have to race to gather evidence and make arrests. If they waited too long, crimes against nature could go unpunished. Before they got to that, he had a whole lot to learn.

Up until then, Jeff had never even seen an alligator egg. Birds, deer, fish—those were more his purview. None of those were liable to eat you alive. *What have I done?* he thought. He wouldn't just have to transform himself in this thing. He wasn't just an actor. He would have to be a damn zookeeper. He would be a set designer and choreographer. The fucking sound technician. He was the whole damn cast and crew. He had to become a new person and then remake the world around him, a fiction real enough to pass for fact even under the scrutiny of those who knew better than him, out of thin air. Then, after all that, Jeff would have to track down as much evidence of alligator poaching as possible. Of course, witnessing the crime of poaching itself, especially if he could catch it on camera, was his prize. They needed enough evidence of each count of crime to prove wrongdoing in court. But evidence that pointed to a wider organized poaching network—that was the holy grail. He wasn't just watching and waiting in costume. He had to become a spy, to dig in places where he didn't belong. That was where the real danger waited, not within reptilian jaws, but among the swamp's most dangerous predators: men.

"We can't give you much money to do this, either," said Lieutenant Wilson. "We really can't give you anything at all. No one should be able to track your finances back to us, so you have to make it yourself."

Shit, Jeff thought.

Of course they would pay him. He'd get the same salary as he always did, akin to that of a public school teacher, in other words, a pittance. The agency had a small fund to get the farm started, too—with money from proceeds from the turtle operation and others like it—but after that, he was on his own. Like most state agencies, FWC lacked adequate funds to accomplish everything they needed to do. To bridge that gap, agents either did without necessities or got creative.

To make matters worse, Wilson explained that another agent had tried this scheme before him. He found the alligator underworld to be closed off and impossible to penetrate. Even the most upright farmers considered the intricacies of their practices to be trade secrets. In place of the usual southern hospitality, the farmers had met him with polite exclusion.

Beginning in 2013, FWC started getting intel that state-licensed alligator farms were paying poachers, laundering eggs, and possibly turning poacher themselves. Hundreds, even thousands, of gators were disappearing. A sizable chunk of the year's predicted hatchlings had vanished. If things got much worse, the species would be in jeopardy, and so would gator country. FWC tried to drum up a sting operation, but it quickly ran into a snag: The alligator farming culture in the state was so exclusive, a veritable good ol' boys' club, that the undercover officer couldn't gain entry. The operation's subsequent plans quickly went awry. Their agent came off as too straitlaced, suspiciously stiff. Tension spread among the farmers, who were already mistrustful of outsiders. They knew someone was poking around. Anyone FWC sent now had to be so seamlessly in character, so convincing, so flawless, that the farmers and the poachers working with them would never know they were a wildlife officer in disguise. He should be charismatic, a flexible changeling who could doff his outer officer and become the character. The agency had seen this in Jeff. What he saw in himself was a different matter.

What was more, that previous officer had blown his cover. Sick of camping out in the trailer, he joined a gym under his false identity so he could shower and work off some of the tension. Then he fell in love. And that, predictably, had been his downfall. Since all women need to have a bit of a sleuth in them, she suspected something was up. She dug a little and found out he wasn't who he said he was. Cover blown, the agency reassigned him.

So Jeff was going into this thing with the odds against him.

"This won't be easy," Lieutenant Wilson said. "But we have a good feeling about you. We chose you for a reason. Just don't go falling in love, okay?"

After saying goodbye to his wife for what felt like the last time for a long while, Jeff set out in his unmarked white pickup into the tangled morass of river country. As he drove out of the city, the concrete and the strip malls and the sea breeze and the swirl and glint of traffic in daybreak's farther edge receded into greenery and shadows. Vehicles peeled off as the highway narrowed from course to trickle. Then finally the long, straight track of the country road shrank into the distance to dissolve against some faraway swamp in a mirage of heat and light.

Jeff knew every back road and waterway in the area. But this time, it felt different to leave town and become submerged in the growth of the forest where the trees almost touched one another over the road and pattered the cracked pavement with remnants of sunlight. It felt brand-new because he was new. Jeff had left himself behind, and in his place, and through his eyes, Blackledge was seeing this world for the first time.

Before he donned that final mask and left, Jeff had visited with his family, a get-together, a family barbecue like any other, except at this one Jeff asked his nieces and his nephews to untag him in pictures on Facebook and not put up any more. Everyone asked questions: "What's up with you lately?" "What's going on?"

"It's for work," he would say, leaving them feeling curious or slighted, yet, after a while, they stopped asking questions. Meanwhile, they speculated among themselves. He would catch whispers of it. Was Jeff getting a divorce? Was he dying? What would make their ebullient Jeff become so taciturn and secretive?

Jeff understood what losing him must feel like, because the loss of them was starting to grind him down. Yet, unlike his family, he knew why he was coming apart. He reassured himself by imagining the day when he would tell them all the truth. He might gather them around at a cookout, teasing like he had a tall tale wound up just for them. *Remember when I was looking a little scruffy?* he might say. *Well, there's a story behind that. Let me tell you.*

In the meantime, he was still fading out. He deleted his profiles from everything, scrubbed the internet clean of himself, not leaving so much as a picture of his face in a crowd. Except for his wife's last name and his adult son, it was as though Jeff Babauta had never existed.

Unbeknownst to his family, new evidence of his life had sprouted in its place. Curtis Blackledge seemed to have always existed, at least according to digital evidence. He was now a real person with a family and friends and a life. There were the pictures to prove it. Facebook, an Instagram, a network of people who knew him. He had lived a more or less ordinary if not slightly disreputable life, and there it was on the internet for anyone who was curious to find it. He owned a condo in Ruskin, which he was trying to sell. He liked dogs, because who didn't? And, of course, he liked to have a drink or two down by the water, taking in the sunset, another escapist on permanent vacation in Florida. Now he was putting paradise to work.

Jeff set about creating an alligator farm out of nothing, Blackledge alongside him like Peter Pan's shadow, starting with a deeper inspection of the raw materials he had to work with. He circled the perimeter of the property, wading through the weeds. Beside the barn, the overgrowth hid a few ponds that Jeff suspected had once been used to farm tilapia. The air around them retained the funkiness of cheap aquaculture. On closer inspection, Jeff would find the fish still living there, and with them turtles, including some softshells. Only one of the ponds was fenced in, and near the entrance to the property, a concrete dome like a holey-roofed igloo hunkered, a chelonian boulder among the foxtails and horseweeds. Building and selling domes like that one was a business venture of the guy, an engineer and entrepreneur, who owned the property. He intended them as mini weather bunkers. The domes were so heavy that even a tornado couldn't rip them off the ground. And therein lay the problem. Made almost entirely of superthick concrete, the domes were a pain to move, and short of hiring cranes and backhoes, they were parked permanently wherever you put them. With his business a bust, the engineer rented out his property, but not without trying to sell Jeff on his business venture first.

The officer who had come before him, the one who had fallen in love, had managed to do a few things around the place, like putting up the fence and equipping the camper. It was a thirty-two-footer with a slide-out that made it bigger inside, but cramped and narrow nonetheless. Otherwise, the place was a shell, a canvas for Jeff's imagination to play. It needed a lot of work, and given his lack of a wealthy, deceased family member, that meant applying elbow grease.

He put in air-conditioning and lights. He fixed anything and everything that was broken. He ran all the electrical himself, mowed down the weeds, fenced in a pond, dusted, cleaned, and made the place not just look livable but like an actual business. He enjoyed working with his hands, but those tasks got lonely quickly. He started borrowing his dogs from home one at a time. If anyone asked—not that anyone else was there yet—Jeff would say he was dog-sitting. Sometimes Mack, his Goldador K-9, attended him, solemnly watching Jeff work or sniffing around, his tail up in a pert wag. Other times it was Ruger, his big, dopey yellow Lab, who would fetch anything he could pick up, even if it seemed too heavy. Then there was Jack, the aptly named Jack Russell, bounding around with his limitless energy, chasing dragonflies, all bark and vigor without a care. He never took Bali, his German shepherd. That breed, he thought, looked too much like a K-9.

Each of the dogs was a piece of home. They eased his loneliness somewhat, though the loss of his usual routines, especially having to sit and wait instead of going out and sleuthing for crimes, made him feel restless and edgy.

In those early days, Lieutenant Wilson allowed him to go home once a week. Spending so much time without his wife left Jeff feeling as if a piece of himself were missing. Just seeing her became a necessary respite. Though they helped his sanity, those returns were also necessary because he needed to file reports, and Lieutenant Wilson didn't allow him to keep his state computer or any personal effects that marked him as Jeff Babauta at the farm.

During that time, Jeff put the finishing touches on Blackledge, too.

Blackledge was what in his younger days in Colorado the locals would call a goat-roper, a rural character who held no allegiance with citified society, who took from the land when he could to make a scratch living. He was a redneck, but also something more, because wasn't everyone more than they appeared to be?

After thirty-something years of failing his folks, drinking and partying and getting into trouble—but not so much trouble that he'd ever crossed hairs with the law—and just getting by on the scarce paycheck from week to week, Blackledge had suddenly and unexpectedly come into some money, so much money that his benefactor, though dead, had believed it would do him more ill than good if the sum didn't come with stipulations. Blackledge had been raised by his aunt out west and then in South Florida, just like Jeff. (All good lies, Jeff knew, contained as much truth as possible. The less he had to fake, the better.) That aunt had taken over raising him from his parents in Saipan. They wanted him to grow up on the mainland where opportunities and jobs weren't quite so limited. He loved this aunt, though in his adolescence his youthful puckishness, which lasted well into his thirties, had brought her much disappointment and irritation. Jeff imagined she was the kind of lady, this auntie, who would scold as much as she would coddle, who would love people by cooking rich meals, who would say, "Everything we've done for you, all the sacrifices we've made, and this is what you turn out to be? Some layabout? Some good-for-nothing?" Sometimes *we* meant "your parents and I." Other times it referred to something bigger than them, a family on a grander scale of centuries of ancestors who had scraped and persevered just to amount to him. And yet, even though all he did was let her down, she still loved him with a fervor that was stronger than any disappointment could ever be.

Prior to his entrance onto the alligator farming scene, Blackledge's auntie had died, leaving him as the heir of a small fortune and a condo on the river. He was not the executor of her will. She didn't trust him that much, a reluctance Blackledge knew he'd earned. He didn't have a steady job. He hadn't settled down with a wife. There were no new little Blackledges on the way to disappoint the family. So it was not surprising that the executor merely told him about the money first instead of handing him a check. This inheritance would only be his when he met certain conditions. He had to show the executor what he would do with the money, and it had to be something worthwhile. No buying yachts or blowing it all on a raucous party in Key West so good that no one in attendance would be able to remember. No, no. To get this money, Blackledge had to submit a business plan. And he thought: *Why not start an alligator farm?* It was just outlandish enough to be worth his while—Blackledge balked at the ordinary, despite having lived such an ordinary life of boozing and malaise up until that point—and it fulfilled the will's demands. The executor left the money with a trustee. Blackledge was now a trust-fund brat, receiving a small sum each month. With it, Blackledge got started.

He had imagined farming alligators would make for a humorous backdrop, and it would give him room and funds enough to live it up. Blackledge quickly found he had been wrong in both regards. Farming alligators was more work than he ever imagined, and not knowing the business, he hardly made ends meet.

Did Jeff need such a rich backstory? He certainly thought so. He wanted to be prepared for any question. In his ideal operation, he would never be caught off guard. He wouldn't learn until later that the average undercover officer never went to such lengths. Jeff didn't see himself as average, so he never paid those kinds of people any mind.

However, Jeff's real life quickly overlapped with Blackledge as he ran into the same difficulties: The farm was eating through cash, and fast, and without a dead auntie and a trust fund, he had to create a working alligator farm from essentially nothing. It really had to make money. He thought about how to do that as he continued cobbling the place together.

At the edges of the ponds, he hammered poles into the earth and topped them with yellow caution signs. NOTICE, they said. KEEP YOUR DISTANCE. This was written around the silhouette of an openmouthed gator. This detail seemed right. *What else?* he thought. He practiced thinking like Blackledge with Jeff as his shadow. Jeff knew too much, but Blackledge knew too little. The wrong missing knowledge here could lose you a hand—or worse. Not that there were alligators in the ponds yet, as far as Jeff knew. Not ones he had put there anyway, but you could never be too sure. More often than not, the odds were in your favor to spot an alligator in any Florida watering hole larger than a puddle.

Before he brought in alligators, the place needed a name. After that, everything would come together. The previous undercover agent had dubbed it Joe's Alligator Farm. That sounded fake to Jeff. And certainly not something Blackledge would use.

As Jeff mowed, he played with word associations in his head, all sorts of permutations on alligators and swamps. Then it occurred to him to hide some sort of Easter egg, give the place a name that had an overt meaning then another covert one, a sort of inside joke with himself, a clue in plain sight that the farm wasn't what it seemed. Florida's tourism board used the slogan "Sunshine State" to make it sound inviting, like a land of endless summer. Sunshine Alligator Farm had a ring to it. The name also held a double meaning for Jeff. He would be investigating wrongdoing, finding poachers and bringing their deeds into the sunlight. Sunshine reminded Jeff of his background motivation, one reason among many to remain meticulous and upright: Florida's Sunshine Laws. Like the national Freedom of Information Act, the Sunshine Laws mandate that state agencies provide information, such as the schedules of political officials or emails made from government accounts, to the public on request. More often than not, "the public" here isn't the average state resident. The people who make Sunshine Law requests are typically lawyers, private investigators, and, of course, journalists like me. Jeff knew it was possible that a journalist might snoop through his files someday, picking over his every action and airing them out to be scrutinized by the jury of public opinion. Everything he did had to be clean, his every move logged.

Keeping honest wasn't so hard for Jeff, though. It was already how he tried to live his life. Don't do anything you wouldn't be proud of. It doesn't matter if no one else sees what you've done. You see it. Who you are in the dark is just who you are. Live like everything is out there in the sunshine.

So Sunshine Alligator Farm would be the name. Jeff made a logo to match, a green alligator opening his mouth as if to bite the word SUNSHINE above his head.

Jeff applied for permits and had received a preliminary go-ahead from the state to start his business. He jumped in. This new venture started to feel real and exciting. It *was* real. It had to be, not just because that would be more convincing, but because there would be real animals involved, real people—all with their own lives and needs.

For now, though, he was just making the set. He cleaned out the old barn, removing the fish food from the previous inhabitants, setting up tables and workstations, wiring up the lights. Back when he was first starting his career with FWC, then called the Florida Game and Freshwater Fish Commission, Jeff had been a fisheries technician. That involved a lot of wading in the muck, collecting water samples, and counting fish to understand how their populations were changing over time. It also meant he knew how to set up and run an aquaculture lab, and he assumed that's what this would be—at least a makeshift one. Although Jeff had hog-tied more than a few nuisance alligators, he had never so much as seen an alligator egg. Luckily, it made more sense for Blackledge not to know what he was doing. Still, that grated on Jeff. He knew himself as the type of guy who checked off every box, who liked to do things right, not a perfectionist necessarily, as nothing in life could ever be perfect. At the very least he was a fastidious realist.

With the barn as done as it would be right now—with metal and pegboard walls and a shined concrete floor, another sign on the outside wall, and secret hiding places for his wallet and phone—Jeff drove to the gate to add some final touches. He installed a new mailbox outside on the fence, and he fastened warning signs to the metal gate: POSTED NO TRESPASSING and BEWARE OF THE DOG.

He leaned a ladder against the arch that framed the entrance, two vertical wooden beams like telephone poles holding a third over the road about fifteen feet in the air. Jeff stamped the ladder's feet into the sand and climbed up, acutely aware that he was doing this—not just hanging the sign but the undercover operation itself—alone. If he fell, if he failed, there would be no one to catch him. The agency would help as they could, but another officer had already flunked out of this gig. There would be no second chances.

He lashed two loops of chain to the crossbeam about a yard apart and climbed down. The ladder creaked with each step. In the lonesomeness, Jeff supposed, this job was like any other he'd been assigned. It recalled solitary nights in the deep woods as a game warden, his only company his dog, the intermittent squawk of his CB radio, and the chorus of frogs that filled up the cool emptiness of the night air. Only now that lonesomeness bled over into the next day and the next, and it left him counting down the days until he could steal away home, kiss his wife, and marinate in the simple, domestic pleasure of being in the easy presence of someone he loved.

Jeff threw a cable over the crossbeam, then connected one end to the trailer hitch of his truck. He looped it around a cable already connected at two points of the sign to make a yoke. The sign sat on the ground face down.

Jeff got behind the wheel, turned the ignition, and idled forward. He craned his head back and watched the sign rise, proclaiming the name of the farm to whoever drove by. When it was high enough, he got out, climbed back up, and secured the chains to the sign. He leaned back and watched it shift in the wind. The chains held.

Back on the ground, Jeff stood at his tailgate and surveyed what he'd done. The farm was finished. Now came the hard part.

6

ALLIGATOR MISSISSIPPIENSIS

The agency gave Jeff a few hundred bucks. With that, they expected him to stock the farm with a reasonable number of gators. It wasn't so different from how the school board gave his wife a minuscule yearly stipend and asked her to work miracles. If it weren't for ingenuity—and dipping into personal funds—not much would get done. The scenario wasn't foreign to Jeff. After growing up poor and then working for the state since his early twenties, Jeff knew how to stretch a dollar.

Knowing that the seed money would run out quickly, Jeff had to finagle a way to start producing revenue fast. He started calling local trappers, both with the state and from private enterprises, on the lookout for some big gators, some real showpiece beasts, so big, he imagined, that no one who saw them would ever doubt Sunshine Alligator Farm was anything but legitimate.

"Hey, this is Curtis Blackledge," he said, the name rolling off his tongue in an unhurried drawl with an easy ownership that no one could question. "I'm opening up a farm. Would you be interested in selling me any of the alligators that you catch?"

They would always say yes, almost without question. Such nonchalance pricked Jeff's investigative instinct, and he made a note to himself to follow these guys a little more closely.

The alligators they trapped had been deemed nuisance animals. They had shown up floating in backyard pools or had basked too long on the wrong golf course. Perhaps they had taken too long to stroll across an intersection that had been built on the mudflat where they'd hatched and grown, or maybe one too many toy poodles went missing near a suburban pond and the trappers chose the first alligator they saw as a convenient scapegoat. One fewer lizard in the neighborhood would keep the residents happy and quiet for a while whether or not he was the real culprit.

Jeff found it ironic that alligators of all animals—living dinosaurs that explorers once called dragons—had become labeled with such a prosaic word as *nuisance*. There once was a time when alligators were oneiric creatures, guardians of that chthonic threshold between the land of the living and the land of the dead. To some Indigenous tribes along the North Atlantic Coastal Plain, the alligator acted as a psychopomp, a spirit guide who protected the dead on their journey into the hereafter. They were syncretic cousins to the ferryman Charon on whose boat souls of the departed cross the River Styx. As part of the Green Corn Dance, a spiritual ritual of purification and thanksgiving each spring, Seminoles and Creeks sang the Alligator Song, invoking the power of this great protector. To these tribes and others like them, alligators were all things life and death and in between. In much the way the tribes of the western plains revered and made use of the bison, tribes of the Southeast ate alligator meat, used their bones, claws, teeth, and hides, and regarded them as so much more than beast.

It's no surprise then that European colonizers would come to view the alligator and its home, the swamp, as adversaries. Ever since Europeans ventured into those same swamps, they associated alligators with the untamable wild. This was not the unspoiled wilderness of the pastoral poet's Eden. Nor was it the transcendentalist's escape. This was no Arcadia. It was more akin to the panic of Pan, a miasmic Styx, a wasteland waiting to be drained, with all the chaos that entailed.

Spanish explorers didn't know what to make of alligators at first. As I've mentioned, alligators draw their name from the Spanish *el lagarto*, the lizard. The Spanish had read of—or perhaps even seen in person—the famous crocs of the River Nile, who had their own place in Egyptian history and myth. But despite the resemblance, alligators are not crocodiles. The two can be as different in stature as alligators and iguanas. Alligators differ most from crocodiles in their temperament. Medieval bestiaries described crocs as "a curse on four legs." Crocodiles are more volatile, more aggressive, more likely to attack, whereas the alligators the first Spanish explorers encountered were more likely to blink at them apathetically before slipping below the surface of their murky pool.

In the 1600s, both Spanish and Huguenot colonists, following the

Timucua Tribe's cue, began hunting and eating alligators. It's hard to imagine seeing a creature as both dragon and dinner, but in desperation, one is willing to eat just about anything, even seemingly mythical beasts.

By the 1700s, the alligator's aura had taken on a much more exotic hue. Naturalist William Bartram, in a fanciful depiction, likened them to living dragons, imbuing their descriptions with fury and smoke. Some of his contemporaries back in Europe criticized his travelogues as ridiculous and overwrought. His was no longer the time of dragons, but the age of humanism, the scientific process, investigation, and taxonomy. Alligators were curiosities, novelties unseen in Europe, yet understood enough that they had lost their magic. They were no longer the creatures they had been in medieval bestiaries. They were predator and scourge, then big-game trophies, stuffed and mounted as décor.

For Edwardian tourists, the hunting of these real-life dragons came into vogue as alligator-skin purses popped up in the hands of socialites as far away as New York City, London, and Paris. Alligator fever swept the globe. Seminoles, forced from their lands into the Everglades, set up roadside tourist attractions featuring live alligator wrestling shows, hoping to make a buck on the white man. Hunters came to shoot their dragons. Settlers carved up the swamp, and within half a century, the American alligator's numbers plummeted toward the brink of extinction.

By the 1960s, biologists doubted that the species would survive. It was about to go the way of the Carolina parakeet, a colorful bird that was abundant in the eastern US before hunting and habitat destruction drove it to extinction in 1904. Desperate to stop such a loss, environmentalists persuaded Congress to protect the Everglades with a series of parks and preserves. That alone seemed not to be enough. But after Congress created the Endangered Species Act of 1973, which barred the capture, killing, or trade of any plant or animal it listed as threatened or endangered, *Alligator mississippiensis* bounced back, almost miraculously so. Their numbers boomed, and in 1987, only fourteen years later, the US Fish and Wildlife Service (FWS) removed them from the endangered species list. About five million alligators call the southeastern United States home, according to estimates by the US Geological Survey. They are so plentiful now that the idea of an alligator being a nuisance—like a squirrel chewing through a telephone line—isn't so bizarre.

Even so, viewing a resource as bottomless is one of the easiest ways for it to not be so bottomless anymore. FWC feared that if poaching was left unchecked, alligator populations might decline once more. Though they seemed plentiful, there was no telling where that tipping point was between plenty and the type of sudden decline that happened seventy years ago.

This, the state's mentality of protection, did little good for the so-called nuisance alligators that Jeff was turning up, who found themselves with their mouths duct-taped shut and their feet trussed up against them in the back of a trapper's pickup truck.

Jeff cocked his head to look at the critter, inspecting the gator as if he knew what he was looking for. It stretched nearly the length of the truck bed, likely over seven feet, with scales like the tread of a semi-truck tire, that is, if a tire could gleam. Its eyes shone like dragonflies in amber. Still, it looked pitiful at this peculiar meeting at the back of a Walmart parking lot.

"Hundred bucks," the trapper said.

"I'll give you fifty."

"How about seventy-five?"

Fine, Jeff thought. At least this wasn't coming out of his own pocket. Rather, Lieutenant Wilson had dipped into a state bank account where revenue made by previous undercover operations accumulated, including money from his softshell turtles. The account wasn't bottomless. Jeff couldn't go hog wild. But it at least gave him cash to grease his introductions and let him start meeting folks at the fringes of the alligator industry.

After they shook hands, Jeff paid, and the trapper helped him transfer the gator to his truck, hoisting it between them, the trapper at the head and Jeff at the tail, and plopping it down on some towels. The whole enterprise felt surreal. This was a majestic creature, a dangerous wild predator, and here they were bartering and trading it like the catch of the day.

Despite the dodgy tinge of the whole affair—with the same feel and setting as many an exchange between poacher and buyer that Jeff had witnessed before—this transaction was completely legal. That was because the trapper was licensed and paid by the state. Jeff, too, or really Blackledge, was a legitimate alligator farmer, and had a license to buy and sell live mature alligators, hides and meat, hatchlings and eggs, as long as all those goods came from an aboveboard source. Dealers ran into trouble when they failed to examine the supply chain that carried these denizens of the swamp to their doors. Or perhaps it wasn't so much that they failed to as they casually looked the other way. Buyers couldn't be held liable for what they didn't know.

Jeff had come by this trapper's name the other way around, however. Lieutenant Wilson had given him a list of people—trappers, farmers, and the like—to investigate while sniffing out poachers. And just by this legal exchange, he couldn't be sure if the trapper was up to no good or not. After Jeff signed the check and placed it in the trapper's hand, he tried to dig a bit deeper.

Blackledge was of course new to the business, but he wanted to do right by his gators and learn as much as possible, especially about how they lived in the wild. That would help him build more comfortable habitats around his ponds, and, he hoped, that would make them more likely to breed.

"You're never gonna get them to breed," the trapper said. "It just don't happen. Most folks harvest their eggs."

Jeff nodded as if this was new information. "Still, I'd like to come out with you if that's all right."

The trapper shrugged and agreed.

Back at the farm, Jeff backed his truck up to the edge of his pond. He climbed into the bed and hoisted the gator up on his shoulders. He fireman-carried it down to the water's edge, where he lay it in the grass, cut the bindings around its legs, then quickly used his knife to slash through the tape that kept those powerful jaws closed, ripped it off like a bandage, and leapt out of the way.

After buying a dozen or so hatchlings from a farmer and adding those to the stock of mature gators—ten females and one bull, with keen hopes on them breeding if for no other reason than to prove the trapper wrong—Jeff had a farm that was beginning to look legitimate.

Solving one problem, however, caused another to pop up in its place. Now he had mouths to feed, and on a budget of exactly zero dollars. What Jeff lacked in cash, he made up for in charisma. He soon befriended the owner of a fish house over in Punta Gorda, a town at the inlet of the Peace River from the Gulf of Mexico, and he agreed to save all his scraps for Jeff, who could have them for free as long as he came to collect them.

It took half an hour for Jeff to reach the docks on the southern coast of Charlotte Harbor off the Gasparilla Sound. He parked next to the fish house and went around back, where he was met by the bloody reek of fish guts. It was coming from enormous five-gallon buckets of the stuff, and not a lid among them. A fish head stared at him glassy-eyed from the muck. *The things I do for my job*, Jeff thought. Grimacing, he lugged the buckets into the back of his truck and packed them in as tightly as he could before starting the foul trek back to Arcadia. No matter how gently he took the turns, carapaces and entrails went flying. There was no such thing as a free lunch.

In the summer months, Jeff tried to feed the alligators a few times per week. This started with the fish parts, but as he made more money—mostly from harvesting and selling alligator eggs—he began frequenting a local market in Arcadia to buy chicken quarters by the case. Each piece cost mere spare change. They felt so cheap they were practically free. He would go out with huge sacks of them, making a squeaking noise like an alligator call as he waited on the pond's bank. The gators were wary of him at first. They would float far out in the pond, watching him. It made sense. Most of them were less than six feet long and typically stood a foot or two off the ground at most, and Jeff, despite not being too great in stature, towered over them. All humans did. And if they'd encountered any humans in the wild, they knew that members of our species can be vicious predators. It was best to stay away.

But after a while, their wariness wore down to familiarity. On any given day, he would go down to the pond and begin his ritual of coaxing, calling out to them in what he hoped sounded like their mother tongue. For some, he would lay the chicken quarters out on the grass. For others, he'd gently place them into the beasts' small jaws. Some swam up calmly to grab their dinner. Others raced, jumping over one another, kicking and thrashing to get to the food, eager and hungry. But never quite so eager as Jeff would expect. He kept them well fed.

One by one they would approach. When he made a sudden movement, some would flinch away or drop their food. He would talk to them, but of course they didn't understand. Or did they? He'd pick up that dropped thigh, moving slowly, and hand it to the gator. *This human isn't so bad*, he wanted them to think.

One alligator lingered in the reeds, munching on her meal and watching him before swimming away. He wondered what she was thinking, and if it took the shape of recognizable thoughts at all.

The bull gator would always come last. He was the biggest, twelve feet or thereabouts, and he always came at his leisure, like a king. His subjects would wait for him. He glided up to the surface and toward Jeff. You had to be old to get that big, so it was possible that this bull gator had been around in the days when the species almost went extinct. Big alligators are survivors. Ornery, old, deserving of respect.

When Jeff saw the bull gator coming, he laid down the chicken parts and stepped back. "Here comes big boy," he said to himself, but it was almost like a heralding, as if a creature so immense and majestic needed to be announced when it arrived. It only felt right. Jeff watched from a safe distance, admiring the bull gator as it devoured its dinner.

Despite keeping them well fed, Jeff worried about his gators. It was his worst fear that one would get sick and die. Not only would that reflect poorly on him—always at the back of his mind was the idea that every move he made would leave a paper trail, and with that paper trail, people could criticize the agency—but having sick gators felt antithetical to his mission, namely helping to defend their species. That's why he got into this whole business in the first place, not just this job in particular but the whole shebang of wildlife protection. When it came to these gators on his farm in particular, he'd started growing attached.

He realized after days of feeding them that they were individuals. They had personalities. Some were skittish by default, others easygoing. His bull gator ruled. All of them would come when Jeff drew near even if he didn't have food. He wondered if they recognized him and had forged a bond or if they just saw him as the delivery guy.

As much as some people seemed to like alligators, Jeff found that most imagined them as dumb beasts with no inner lives. Perhaps it was because they cast such forbidding and alien figures, covered in scales instead of fur or feathers.

We grant such rich and intelligent lives to birds, who share a common lineage with alligators. Bowerbirds build complex collections, and Corvidae such as crows and Florida scrub-jays forge relationships with their favorite humans, sometimes bringing them shiny little gifts like thimbles and bottle caps. Birds remember us. Some, such as macaws, even learn and mimic human speech. Jeff's own parrot back home swore a blue streak, having picked up a few too many expletives from sitting next to his wife as she yelled at football games on TV. Other birds have recognized themselves in their reflections, leading scientists to postulate that they may possess self-awareness, consciousness. Why not alligators?

Neurological studies have shown that the brains of many non-human animals release the same neurochemicals as the ones we associate with strikingly human emotions and concepts: fear and sadness, of course, but also kinship, friendship, and love. This isn't just primates, either. Comparative neurological studies have found that even though the brains of animals traditionally associated with intelligence, such as the higher orders of primates and dolphins, are structurally more similar to those of humans, in terms of emotional resemblance it's dogs who are our closest kin. We are not anthropomorphizing our dogs when we say, for example, *He missed me*, as Jeff's did when he had to leave them behind to go undercover. They really did seem joyful when they came to visit the farm. Dogs can grieve. Dogs really do love us. Does your dog experience cognition in the same way you do? Probably not, but it's possible that animals experience emotions and cognitive schemes that *we* can't comprehend. Animals may think in esoteric signs and symbols. They may replay images of the world inside their minds. Hell, they might cogitate in an intricate language based entirely on smells.

To call someone a "birdbrain" is actually a great compliment, as the mass-to-cognitive-power ratio of a bird's brain is one of the highest in the animal world. It's not the size. It's what you do with it, or in this case, your neuronal density. Birds can solve complex problems and have intricate social structures. They have rituals and preoccupations. Alligators are similar problem solvers. They climb fences, break out of cages, sneak into backyard pools like navigating a maze. They have personalities.

People who work with animals can see, have witnessed repeatedly, that animals exhibit behaviors that the pedants of the world seem to only think exist for humans. Jeff had already gotten a taste of this in his short time as an alligator farmer. He looked into their eyes and experienced a connection. He wasn't just the guy who brought their supper. They knew him. They were individuals. Alligators—all animals, really—are so much more than we imagine. Assuming we know everything robs the world of wonder.

Jeff was learning that. He took very good care of his gators, motivated by his natural empathy and his growing relationships with them. That meant he was ready to do whatever was necessary to keep them healthy, even pumping water into the ponds when the weather got dry. It seemed like there was always work to be done, and there was always something new to learn.

In watching his gators and seeing their distinct behaviors, Jeff began to wonder: Why don't we grant the same depth of possibility to birds' scalier cousins, the alligators? He mused that perhaps we fail to allow alligators to have inner lives because we categorize them as frightening, the ancient, the other. We don't see our own faces in the shape of theirs, and this is one of the problems that hinders their conservation.

If I could change people's minds, he thought, *and make them see alligators for what they're really like, they would understand what makes them worth saving.*

Knowing his gators, too, helped him forge ahead through the coming trials. As his mission began to seem more and more impossible, he would look out at the reptilian eyes peeping at him from the surface of the pond, realize that they were watching him, and remember his purpose: to save the forgotten creatures, the ugly things, the scaly things, the things it seemed no one loved except for him.

7

MERMAID IVORY

Chokoloskee, Florida, is a small village on an island within the Ten Thousand Islands chain, a many-faceted archipelago of tangled mangroves, sloughs, and flows with evocative names like Lostmans River, Hell Gate, and Blackwater Bay. Peg Brown reigned as a legendary alligator poacher for decades in the Ten Thousand Islands before hanging up his bang stick in the 1960s or 1970s. Knowing that I liked tales of that sort, an editor at the *Miami Herald* had given me a tip. He had grown up with Peg, knew him a bit but not well, though it seemed everyone down there knew his legend. The editor told me I should look into contacting Peg's family, but first I had to read a particular story in *Tropic*, a defunct magazine insert of the *Herald* that ceased printing decades ago. No physical copies of the story seemed to exist, not even in microfiche. But there was one scanned copy in an archive. I read it, and I wanted more. It was just a taste of the story that was to come.

"Truth to tell, there's nothing much you can do with alligator hides anymore, the future having dropped slap off that particular dodge some few years ago. But the old ways die hard, and there is probably no such thing as a truly retired poacher," John Rothchild wrote in *Tropic*. These two sentences open Rothchild's story "Poacher," published June 18, 1978. I became obsessed with these two lines. Their commanding, eccentric voice smacks with the golden age of gonzo journalism. I'm ready to jump in, and then it just keeps getting better.

"Peg Brown, they say, is the most outrageous alligator poacher who ever lived," Rothchild continued. "And now that the statute of limitations has run out on anything he is alleged to have done in his time, he'll modestly concede that he's sent probably 10,000 gators to the promised land."

Peg snuck around the swamp, bamboozling rangers, barely scraping out of danger, always ready to dupe his pursuers but never firing a single shot their way. Even poachers have standards. Peg seemed larger than life, by degrees a classic rogue and an archetypal trickster. The stories of him had transcended mere rumor and cast him squarely in the level of legend. He was a folk hero. All Peg Brown stories, I began to see, took the same shape as traditional trickster folktales: one wily hero, for better or worse, against the powers that be. Although he could have beaten the rangers with violence, he battled them with cunning and humor instead. He was a stand-in for the little man, giving him hope that one day he, too, could face impossible odds and win.

By the late 1960s, rangers were making regular overnight patrols. They caught some alligator poachers, but others, they knew, were still at large. They chased after them by boat and by chopper. They had even heard the stories of Peg Brown, the same tales in which they played sheriffs of Nottingham to his Robin Hood and Merry Men. I wondered what they thought about being the villains in these powerful tales of an underdog's triumph. No doubt they felt as Jeff did about his job, that they were following a righteous calling to protect the wild. That feeling of righteousness can be dangerous. Though not without difficulty, Jeff was able to hold that calling in his head in harmony with his compassion for those people committing crimes. Countless others in wildlife law enforcement resist such empathy for their fellow man, considering it at odds with their duty. They begin to see the world under a false pall of black and white, full of good guys and bad guys instead of real people making hard decisions to stay alive. When you lose sight of that, righteous thinking can justify the worst kinds of evils.

In that view, the escalation of force against Peg and his compatriots seems unfair. Facing those odds is also what made him an underdog in the first place. Rather than a villain, he was a renegade outlaw sticking up for his community and working to feed his family. By night, he faced down all of the park service's firepower. Yet they never caught him.

Of course, no matter how good "Poacher" was, it wasn't enough to satisfy my obsession. "There are so many Peg Brown stories in currency that at this point they all have names," wrote Rothchild. I wanted to hear every last one of them. Not only would understanding these stories—and the people behind them—give me deeper insight into the culture of the Everglades, but discovering the real history behind the Peg Brown tales would also grant me an unbeatable look into the hearts and minds of the poachers of the past and the ones in the present who had taken up their mantle as latter-day Robin Hoods and tellers of tales. It was hard to tell where Peg Brown's legend stopped and the man began, so I knew the truth had to be one hell of a story.

I started digging. I found almost nothing else about Peg other than a few fishing tournament wins, and a mention or two in his brother's book, *Totch: A Life in the Everglades*. A veteran journalist friend of mine swore up and down that that brother, Loren "Totch" Brown, was the real alligator poacher in the family. As good a journalist as my friend was, I had my doubts. The story was missing something, and now it had conflict. It seemed as though the family had room for only one major alligator poacher. That meant one of them was a legend and the other was a liar. I had to know who. I reached out to the Browns. Over the past few years, rural journalism has gotten all the more difficult as propaganda has surged through the internet and turned mild distrust for journalists into outright hatred. I have been cussed out and threatened and stalked, all for doing little more than introducing myself. I can usually turn people around: In person, I don't exactly look threatening. A smile and a sincere handshake go a long way. But having noticed the distrust for society in general borne by the people of the Everglades, I knew I would need to get down to Chokoloskee and show them I was sincere.

I was surprised that it wasn't too hard to get in touch with Peg's surviving relatives. Nearly one in three people in the town, it seemed, had the surname Brown. Even some of the ones who weren't named Brown were family, too. After a series of calls, everyone referred me to Kent Daniels, whose business card, if he had one, would say RACONTEUR. Kent was the unofficial mayor, press officer, historian, and one-person welcoming committee for Chokoloskee. Kent was half Seminole, but he didn't belong to the tribe. He didn't really take a shine to being told what to do. To him, the tribe was just another form of authority to avoid. Kent offered to introduce me to Chokoloskee and that lower edge of the Everglades, give me a tour and tell me the stories behind everything we saw, including and especially the legends of Peg Brown. He could also give me invaluable insight from the Native perspective without having to pass through the tribal council's filter. I hoped his stories would help me see the other side of Jeff's operation, understand the alleged poachers' motivation beyond just money in a way those particular men themselves could not have put into words. They were too close to what happened. Some of the other men I talked to in Chokoloskee, alleged poachers themselves, had no skin in that game. And contrary to the men Jeff ran into, these guys wore the name *poacher* as a badge of honor and tacked on *alleged* with a wink and a nudge. I would meet up with them later so I could see the wilderness from their viewpoint without getting tangled up in the law.

Kent said when I got down there—essentially a straight shot down the middle of Florida from where I lived in Orlando—I could find him in the lobby of a little waterside motel called Outdoor Resorts of Chokoloskee, an establishment owned by—you guessed it—more Browns. When I walked in, I looked around, confused at how it seemed there was a small, poorly lit convenience store and tackle shop attached to the lobby without a partition. The men sitting around the front table all gave me a look like I didn't belong there. I went up to the desk to introduce myself and ask after Kent.

"I'm Kent," one of the men behind me called. "You must be Rebecca Renner."

"Guilty as charged," I said. The group of chatters' expressions had changed, opened up, welcoming. One gave up his seat, and they invited me to talk with them before Kent and I set out. When they heard why I was there, they took turns exchanging stories. It was like being back home, before so many of my family members had died, in a time when we'd sit on my grandmother's dock and the old folks would tell stories about the river and the ocean, and how the past had played out along the sandy banks. That was perhaps why I became so taken with Chokoloskee, its stories, its people: They reminded me of a home that I thought only existed in my memory, one that I believed I would never see again, because the swamps were razed, developed, and polluted, and as the estuaries faded, the stories faded with them until it seemed the only one who remembered them was me. As I listened to them, I heard the long-lost kin of my own history, a missing part of myself that I hadn't realized was gone.

Each of the men took a turn telling me a related story until they all seemed to coalesce into a single yarn spun with Craig Daniels, Kent's younger relative, at the lead. Craig is the type of character you can't get away with in fiction. He is just too much to be true, and yet there he was, sitting right there before me: a local pastor who was missing a finger, who had been shot and gone to prison, who preached with the same panache he used in telling poaching stories. He said a gator took his finger. He was Peg Brown's grandson. It was Sunday morning, and he was about to leave to lead his congregation, but first he had to regale me with a little violent family history.

When the national park came in, it pushed everyone there off their land, the Brown and Daniels families included. Even if they hadn't lived within that tract, they had all fished or hunted there, and with the nearest dose of civilization apart from the hamlet of Everglades City about forty miles away in Naples, most made their livelihood off the land. The Browns made most of their money fishing and hunting, so they kept on doing just that with the additional obstacle of running from the law while they were at it. They were a hardy and raucous bunch, stubborn the same way that was in my blood. (My own apocryphal family story says that my great-great-uncle disappeared into the swamp in those same days and went south, perhaps to Everglades City. Wherever he went, no one in the family heard from him again, so there's no telling where he turned up, if he turned up at all.)

"Tell her the one with the hammer," Kent said, gesturing at Craig.

"Oh, that one," Craig said. "Are you sure she can handle it?"

I see what you're doing, I thought. They were baiting the story, tag-team style. I knew how this went. I was supposed to say, "I can handle anything." And so I did.

"Are you sure?" Craig said. "This one's not for the faint of heart."

"Good thing there's nobody like that here," I said.

Craig grinned. He seemed tickled that I was in on the show. "All right. Once, maybe thirty years ago, my uncle—his name was Floyd Brown—was out hunting. Killing gators. Where he was, there were so many that they'd been watching him as he did it. Hundreds of eyes watching him from the water. Every time he'd kill one, another would jump out. Bang! He'd have to shoot it. They were nearly on top of him. There were so many he was running out of ammunition."

"How many were there?" I asked, knowing that was my next line, too.

"Oh, hundreds," Craig said.

"At least," Kent said. "Over a thousand."

"He had to keep going, or he was going to get ripped to pieces," Craig said. "Jump, bang, jump, bang!—and then he ran out of bullets."

Had I been anyone else, I would have thought they were lying to me just to yank my chain. But I knew better. In the storytelling tradition that I come from, yarn spinners employ hyperbole to create evocative and memorable images, and to get the visceral feeling of the story across.

"And then he used a hammer?" I asked.

"Yep, it was the only thing he had," Craig said. "If he didn't think of something, they were gonna eat him alive. So he looks around his pitpan and sees the ball-peen hammer, and knows that's what's gonna save his life."

"How's that work?" I asked. "How do you kill a gator with a ball-peen hammer?"

Craig swung his hand, wielding an invisible hammer at Kent's head. "Whack! You put its lights out."

"But that made 'em madder, didn't it?" Kent asked.

"Absolutely," Craig said. "They were mad as hell. They started coming faster. But Floyd was a machine. He just kept going. Jump, whack, jump, whack! Thousands of them."

How many gators did Floyd really kill? The number didn't matter, but Floyd's resourcefulness did, and the hyperbole amplified that. He was overwhelmed. But he made do with what he had. There was a stubbornness in this family. And that wasn't the end of it.

In those days, the men said, taking turns filling in the story, just seeing a man committing a crime wasn't enough to arrest him. Rangers had to physically catch poachers to bring them in. When the rangers spotted him, Floyd had to leave the thousands of alligators he'd just killed with only a ball-peen hammer behind. That happened with many a story, the law always on the tail of the heroes, who made it just in the nick of time. The heroes were nefarious, but they were still good folks, deep down. They had their reasons. They also had their standards. In this family, poaching was fine, but you didn't steal from your neighbor.

All these stories orbited around kernels of truth. The most ridiculous parts of them were liable to be true. Obvious hyperbole aside, spinning yarns takes sanding down the edges of a story to make it easier to swallow, not adding outlandish things that don't belong. Though sometimes you meet someone who abides by a different tradition of backwoods storytelling: When at all possible do as Peg did with his high jinks, and bamboozle the outsider. I knew how to spot it when it came along, of course. I'd done it before, myself.

After their stories petered out, Kent assumed his role as my tour guide. He insisted that we take my Honda Civic and that I drive, something I warned would not make for a comfortable ride, not to mention that I wouldn't be able to take notes, but my complaints went unanswered. He should have known better when we reached my car, and he saw that an empty cylinder remained where the driver's-side lock had once been. But there was no changing his mind. Too stubborn, I guessed. I reassured myself that it would be okay. I would figure it out. I always did. So we boarded my jalopy and set off in search of his tales of the Everglades and other yarn spinners who would pick up the story along the way.

Kent gave me verbal directions and nagged me to follow the speed limit. We cruised back through the mangroves to the mainland, where we pulled into the Rod & Gun Club, a hotel with a bar and restaurant that looked like the kind of place Hemingway would have frequented. A twelve-foot gator skin stretched across the wall over the billiard table. In the gleaming cherrywood of a small back barroom, Kent gestured to the bar and said this was where the storytelling magic happened. All the poachers would come here, drink, and exchange tales of pulling one over on the law. Though Kent was a yarn spinner and perhaps a long-retired smuggler, he had never been a poacher himself. He didn't seem like the type who would have liked killing things, even out of necessity. Later one of the men who had been a poacher back in the day refuted Kent's claim that they frequented the Rod & Gun. That place was for Yankees and tourists, he said. Celebrities went there. The poachers went for something with rougher edges and lower prices. They frequented a pub called the Oyster Bar, which had long since gone belly-up but lived on in the stories of the stories that were spun there.

As Kent shot the breeze with a woman in the kitchen, I listened, just taking everything in. They talked about local businesses on hard times. The woman, Patty, mistook me for the daughter of a local, and I thought about that long-lost great-uncle of mine, and I wondered if when he'd allegedly disappeared into the swamp he'd wound up down in Everglades City. In these parts, it wasn't outside the realm of possibility.

With his social call over, Kent led me back to my car and directed me to drive farther inland. I obeyed, interviewing him along the way with my digital recorder rolling in the cupholder so I could keep my hands on the wheel.

Some interviews, you have to ask a lot of questions. But Kent seemed to need no prompting. He directed me to drive toward the swamp, noting landmarks along the way so I could come back later. As we ventured deeper into Big Cypress Swamp, passing the ranger station into the national preserve, flat marshes of sawgrass, wire grass, bulrushes, and canebrake extended past the road in seemingly endless plains. Far off, a line of slash pines bristled from the saw palm scrub. We passed the "official" skunk ape research headquarters, an exhibit dedicated to Florida's odoriferous answer to Bigfoot. Islands of cabbage palm or larger cypress domes sprang up in the middle of these wetlands where the water belowground gathered in deeper pools in the limestone. Gradually, this more majestic growth overtook us, and we entered the swamp proper. Big Cypress National Preserve is larger than the state of Rhode Island. The entirety of New York City could fit inside it three times over, and there would still be room.

Hardwood hammocks like rain forests cast the rich understory into a tranquil gloom. An exuberance of bromeliads issued from the boughs of trees like fireworks. I would later venture deeper there on my own and sit beside a pool that had collected in the shadows where a dozen or so alligators swam, undulating away out of sight, or drifted, sleeping. Some watched me as if expecting food. Overcome by the peace of the place, I sat and listened as the purple cast of gloaming shifted into the evening dark, and the hot buzz of katydids gave way to the thousand voices of frogs and toads in chorus. It met the shimmer of the crickets' song and the mysterious plink of drops into water. I wanted to be like Jeff, to be able to recognize every voice in the night music. To know each name was to know the swamp itself. I wasn't there yet. But I recorded the enchanting songs so I could figure it out when I once again returned to the electric world of Wi-Fi. There was something extraordinary in the wonder I felt in hearing those enigmatic calls. I wanted to know everything, but I couldn't let answers wash away my sense of wonder.

That trek would all happen much later. Right then, me and my Honda Civic were about to be in trouble.

"Turn here," Kent said, pointing to a dirt road, one that had no sign that I could see.

"Are you sure?" I asked.

"Would I lead you wrong?" Kent said.

I don't know, would you? I thought. "Where are we going?" I asked as I turned.

"Through the swamp," he said. "I want to show you something."

Something about tomatoes. He was talking so fast I could barely register one idea before he jumped to the next. The canal along that trail existed because of the tomato farmers, he said. I was willing to believe him, but I saw no tomato farms there, just pine and palms in scrubland as far as the eye could see—except for the road, if you could call it that. A trail of calcified shells ground into bone-white sand stretched on into the distance until it dissolved at the horizon in a billowing white sandstorm. There was no way to tell where we were going or how far away from there we would reach the end. If there was an end.

The turbulent ground under my tires jarred the car so violently that it threatened to knock something loose. I can drive in just about any conditions, but at a certain point I, too, succumb to the limits of logic and physics. By then, we were several miles outside of cell contact from anyone who might come to the rescue. At every clank, I imagined something important falling from the undercarriage, like a rear axle or my entire engine block, and I knew that if we broke down there, I would be walking back to the ranger station by myself in that vengeful summer heat, regretting every decision I'd ever made that led me up to that moment. Tropical heat has that effect on people.

Unperturbed, Kent kept talking. I never had to ask a question. He never left any dead air. He talked about the effects of farming and the parks on the people. There was oil drilling, too. Every manner of industry was allowed in the glades, as long as you had enough money to do it. Anything was legal if you knew which palms to grease.

But the changes to Florida really started with the Spanish conquest, he said.

I nodded, interested. That was just the kind of thing I wanted to hear about, conquest from the Seminole perspective. I didn't dare look at him, afraid he'd stop talking to scold me about keeping my eyes on the road.

The Spanish even changed the environment, he said. I knew they'd logged to build ships, as did other settlers all along the coasts for centuries. Magnificent bald cypress groves had fallen to become masts and planks, dock pilings, shingles, caskets.

"Here's something you might not know," Kent said. "Manatees are an invasive species! The Spanish brought them along for food, used them like livestock. Tastes like pork."

Huh?

I had to interrupt him there. "I'm sorry, what? Manatees?" The Spanish had released a variety of invasive species upon their so-called New World, among them the mustang horses of the West and the wild boars whose populations have boomed across the southeastern United States and California, plus regions of Chile, Argentina, Uruguay, Paraguay, and Brazil. (Tenacious and destructive boogers. Well traveled, too.) But manatees? *That's not right*, I thought.

"Yeah, manatee steak," Kent said. "Great on the grill." Not that he would shoot one, he said, because the animals were protected, but Kent thought they shouldn't be, and it was a conspiracy that they were.

"But—but manatees are from here," I said. When I'm interviewing, I try not to interrupt. I'd rather be a fly on the wall and listen, getting the unadulterated tale from my subject, whatever that tale may be. That meant learning to let people be wrong. But I have my limits.

"Manatees are from the West Indies," Kent said pointedly. "Their full name is the West Indian manatee. They're from India."

The West Indies is the Caribbean, I thought. I shot him a confused and beseeching look before quickly returning my gaze to the dust-clouded road. Kent was such a knowledgeable fellow. He'd seemed so smart up until then. *He can't actually believe this*, I thought. *Is he trying to screw with me?*

I had read a few other magazine articles reported from Chokoloskee before I'd ventured down there, and in every last one, there had been major gaffes in fact, real howlers clearly gleaned from local sources that any journalist familiar with South Florida would know to be untrue. Although they may not have hoodwinked visitors anymore, as tourism had become Chokoloskee's lifeline and main industry, it seemed that bamboozling writers had remained a time-honored tradition here. The only story I read that passed was from Peter Matthiessen, the author of the award-winning novel *Shadow Country*. Ironically, I would end up working in Matthiessen's shadow, as several of the old-timers whom I interviewed said that I was the second journalist they'd ever talked to, the first being Matthiessen himself nearly half a century ago.

Kent went on, deriding manatees, saying people should be able to hunt them. Hunters would come in droves if they had any idea how much mermaid ivory was worth. According to Kent, mermaid ivory was the name for the ivory derived from manatee bones, which he said was worth hundreds of dollars per piece. A single manatee could bring in thousands.

Mermaid ivory? I thought, incredulous and a bit offended. *Do I look like I just fell off the turnip truck?*

"Yes, there's so much people from outside don't know," Kent said. "Such as, mangroves are invasive, too."

What? I went into this interview knowing Kent had a propensity for embellishment, but at that point I knew I'd have to sit down and comb through his assertions one by one to disentangle the facts from the shenanigans. *Man, you are giving me more work than you realize.*

"The whole Everglades has changed," he said. "People who aren't from here don't realize. The whole place is unrecognizable. Nothing looks like it did fifty years ago. If you showed me a picture of all this back then, I wouldn't know the place." The big trees had disappeared. The mangroves had migrated. I'd never heard anything about that, but just because I hadn't heard of it before didn't mean it wasn't true. I reminded myself to withhold judgment.

A thick cloud of sand descended upon us, completely whiting out my windshield. Wary of continuing forward, I slowed to a crawl and put my wipers on. Their rubber strips proceeded to unravel from the blades, and they screeched back and forth across the glass, smearing the sand, tatters flapping in the wind.

Oh, for fuck's sake, I thought.

I sighed and looked at Kent. "It'll be okay," I said, my tone falsely sunny.

"You need new windshield wipers," he said.

No, really? I thought. I rolled down my window and stuck my head out so I could see, and we set off again. Out of the corner of my eye, I could see him staring at me, judgmental and vaguely horrified.

I had gone down there to get to know the people by seeing past the Florida Man clichés. Now here I was acting like a Florida Woman.

"Turn those things off," Kent said. "You're gonna damage your glass."

He was right. I turned off the wipers, parked the car, and got out to clean the windshield with a rag as best I could. When I got back in, he told me to drive to Naples to get new wipers and to do so before it rained or I was in real trouble. He said he wouldn't take me anywhere else until I did that, which, okay, I admit was reasonable.

Several hours later, we made it out of the glades more or less intact, I treated Kent to dinner, and then, after dark, retired to my dockside motel room, exhausted, where I copied down notes from the day and started fact-checking. Manatees, of course, are endemic to Florida and the Caribbean. As are mangroves, but I had more questions there: Could mangroves have migrated into that portion of the glades? It didn't seem impossible. Kudzu had spread across the Southeast within a generation. But if mangroves were endemic, what could cause such a mass migration? To my surprise, the most outlandish of Kent's claims was true. Mermaid ivory is real.

Although it bears a mythical name, mermaid ivory comes from the bones of real animals in the order Sirenia, a name derived from the Greek Σειρῆνες, the Sirens who transfix sailors with their beguiling songs and lure them to their deaths in the deep. By the time they appeared in medieval bestiaries, these Sirens had become mermaids much as we know them today. According to legend, sailors mistook manatees for mermaids. Anyone who has seen these Rubenesque mammals up close knows those delightful tales are questionable at best. Nonetheless, it follows that their bones would take on a florid name like mermaid ivory. Most of the mermaid ivory on the market comes from fossils of the Steller's sea cow, another member of the Sirenia order that went extinct in 1768. Because the animal is extinct, trade of this mermaid ivory is legal. However, trade of manatee bones is not, as they're protected internationally under the Convention on International Trade in Endangered Species of Wild Fauna and Flora (CITES) and in the US under the Marine Mammal Protection Act, the Endangered Species Act, and others. Some of the first-ever conservation laws were ratified to protect manatees.

Mermaid ivory, who would have thought. I was so excited to learn something new, even if it wasn't the story I was chasing. I went to sleep in that blessèd air-conditioning, imagining what other new discoveries the next day's adventures had in store.

The next morning as storm clouds darkened the skies, I made the hour trek from Chokoloskee to Naples, the closest city and my most realistic hope of resuscitating my car. By the time I made it back to the Ten Thousand Islands, a wet wind told me the storms would blow over. I called Kent. As the sun peeked out from behind the clouds, he insisted it was going to pour. If I was dead set on getting wet, he said, I could talk to someone else. But, he added, "Call me if you run into any trouble, and I'll get you sorted out."

I think he's done with me, I thought.

So I called Jonnie Brown. Jonnie was one of Peg's many sons, and so he had firsthand stories of that legendary poacher. If Kent had been the keeper of the tall tales, Jonnie was my closest hope to seeing past the tales to the real man who had inspired them. Though I'd talked to him several times on the phone, I hadn't met him in person yet. I enjoyed the sound of his voice, a throaty drawl particular to the backwoods of Florida. He sounded like a large, imposing man. He reminded me of my father, especially when he checked in on me and said things like, "Everybody's being nice to you, *right*?"—the implication being that he'd knock their heads together if they weren't.

When the phone rang, he answered fairly quickly, happy to hear from me. I told him what was up, what I'd done the day before, and how Kent had canceled our plans and left me with the day open.

"You know he's a *bullshitter*, right?" Jonnie said.

I had to laugh.

"I'm aware that Kent is an—expert embellisher."

Jonnie laughed, too.

We'd gotten lucky, he said. He happened to be free all day, and we made plans to go out on an adventure. This time, thank God, we'd take his 4x4 truck.

Together we would delve into the Everglades and into the past, and I would come to see Peg as his son saw him, as a man of many opposites: a quiet man and a storyteller, a rough customer and a smooth talker, a moonshiner and a war hero, a poacher and an outdoorsman, an adventurer and a dad. Jonnie would also offer me a glimpse of the wild from the poachers' perspective. Though far from legendary, he had followed in his father's footsteps. Surrounded by the true places from the legends, I would become a part of their story in a way that I could never have predicted.

8

GOLDEN EGGS

Moths and beetles flicked around the yellow-tinged light above the barn door. Despite the season, winter by then, the night was always alive—especially the air, which teemed with every manner of biting and stinging thing. Jeff and Lieutenant Wilson ducked under that winged cloud and into the coolness of the barn. With its concrete-block walls, the air always felt a little wet, but it was welcome nonetheless. They chitchatted back and forth about what Jeff had been doing.

"How far have you gotten on your list?" Lieutenant Wilson asked.

The most crucial, but still frustrating, tool in Jeff's arsenal was his list of names. They were people who'd applied for permits, people who'd once been arrested for alligator and alligator-adjacent crimes, and other folks who handled alligators, like trappers, who may have had ample opportunity to do some illegal sales or smuggling just by the nature of their jobs. Had they already? Who knew. It was Jeff's job to find out.

"I've gone out with a few trappers," Jeff said, "nobody I've seen doing anything illegal."

Lieutenant Wilson nodded, his expression businesslike. "And the farmers?"

"That's where I'm having some trouble," Jeff said. "Lot of doors slammed in my face, both figuratively and actually."

Jeff had started cold-calling the people on the list, working his way down. No one wanted to talk. On some calls, the person on the other end hung up immediately. After going through nearly the whole list like that, Jeff realized he needed a better plan.

"Do they suspect anything?" Lieutenant Wilson asked.

"Not as far as I can tell," Jeff said. The possibility of being found out, the fear even, always lingered at the back of his mind.

"Well, keep trying," Lieutenant Wilson said. "That's not why I'm here tonight. I'm here to discuss a concern with you." *Oh shit*, Jeff thought.

A previous visitor, a higher-up from FWC, had raised a potential issue: If the neighborhood kids climbed Jeff's outer fence, then the fence around the pond, they could be killed by a gator. A death—anyone's death—would put an end to Sunshine Alligator Farm and possibly to the investigation entirely.

As far-fetched as the possibility seemed, it started the gears of worry turning in Jeff's brain. He'd been so focused on the gators that he hadn't considered that anyone might want to break into an alligator farm. But "Florida Man Brandishes Alligator at Walmart Checkout Counter" has to get his gators from somewhere. While it was possible that teenagers might sneak into the farm, as teenagers in the middle of nowhere will be teenagers in the middle of nowhere, Jeff's greater concerns were meth addicts, weirdos, and anyone else who'd wised up to the fact that the price of alligator eggs and skins was skyrocketing.

In the previous year, flooding along the Lower Mississippi Delta caused thousands of alligator nests to become unviable. Just as in Florida, Louisiana alligator farmers relied on permits to harvest wild alligator eggs to maintain their stocks of hatchlings. As the number of eggs and hatchlings coming in dwindled, Louisiana farmers turned to other sources and were ready to pay ten times what they had before for these now golden eggs. The rumor around the industry was that many farmers relied on poachers. But if they could prove they didn't know the origin of the eggs, they could escape prosecution, even if their poacher—or thief—suppliers got caught. So poachers got in the habit of falsifying harvesting or farming documents, or bills of sale, and the most unscrupulous among the farmers stopped asking questions.

It was no surprise then that other farmers across South Florida had seen an influx in alligator thieves. By night, camouflaged shadows would cut fence wires and duck in. Hunters in their normal lives, they would sneak by the light of headlamps to grab eggs by the tray and baby gators by the dozen. They already had all the equipment they needed for backcountry espionage. They had the waders and the guns and the ammunition. They had the boots. They had the false foliage to lay over themselves, becoming part of the brush. More often than not, they were also packing enough desperation to do something stupid in the name of quick cash in their wallets. Learning this, Jeff knew he couldn't be too careful.

On that visit, Lieutenant Wilson helped Jeff devise a series of listening and recording devices to place around the farm.

"You won't be seeing as much of me anymore," Lieutenant Wilson said as he was getting into his own truck to leave. "I'll be dropping information packets in your mailbox. Otherwise, you're on your own."

The next day, Jeff put up game cams, also known as trail cams: small, weatherproof surveillance cameras made to record outdoors. They were especially useful at night, when they were designed to pick up the smallest movements on a dark trail. He stationed them so they observed the exterior doors, and then he put one at the gate so that it might track movements out there, even cars that pulled in to turn around. It all served to keep him wary. He never knew when the short flash of a pickup truck might be thieves casing the place for later. He became vigilant about break-ins and keenly aware, in the quiet of the night, just how alone he really was out there. The cameras could only do so much. The real deterrent was him, his lights on in the camper, his silhouette against the dark, his dog barking from inside, the low growl that warned about its ready jaws.

As the farm grew, his work there became less and less of a charade. He finagled an official permit for his alligator farm, evading the inspector (a man whom he knew from the agency) in the process. Get recognized by just one person from your old life, and the mission would be over. He disguised his voice over the phone like some cartoon villain. He made excuses not to be at the farm while the inspector came around. Now on to the little details. He needed it to look like a real business. He made business cards that said SUNSHINE ALLIGATOR FARM, along with the farm's contact details. He concocted a website. He got into designing the whole thing, exactly, he felt, like a real business owner would.

He wanted T-shirts, mugs! *Calm down, Jeff,* he told himself. *Don't start bleeding money before you've gotten the show on the road.* So instead, he did the sober thing and drove around town, tacking the card to the community boards at the feed stores and the Tractor Supply. He wanted people to know the farm existed. He was open for business, no trap set yet. He needed to get a lay of the land first.

And just like that, Sunshine became a real alligator farm. The perfectionist in Jeff grated at how haphazard the farm looked, but as he invested deeper, he came to understand how the farm's imperfections weren't flaws but, oddly, details that made it look more real. The more perfect it seemed, the less realistic it would be. So finally, flaws and all, his farm, his set, had come to fruition, complete with real bills to pay.

The agency wasn't about to cough up for any of that: They couldn't. It wasn't just that such a paper trail would have blown Jeff's cover, and paying in cash would have raised suspicion; the agency didn't have any money to spare.

What he needed more than anything was help from people who knew better. If he could make a connection with an alligator farmer, just one person who knew how to make this all work, he could overcome all the worries he had about taking care of his gators and really start digging into his investigation in earnest. Such help, however, had not appeared.

As one would expect in a subculture so entrenched in the moneyed Old South, the alligator industry was not exactly welcoming to outsiders. Jeff continued to reach out to farms, cold-calling them or chatting up their managers at meetings the state held to apprise the farmers of the current state of the wild alligator population—and how many eggs the law entitled them to harvest that season. They would smile and shake hands, ever polite and cordial. As my father, in his life an old southern man himself, would say: They had cultivated a talent for so gracefully telling a man to go to hell that he left looking forward to the trip.

Desperate to make connections, Jeff began frequenting local bars. While he wouldn't exactly have called himself a city slicker, these weren't the kinds of establishments he was used to. A man of Jeff's age greatly preferred his own backyard or a family cookout to the watering holes in

Arcadia, with their Western-style saloon signs, polished wood paneling, and colored-glass lamps that hung over the tables. The crack of billiard balls punctuated the laments of country songs on the radio.

Jeff didn't do any drinking. Things got tricky if you let your faculties fog over with even a few beers. Still, he had to make it look real. He'd order a longneck and nurse it, making conversation and taking mental notes for a while. Then he'd head to the bathroom, taking his beer with him. He'd pour it out and replace what he'd spilled out with water. Always a little on edge, he'd look around again then head back to his conversation. If he was there long enough, he'd have to imagine the alcohol he hadn't drunk loosening his tongue. *Talk too much. Make it realistic. But always be ready with an ear for someone to divulge his secrets.*

Still, for all that work, the leads he found this way dwindled into nothing.

It was more than just an unwillingness to reveal trade secrets. It was that Jeff was not one of them. He was an unknown commodity. An outsider. And no matter how kind and hospitable you are to an outsider, wisdom said not to trust him—that is, until he showed you who he was. The more doors shut in his face, the more Jeff began to wonder if they detected, even if they couldn't put it into words, that something was off about him. People were perceptive that way, Jeff had learned after a lifetime of studying them in his encounters with poachers and hunters in the field. It was the same way a doe might scent a threat on the wind, a hunter watching in a blind, still as can be yet human and alive and breathing.

Jeff *wasn't* who he said he was. There *was* something off about him. And when it came down to it, he couldn't go any deeper, couldn't slough off his memories, his duties, his former life—could he?

The next weekend, Jeff went home, and as they always did, he and his wife, Sandy, traded war stories, tales from the trenches of their jobs. She detailed her students' antics. He talked about how he was up against the impossible, and he had even more work now that Lieutenant Wilson wanted him to not only keep a log but file a report on nearly every move he made.

"Wipe your ass?" Jeff joked. "Write a report on it."

Sandy laughed. She was chopping vegetables for their dinner as the dogs ganged around their feet and the parrot squawked in the living room, knowing it was nearly dinnertime.

"What's worse is that he expects me to do it all on this damn thing," Jeff said, gesturing to his state laptop where he sat at their kitchen island. "But I'm not allowed to keep it at the farm. Oh no, they're not allowed to make things that easy on me. Instead I have to waste my precious time with you doing this." He would have preferred to be cooking with her instead of sitting around typing.

"It's all right," Sandy said. "But what if—you did bring it with you?"

"George said I can't," Jeff answered, referring to Lieutenant Wilson by his first name. They had become that familiar by then. "Somebody might find it."

"You've hidden a bunch of other things," she said. "Why not that? It's not like he's there looking over your shoulder."

She was always his voice of reason. He'd already thought of bringing his computer, of course, but had balked at this small act of disobedience. Turned out, all he needed was a little push.

When Jeff returned to the farm, he snooped around for another "hidey-hole," as he called them. He hollowed out a section like a shelf behind a pegboard wall and tucked his laptop inside. Guilt nagged at him about disobeying Lieutenant Wilson like that, but every time he needed to write a report and the computer was right there, pragmatism and relief won out, and he shooed the guilt away.

Over the months, he and Lieutenant Wilson had developed an increasingly complicated relationship. Jeff liked the man and trusted him completely. He could say that in all honesty. When this was over, and the lieutenant was no longer his commanding officer, he could see them being friends. Yet as the operation went on, it became apparent that they didn't see the world the same way. Lieutenant Wilson saw things as black-and-white, the "good guys" versus the "bad guys." Jeff knew reality fell in shades of gray, that the "bad guy" you met in the woods could be a decent fellow having a bad day. Lieutenant Wilson expected unfailing perfection. As perfect as Jeff wanted to be—and he strived to do everything in his job and in his life by the letter—reality often reminded him of his martial arts training: The strongest men are like bamboo. When adversity pushes against them, they bend, because if you don't bend, you break. The agent who had come before him in the operation had broken and then failed. Jeff couldn't be like him. He had to bend. So he hid the computer. Even though he went home less and less as the investigation picked up, the time he spent there was his lifeline. Without having to write reports, he could be fully present. He could remember who he was. Jeff Babauta.

On the other side of that coin, he could be fully present at the farm, too. He could inhabit the essence of Curtis Blackledge. That was increasingly important, as Blackledge really had some work to do. Running a farm was a never-ending cycle. As soon as money came in, it seemed to go out.

If he didn't think of something, he'd have to dip into his own funds to feed his gators. As an alligator farmer, he did have one option. He could legally go out into the swamps and harvest alligator eggs, but that was risky without anyone willing to teach him. His best resource ended up being an episode of *Dirty Jobs*, a show that revealed the greasiest, the muddiest, the filthiest, and the grittiest careers America had to offer. As he hunched in the glow of his laptop screen in the camper, watching the show's host wade through the filth, Jeff looked on the bright side that at least now there wouldn't be any surprises. Or so he hoped. What choice did he have?

When the summer months came, Jeff woke on a misty morning, when sawgrass pierced those earthbound clouds, humidity so thick in the air you could drink it, and condensation beaded on the cold camper panes like the outside of a glass of iced tea. It was finally nesting season. He packed up his truck and headed low into the wetlands, whispers of the night's rhythm parting for the new day's pulse, the nocturnal chorus giving way to solitary singing somewhere high in the loblolly pines from a seven-story vantage over the savanna, a lonesome sentinel to the daybreak.

Permit in hand, Jeff joined two plainclothes officers, and together they worked methodically over the marshy terrain in search of alligator nests. This had to be careful work. Despite all that ambient serenity, danger hovered, too, at ground level with the mist. There were your usual hazards: wild boars, poison ivy, rattlesnakes shivering out a warning from their hideouts in the brush. A checklist of these occupied a space at the back of Jeff's mind, not a worry so much as a readiness. He knew from years of practice that the swamp only posed a threat to the uninformed, the unprepared.

But wasn't he one of the nearly clueless now, out there picking through the weeds? Seeking out the stinking lairs of these armor-clad anachronisms and hoping Mama Gator wasn't there to protect her eggs? It seemed like a bad idea all around, but he had to do it.

Back when he was Jeff Babauta, if someone like a park visitor or a friend from up north had asked him how to stay safe around alligators, he would have said: *You don't* stay *around them at all.* See a gator and get out of its way. It seemed obvious, really, and it was more or less the natural reaction visitors—and most people—had to the reptile. It's no surprise then that alligator attacks account for an average of one death per year in the United States. Just one. Bees—yes, *bees*—are significantly more deadly. That isn't to say that people ought to cozy up to wild alligators—that would probably change those statistics entirely. Sometimes a little bit of healthy fear is a good thing. It stops you from doing something stupid. As he rooted through the weeds on what felt like the riskiest of Easter egg hunts, Jeff had a distinct worry he would be that one person this year.

Alligators rarely attack humans unprovoked. The keyword there is *unprovoked.* Invading one's nest and absconding with her unborn children felt like the very definition of provocation.

Jeff recognized that he was out there both literally and figuratively looking for trouble. As he traipsed along the path—if you could call it that; it was barely more than a line of pine needles, a narrow gully in the rough sawgrass waves that the habits of deer had traced over time—he memorized the sounds of his own footfalls, his ears perked to the wetlands, ready for a new disturbance to cut across the placid whispers of the morning. He was keeping an ear out for the louder and more sudden sound of an object splashing in the river.

Using a snake hook, Jeff combed through the brush, purposeful and methodical, pretending to know exactly what he was doing. The other half of his attention remained in cervine alertness to his surroundings.

Jeff continued along in his search, watching as the new and trepidatious day unfolded along the forest floor with unassuming splendor. The resurrection ferns along the oak boughs began to curl and close, protecting their night-caught moisture, and the creeping things and the slithering things and the clawing things and the flitting things, all of nature's wonderful myriad of ugly and beautiful creatures, began to stir. A Carolina wren trilled an exuberant song, hidden in the architecture of the canopy. A woodpecker tapped a cadence on the spindle of a hollowed pine. Even as the fog rose with the dawn, the dew-cooled morning lingered on that shady trail, a brief reprieve from the dense summer heat. Golden orb spiders poised themselves, anticipating insect rush hour in their droplet-strung hammocks. The night's mosquitoes had retired to their mysterious homes to lie dormant until their next dusk hunt, but the bluebottle flies and the gnats had yet to arrive at their persistent duty of annoyance, giving the air a quality of repose, a transient and peaceful waiting into which the wilderness would pour its full vigor in time. Far below, much nearer, unexpected, palmetto fronds shook as an armadillo hopped and scurried through the scrub, leaving its trail rustling. Once it reached a safe distance, it stood up on its hind legs and observed Jeff for a moment before it turned and bounded away.

It didn't take long for Jeff to find a nest. At first, he thought nests would be hard to find. Then the smell hit him. Alligator feces has a distinct stench, one he had come to recognize after these months of keeping the farm. It was like a chicken farm mixed with a shallow oyster bed that had grown hot in the sun. Earthy and gamey and funky. The stench put him on alert. Not only did it mean a nest was nearby; it was more than likely that the nest's owner was around, too.

Scanning the area, Jeff followed the smell to a low-lying thicket. Behind it was an alligator slide, a strip of mud remembering the repeated impression of an alligator's belly as it slid down into the water. And in the middle of the thicket, there was a dark, wet mound—about a yard in diameter—constructed of pine needles and leaves, twigs and mud, and the ripest dung. Jeff grimaced at the smell, but there was no use in being squeamish about it. He took one more look around to check for Mama Gator. Then he lifted the thatch of mire that roofed in the nest. The inside exuded a fetid heat. Jackpot. The stark white curves of eggs poked out from the rank compost.

The law said he could only open a designated number of nests, only take a certain number of eggs. Open more, and anything you took after that was poaching. This way, a considerable number of nests would remain undisturbed, protecting wild alligators from the threat of population decline. For alligator farmers and anyone else with an egg-collecting permit, such a law meant that if they opened their set number of nests and none of them contained eggs, they would go home empty-handed. The law-abiding among them would, at least.

With another quick look around, Jeff squatted to pick up an egg. It was warm, alive. His first alligator egg. He paused, drinking in that poignant moment. It felt momentous, but he didn't know why.

He marked the egg's upward-facing side with a Sharpie, put it in the box of soil he'd carried with him for this purpose, and then recorded the egg with a tally mark on his sheet. Mama Gator hadn't shown up, but Jeff wasn't going to wait around for her. He packed up those unformed creatures in their dirty little pods, visited other nests to collect more, and then spirited them all back to the farm, reporting his numbers to the state by phone as he went. He was careful to keep them warm and alive, even though he didn't plan to hold on to them for very long. As soon as the new day came, he hustled to turn those eggs into money. A single day's harvest like this could net between $3,000 and $5,000, straight into the farm's account, keeping the rent paid and the lights on and chicken in his alligators' bellies. Or at least, that's what he was doing as Curtis Blackledge.

Under his new farmer guise, Jeff went out to catch an egg launderer. In this context, laundering meant passing off illegally harvested eggs for legal ones—and reaping the profits. It works like this:

The farmer who bought fifty-three eggs from Jeff recorded that he purchased only thirty. That left space in his logs for him to fill with twenty-three eggs he'd gotten from anywhere, including ones poached from the wild. Why would someone do that? Well, if you could buy illegal eggs from poachers for pennies on the dollar, but then turn around and sell those eggs, or the little alligators that hatch from them, for the same price as legal ones, you could make a profit, one that added up quickly in those days when alligator eggs sold for upward of $60 apiece.

That farmer paid Jeff only five bucks an egg. As Blackledge, he felt slighted. As Officer Babauta, on the other hand, the discrepancy between the number of eggs he'd sold and what the farmer reported constituted damning evidence that would land the farmer in court.

FWC saw that kind of thing going on all across the state. Laundering was rampant. The agency suspected a larger organized crime ring waited in the shadows. That's what Jeff was after. Finding the ledgers, false books that kept track of their illicit sales, would be his holy grail.

Still, that could wait. With his current paltry sum, he needed to feed his gators. Somehow, in just a matter of months, Jeff's gators had gone from accessories in his operation to true companions. The protectiveness he felt for his family and faithful dog Mack had found its way to his gators. Was it Blackledge who insisted he did what he could to provide for them? Or was it Jeff? The lines were blurry. The longer he spent in the field under the guise of his character, the more it seemed they were blending together. He was losing his identity so gradually that he didn't realize until a piece of it felt missing.

He was past due for a break.

He drove back to his wife—his real home—in his unmarked unit, the white pickup truck. The closer he got to the realm where his life as Jeff Babauta resided, the more anxious he became that someone was watching him. He caught himself looking over his shoulder constantly. That truck in his rearview mirror—how long had it been following him?

Jeff was no stranger to this well-founded paranoia. In his days as a uniformed officer, he frequently saw folks he'd arrested around town.

Even before this, he used to leave home for days at a time for other work assignments. He always worried about his family's safety, and for good reason. His wife's long days as a third-grade teacher left her preoccupied and vulnerable. One incident in particular stuck with him. There had been a big takedown of a poacher, someone who knew not only Jeff but also his family. The man could have picked Jeff's wife out of a crowd. He had targeted another officer and his family before. This sent Jeff into a panic. His son, in high school at the time, was frantic as well.

If something goes wrong, Jeff thought, *if something happens to them—or God forbid, her students—it'll be my fault.*

Worries like this haunted him. He was meticulous for a reason. When you fucked up, when you forgot something, people could get hurt. Sometimes those people were the ones you loved most.

I'm the one who agreed to do this, he would think. *Not them. This isn't their fault. Don't target them. You know better, don't you?*

Just because someone had committed a crime, or even several, that didn't make them a bad person. It wasn't who they were. This belief never stopped him from worrying. What if people like Lieutenant Wilson were right? What if there really were "bad guys"? Jeff liked to think the best of people. He had to. It was the only way he could get by in a job like his. *But what if?*—the thought always nagged him. What if wanting to believe the best in people was the flaw that would lead him to getting burned? What if he let his guard down for the wrong person?

After the takedown of that poacher, his fears of reprisal climbed. That night, Jeff had sat his son down in the living room of their home, their dogs' paws tapping on the linoleum, the parrot uttering minced oaths like a jambalaya of his wife's favorite curse words. This was their safe space, his little kingdom in the suburbs, but now here he was, saying out loud the worries he turned over in his mind on long drives—and how he dealt with them.

"I just know somebody's going to target me," his son had said.

"They're after me, not you," Jeff had tried to reassure him. But the worry still nagged at Jeff that he might be wrong. "That said, you never know. Be vigilant. When you're out, be aware of your surroundings. Look around and make sure nobody's going to jump out from behind something. Lock your car doors when you get in." Noting the panicked look on his son's face, Jeff had added, "But, you know, the people I deal with, I don't believe that they would do anything like that. But you just don't ever know. So just stay vigilant and keep your eyes open. Be careful what you say on the web."

At his son's high school, everyone knew Jeff was the game warden. His son ran in a crowd of guys who hunted and fished, and they'd razz him sometimes. *Your dad busted my cousin*, a friend might say. If it wasn't a cousin, it was someone else's dad. To that, his son would say matter-of-factly that Jeff must've thought he was doing something illegal. Don't do the crime if you're going to gripe about the consequences. His son was used to being a little extra vigilant. But none of those folks had ever made them feel scared until then.

The poacher-lawman dichotomy was just the way of the world. To step outside of it, to treat either man as an out-and-out villain, was to cross the line of taboo. They played each other's antagonists. Regardless of the archetypes embodied by each group in fiction, the roles they played in reality were something different entirely. In the narratives of their lives, the poacher and the lawman were each other's punch-clock villains: They could face off on the clock, but afterward they could sit side by side at the same dive bar, drink the same shitty beer, and share fish stories.

Not that Jeff did, though. In the past, Jeff and his family would have to leave a bar if they saw someone he'd previously arrested. Still, nobody ever confronted him. People seemed to like him, even the ones he arrested. He once heard someone say, "If you ever get confronted by Jeff, you better go ahead and tell him the truth. He'll know you're lying. Either way, he'll deal with you. So you just tell him the truth and keep it friendly." Those were guys catching the wrong kind of fish or bagging deer out of season. They were poaching by opportunity. But an entire poaching operation, an organized one with money to throw around, as FWC had suspected existed in the shadows—that was a whole different ball game. As the stakes grew higher, so did the danger. The poachers had much more to lose.

Jeff turned all this over in his mind as he drove home. He parked his truck under his utility shed and pulled down the tarpaulin cover. No one, not even his neighbors, would see it.

As he unlocked the door, the dogs barked and howled. They nearly mauled him with kisses once he got inside. Then they cleared the way for Sandy, who got her own kiss, too.

Jeff raises the sign at Sunshine Alligator Farm. *(Courtesy of Jeff Babauta)*

Jeff had business cards printed for Sunshine Alligator Farm, a necessary detail he hoped would bring possible suspects his way. *(Courtesy of Jeff Babauta)*

Picturesque royal palms—a species of tropical palm tree native to South Florida, Mexico, and the Caribbean—mark the trailhead at the Fakahatchee Strand.

A trail of crushed shells leads into the thick of the Fakahatchee's eponymous strand swamp, a type of swamp that grows lush because of the linear stream of water that flows through the limestone beneath it.

A boardwalk winds through head-high ferns and palm trees, part of the Royal Palm Hammock Trail in Collier-Seminole State Park.

An alligator hide hearkens to Everglades City's rugged past in the billiard room of the Everglades Rod & Gun Club.

A small lighthouse lantern, hurricane lamps, and other artifacts of Floridiana decorate the Everglades Rod & Gun Club's quiet back barroom.

The alligators line up for their supper at Sunshine Alligator Farm. Jeff learned how to mimic a hatchling's chirp, and he used the call to beckon his alligators to feeding time. *(Courtesy of Jeff Babauta)*

Fresh tire tracks cut through the mud in Big Cypress National Preserve. Perhaps they belonged to a hunter. Unlike in the national park, hunting is legal (with regulations) in the preserve.

The golden hour illuminates the understory of a cypress dome in Big Cypress National Preserve. Cypress domes are unique habitats where water pools deeper in the limestone bedrock, allowing taller trees such as cypresses to grow and provide shelter for abundant life on the forest floor.

Nicknamed the Fakahatchee Hilton by backpackers, this way-stop on the many miles of the Fakahatchee Strand's backcountry trails acts as a location marker so visitors know they're not totally lost.

Another angle of the Fakahatchee Hilton. Rustic homesteads like this one served as hideouts for alligator poachers in the Everglades' not-too-distant past.

The crew from Sunshine Alligator Farm prepares to hunt for eggs by land, water, and air. *(Courtesy of Jeff Babauta)*

Suspicious of covert work going on at the farm at night, Jeff installed trail cams. Here, one captures a secretive delivery of alligator eggs. *(Courtesy of Jeff Babauta)*

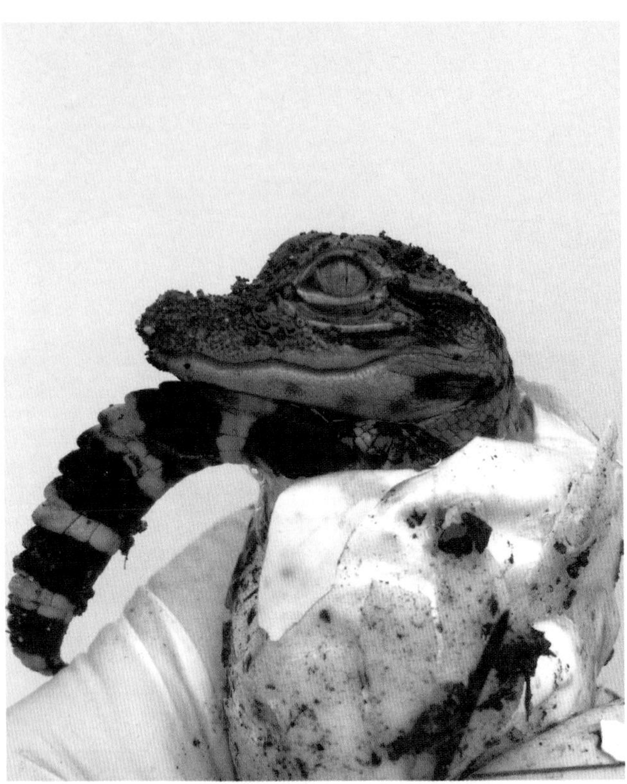

Hatching season has arrived at the farm. Here, a hatchling emerges from its shell. *(Courtesy of Jef Babauta)*

In the area Jeff called Sunshine Daycare, kiddie pools serve as makeshift nurseries for newly hatched alligators. *(Courtesy of Jeff Babauta)*

Mangroves in Ten Thousand Islands National Wildlife Refuge offer shelter for marine life such as the smalltooth sawfish, a critically endangered ray with a chain-saw-like snout.

The Smallwood Store of Chokoloskee came into existence as a trading post and general store in 1906. Today, the Smallwood Store is a museum, offering visitors a glimpse into Florida's past.

Alligator scutes, or osteoderms, make up a bony layer under the crocodilian's skin that serves as armor.

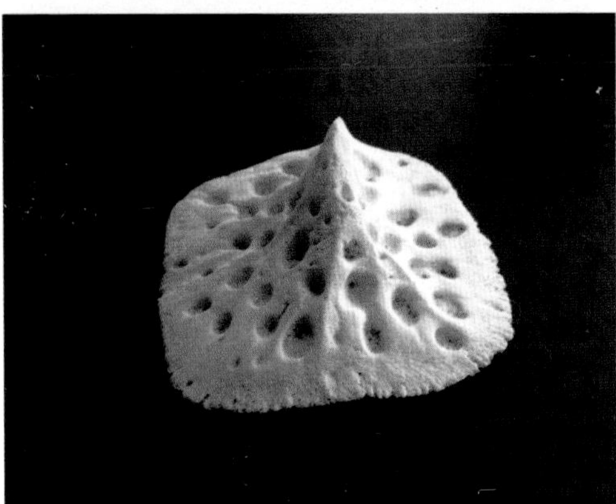

Some gator country cultures use alligator scutes as talismans in folk magic practices. Gladesmen gave this one to me on my journey in the Ten Thousand Islands.

Spanish moss, a type of air plant related to bromeliads, hangs from gnarled oaks in Merritt Island National Wildlife Refuge.

"It's been a while," she said.

"Sorry," Jeff said. "I got a little wrapped up in things."

More like I lost myself there for a second, he thought. On the way there, he had swiped his hand over his face like an actor preparing for a scene. "Jeff Babauta," he had said. "Jeff Babauta. Jeff Babauta. Jeff Babauta."

"I understand," Sandy said. "This is important. Don't worry. I have plenty of work for you to do here, too." She gave him his honey-do list.

Jeff smiled and shook his head. He both loved and hated fixing things and working in the yard. But now these tasks served another purpose. Curtis Blackledge did not have a wife. Curtis Blackledge didn't have a yard to keep up. Curtis Blackledge didn't know the satisfaction of trimmed bushes and cleaned gutters. Curtis Blackledge didn't like firing up the grill with his family. Jeff Babauta did.

Jeff Babauta, he thought as he started the lawn mower. *Jeff Babauta. Jeff Babauta. Jeff Babauta.*

9

THE INNER CIRCLE

All too soon, Jeff was back at the farm again. The bills were paid, but he'd hardly made any headway in the investigation. Jeff kept up the cold-calling. He got more aggressive with his friendliness. The more he did all this, the more Jeff began to realize that acting a fool, even when he didn't know things and needed to learn, was embarrassing. So just as with everything else, he got in front of the mirror and practiced. Like an actor doing rehearsals and loosening up before a scene, the more he practiced, the more he went out into the world as Blackledge, the easier it became to flow into that persona, to settle into the idea of not knowing, to be comfortable enough in his foolishness to ask questions. And that was how you learned, wasn't it? Perhaps Blackledge wasn't such a fool at all.

Swallowing that pride, he pursued his leads with more intention. When calling didn't work, he knocked on doors. He drove out into the country where kudzu made battlements out of fences, and the canopy of wild old oaks concealed farms, some just as old, back in their shade. He began to recognize the fetid smell of an alligator farm. He knew one was there, even when he couldn't see it. People started opening up. Pressed for hospitality, they eventually gave it.

"Hi, I'm Curtis Blackledge," he would say. "Most people call me Jeff. I know it's weird, but that's what my aunt always called me, and she raised me." When undercover, it's best to move toward using your real name as quickly as possible, Lieutenant Wilson had explained. That way, if someone shouts your name in public, they won't compromise your mission. "I started an alligator farm of my own, and I'm hoping to learn more about doing it right. I can already tell you have a top-notch facility here. Mind if I come in and tour the place? Really see how things are done?"

And—it worked. Persistence had been his welcome mat.

Perhaps they thought, *Anyone who cares this much is worthy of the inner circle*. Or maybe it was something else. He had spent so much time setting his own trap that he couldn't help but wonder if he was walking into a trap himself.

These farmers, salt-of-the-earth folks, had him over for lunch. He toured their facilities, cracking jokes and making them smile, humor the most effective tool in his kit. The look in their eyes said he'd made a connection. They were glad they'd let him in.

Then there were the ones with old money who remained stubborn as the swamp.

He would launch into the same introduction. These were the same people who had hung up on him at first. Now he wasn't going to take no for an answer. He decided to use a little psychology on them. He talked to them with familiarity, as if he had already succeeded in winning them over. Perhaps they were confused. Maybe they actually liked him. Either way, they stayed on the line and made excuses.

"Fuck you," he said once. "I'm coming to your place."

He showed up at their farm, jovial and charming. Faced with his disarming grin, they seemed to change their minds.

The more farms he toured, the more Jeff realized how great a spectrum there was from the best to the worst. Even without much money or training, Jeff's own farm sat squarely in the middle. He felt pride that he had done much better than he could really afford. He wanted to do better. He always wanted to do better. But he knew that he needed to find the sweet spot between having what was best for the gators and keeping a place that looked shabby enough to be real. So he kept touring, both to learn and, hopefully, to sniff out poachers.

By midsummer, Jeff's pestering opened the door at Shady Creek, an Arcadia alligator farm under the shade of river country's moss-heavy oaks.

Jeff had already tried to get a tour there. A few weeks before, when he'd first started knocking on doors and cold-calling, Jeff had driven over to the farm, which wasn't too far away from his own, and they had greeted him with the same general indifference as everyone else. The person who met him at the fence said they were about to have a business meeting. "Why don't you come back some other time," he'd said, an amiable way of saying *Get lost*.

After the gatekeeper deserted him, Jeff had craned to see through the foliage to the inner workings of the farm. The place seemed very official, put together. It wasn't just some hole in the ground beside a barn. There were various pools and what looked like the entrance to a clean workroom. Jeff caught the scent of bleach alongside the fishy smell of the tanks and the mossy scent of running water. There were only about five employees, and it looked like they were getting ready to huddle. They really were having a business meeting. They had official T-shirts and everything Jeff had wanted for his own business.

Now he was finally getting in.

A bright-yellow sign with the farm's name encircling a grinning alligator marked the entrance to a long driveway that led Jeff into the swamp. Jeff parked by their barn and greeted the man he'd spoken to on the phone, a square-jawed fellow named Robert.

"Jeff Blackledge," Jeff said, shaking Robert's hand. "Pleasure to meet you."

"Likewise," Robert replied with a curt nod. As they started into the facility, Jeff sized Robert up. He had short light-brown hair, looked like he kept in shape, cared about his appearance, like in another life, he could have been an actor. He spoke, too, with a quiet, nonchalant intelligence. It was clear to Jeff that Robert wasn't like so many of the people he'd met out there in the boondocks. Robert had depth. Yet he had no desire to flaunt it.

When he was making his initial overview of the list, the case agent had said they'd worked him already, meaning Jeff's predecessor had checked in with Robert's operation and found nothing out of the ordinary.

No way this guy's breaking the law, Jeff thought. Still, Robert seemed distracted, irritated even. Something was on his mind, and it had nothing to do with Jeff.

Robert guided Jeff to the facility's back entrance, where he motioned to a shallow pan like a paint tray in the St. Augustine grass beside the walkway. The water in it smelled like bleach. Robert directed Jeff to dip the soles of his shoes and wash them off before they could move on. The formality of this act, and the whiff of science-backed agriculture that attended it, impressed Jeff. *This isn't just some backyard rodeo,* Jeff thought. *This is some agriculture-department-grade rule following.*

While he slipped the soles of his boots through the caustic water, Jeff's admiration gave way to myriad questions. *Is this something I should be doing at Sunshine?* he thought. *How terrible is it not to have one of these?*

"What's this all about?" Jeff asked. "Because, you know, if I need to do this in my facility, then I don't know nothing about it."

"Oh, the Department of Agriculture guy was here last week," Robert said with a tone of complaint.

So that's what's on his mind, Jeff thought. *I knew he was distracted.*

"He told me I need to make some changes," Robert explained. "To keep bacteria from entering the building, you have to be cleansed. Or like how in the butcher shop, you have to wear hairnets for example. Things like that. You already know a lot of it. It's common sense."

"But you weren't doing it," Jeff said with a grin. If Jeff had learned one thing from his career in Florida wildlife law enforcement, it was that *common sense* was an oxymoron.

"Oh, we were." Robert cracked a smile for the first time in their conversation. "We just weren't doing it to the nth degree. They want this place spotless. If that's what they want, that's what we'll do." He said it with a tone of honest piety, like deep down he enjoyed the work it took to follow the rules.

This fellow's got a good aura about him, Jeff mused. To Jeff, Robert seemed upstanding, a man he could trust. He wore a crucifix on a chain around his neck. As a Catholic himself, though not an especially devout one, Jeff saw Robert's faith as another vote in his favor. Jeff believed he could learn a lot just from basking in his farm's proverbial glow. Perhaps Robert could someday count as a friend to lighten the burden of Jeff's loneliness, too.

Even though Jeff's facility, at this point, wasn't putting out any products, and its true mission was to act as a backdrop, he wanted it to be functional. And it wouldn't hurt if he was eventually turning a profit. He wasn't doing any butchering. His gators lived in the fenced-in ponds, not inside any sort of facility, so they were frolicking in whatever bacteria nature had to offer. Jeff didn't need this stuff. And yet—here came his impulse to do everything to the letter barreling in. Here were boxes he hadn't checked off. He made a mental note to tackle them when he got home. *No, not home*, he thought. *The farm. The farm isn't your home.*

After Robert sloshed his feet through the pan as well, he led Jeff inside, where he gestured to long tanks like raised lap pools where baby alligators, dozens of them, most no more than a foot long, swam in the same undulating motion as their much larger elders did: on the pivot of their head where it projected through the surface. Others fought and rolled around with one another. More lounged on Styrofoam islands. They squeaked and peeped at the sight of the men. Robert called these tanks raceways. Each was twenty feet long and five feet across.

"We use them for grading," Robert explained. He indicated the dams that blocked off the ends of the raceways. Each had a hole in it big enough for a baby alligator to squeeze through. The hole in each consecutive dam was of a progressively smaller size, so only the smallest alligators could fit into the last tank. Thus the alligators "graded" themselves by size without the farmers needing a ruler or a scale, or to handle them at all for that matter. This was an aquaculture concept. Not every facility had such a thing. Having visited an increasing number of farms, Jeff was quickly learning that farmers implemented whatever technology, both low and high, they could afford. The ones with shallower pockets made do with more MacGyvered solutions, like the place down in Moore Haven that used shipping crates and pallets for egg candling.

Robert opened the door to their butchering room, and a puff of clean, cool air washed over them. Jeff studied the shine of the concrete floor, the coolness of the concrete-block walls, the stainless-steel tables that looked untouched but weren't. The place was spotless. Alligator meat is relatively cheap, more of a by-product than a main source of profit. (Although when you can find it in the grocery store, the prices vary wildly, ranging from the cost of chicken breast to the wallet load of a decent steak, with most of this price due to the middlemen. Purchase gator meat closer to the source, and it can run as low as a few bucks a pound.) The real profit comes from the skins, which often go for hundreds of dollars for unblemished, high-quality hides.

From the sheen and hygiene of Robert's facility, it was obvious that the owners had money. Had Jeff been back in his real persona as Officer Babauta, he might have assumed that they'd scrubbed the place down before he arrived. But he wasn't. And they hadn't. Jeff was nobody. They didn't care what he saw. Sure, they were making improvements for inspections, but a farm didn't get this good overnight. Their facility was just like this. That's how Jeff wanted his to be.

In terms of the case, not only was Jeff learning, he was also trying to spy clues of wrongdoing. He knew no one would likely keep obvious displays of poaching or laundering out in the open, but if something was going on, there would be hints of it. He looked for something off, like one unlabeled box amid labeled ones, loose CITES tags, mess, or disorganization. Even if nothing overt called his attention, Jeff's gut would tell him something was off. Jeff's gut had a career's worth of practice. By now, he knew he should trust it.

Jeff's gut said that Robert and Shady Creek were aboveboard. More than aboveboard. Shining examples of what he aspired to be. Jeff could have inspected every inch of the place for hours, but the tour came to a close all too quickly. In less than an hour, it seemed like they were shooing him out the door. Jeff understood, though. As someone often preoccupied with perfecting his own work, Jeff saw the same in Robert, and so he could forgive his brusque demeanor and short tour. He wanted to return to Shady Creek. Yet he had a feeling he wouldn't be back again. There were no problems there that he could see, and they had no time for him. You win some. You lose some.

Still, this new window to the inside had whetted Jeff's appetite. He wanted more tours, more calls. He wasn't quite ready to call this one a draw.

A few weeks later, in the midst of summer nesting season, the idea to call Robert sprang into Jeff's head. As a farm manager, Robert would likely be going out to collect eggs, and maybe if Jeff asked, Robert would let him join in.

Standing outside the camper, leaning against the side, watching the sunset turn the treetops into shadows, Jeff called Robert. The line rang itself out then went to voicemail. Jeff left a message. *Oh well*, he thought. He went inside, removed his laptop from its secret compartment in the wall, and got cracking on some paperwork.

About an hour later, his phone rang. It was Robert. A small miracle.

"Hey, how ya doing?" Jeff said, genuine warmth in his voice. "Didn't think you would call me back."

"I would have picked up in the first place, but I'm already in Okeechobee collecting eggs, and you know how it is down here," Robert said.

"That's what I called to talk to you about," Jeff said. "I'd sure like to tag along and learn a thing or two. You don't need to pay me nothing. I'd just like to see how this operation works. Hell, I'll even pay for my own hotel room. I'll meet you down there."

"Sure, sounds great," Robert said. "I'll call you tomorrow and see what we can work out." He hung up before Jeff could say another word.

Jeff finished his work. He read a chapter of a novel and went to bed. The next day, Jeff kept his phone close. As he finished various chores around the farm, he would pull it out and look at the screen, thinking maybe Robert had called, and Jeff just hadn't heard the ring. Nope. Nothing.

He just wanted to get me off the damn phone, Jeff thought, frowning and shaking his head.

On the third day, Jeff called again.

"Hey, man, I thought you were going to call me," Jeff said. "I was all ready to come help you."

"Sorry, I got caught up in the harvest," Robert said.

"I'm all packed," Jeff said. "I can still come."

"Unfortunately, we're done," Robert replied.

"Done for the day?"

"Done for the season. Maybe next year. Keep in touch."

Jeff put his phone down on the counter of the barn workroom and sighed. He wanted to like Robert, but the more he worked, and the more he thought about his brief glimpse inside the upper echelon of alligator farming, the more Robert's cordial dismissiveness hurt. It put a nick in the farm manager's otherwise golden sheen.

No use dwelling, Jeff thought. He told himself to put Robert out of his mind and keep moving forward.

It was time to pick up more fish guts.

Jeff had managed to dodge the agency inspector when he came by the farm. When the man called again, Jeff deepened his voice, hoping the inspector, a man he had known for years, would not recognize it.

"Everything shipshape?" Jeff asked.

"The place is coming along," the inspector said.

The noncommittal answer made Jeff's heart sink.

"I want this place to be perfect," Jeff said. "What am I missing?"

"You need more square footage to bring you up to code," the inspector said. "Meaning, you need more room for the gators, even though you don't have them all yet."

"So the kiddie pools are all right?" Jeff asked. The previous agent took a few steps toward creating the farm before he got burned, buying kiddie pools for the hatchlings, among other things. In lieu of concrete raceway tanks like at Shady Creek, several of the less well-heeled farms Jeff toured used kiddie pools, the cheap and ubiquitous plastic lounges of childhood summer, as nurseries for their tiny gators. Jeff planned to use these, too. Stacks of them sat in the barn, giving off the hot smell of plastic.

"They're fine," the inspector said. "But you're going to need more of them."

More? I already have a bunch.

"How many more, you think?" Jeff asked.

"Oh, a dozen or so ought to do it," the inspector said.

Jeff thanked the inspector, and afterward, he drove into town, hitting every store he could think of that might possibly stock kiddie pools. He was well aware the whole scenario was ridiculous.

You can't make this shit up, he thought, shaking his head and smiling at the absurdity as he stacked kiddie pools onto a cart.

At one checkout counter, the cashier looked at his stack of pools and said, "Damn, you have this many kids?"

"No," Jeff responded, amused with himself. "I'm an alligator farmer."

"Oh," the cashier said, as if enlightened by Jeff's answer. He craned his head over the checkout counter to watch Jeff leave.

At Jeff's next stop, the hardware store, he spied a familiar face at the end of the aisle. "Well, look who it is!" Jeff called out as he approached.

Robert turned from the tools wearing an irritated frown. When his eyes landed on Jeff, he conjured up a closed-lip smile. "Fancy seeing you here," he said, shaking Jeff's hand. "How's the farm coming?"

"It's really coming along," Jeff said. He gestured at the kiddie pools. "I have my own inspector problems." Jeff explained, and Robert's forced expression gradually gave way to one of genuine, albeit light, amusement.

"Whatever works," Robert said. "I'm buying some things for the farm myself. I have to get the place well situated before the family and I go up to the mountains for our annual hunting trip."

"What do you like to hunt?" Jeff asked. *Finally, something we have in common*, he thought.

They chatted about hunting, Robert's family, and their farms; and by the end of the conversation, Jeff had felt Robert warm to him. Or, if he hadn't warmed, he'd at least thawed.

"We should go hunting together sometime," Jeff offered.

"You bet," Robert said as he walked away. "I'll call you."

By the end of the day, Sunshine Alligator Farm sported some forty or fifty pools, all ready for hatchlings. Jeff himself sported a new hope that he had found a way in.

When days and then weeks passed, and Robert hadn't called, Jeff shrugged. He could have called Robert himself, but what was the point? *I can take a hint*, he thought. So he got on with his life.

Jeff's days, like most farmers', started early. Before he ate breakfast, Jeff would get dressed and take a quick turn around his farm, observing every gator, making sure they were all well fed and looked healthy. He would check the temperatures of the ponds as well as the water level. In the summer, alligators would spend a great deal of each day either in or under the water to keep cool. During cooler months, the gators would spend more time basking to bring their temperatures up. Jeff mowed and used the Weedwacker around the ponds to keep their basking space open. Sometimes when he got bored, he'd train them like dogs.

He threw a soft Frisbee toy toward the pond. "Here boy," he called out.

To Jeff's surprise, the Frisbee flew just close enough to the gator that it chomped down and—kind of—caught it.

"Fetch?" Jeff said. *I didn't think this through.* "Or, you know what? Maybe just keep it."

A real alligator farming operation hires people to do all of these things. The more alligators they have, the more people they bring in to maintain them. There's someone for everything: a food specialist, a veterinarian, a butcher, a skinner. When the alligators reach maturity, they'll skin them. While the butcher processes the meat, the skinner will soften the hides enough so they'll roll like vellum. If prices for skins are too low, he might stash this set in the freezer and sell them when the price goes back up again. Butchers at big enough farms have deals with supermarkets and specialty meat distributors. Smaller farms sell straight from their own shops. In the right parts of Florida, it's not unheard of to spot hand-painted signs along the roadside enticing drivers to pull over and partake in some alligator jerky. (Who thought it was a good idea to take an animal whose meat is already tough and stringy and make it even tougher and stringier?) Some facilities make money on the heads and claws, sending them to a taxidermist's shop. They then go on to roadside orange stands and tourist shops in greasy gas stations stocked with useless Florida bric-a-brac. The alligator skulls will persist there, cultivating a layer of grime, languishing under the fluorescent lights and bathed in the unctuous odor of the fossilized taquitos that have been turning on the roller grill since the beginning of time.

In the corners of gator country, folk magic practitioners incorporate alligator claws and teeth into their rituals, which seems a more fitting end for these majestic beasts. At the very least, it's one that does not denude them of their power after death. Though, as the owner of an alligator scute once given to me by a gladesman as a talisman of protection, maybe I'm a little biased.

Jeff wasn't doing any of these things. Knowing he would soon have to part with them, he refrained from naming his gators. Yet he loved them enough to leave them intact. It pained him to think of them as a commodity to be bought and sold.

He watched over them that January as the weather grew cool. In the depths of winter, alligators' metabolisms slow down. If it gets cold enough, they'll go into brumation, the reptilian version of hibernation. They don't eat much during the winter, so Jeff spent less on food. He needed less money to run the farm. Everything seemed to slow down. These doldrums just stretched on and on. Jeff was beginning to feel like a weather-chilled alligator: The world kept moving around him, but here he was, standing still.

Yet, on the other side of every winter, spring arrives to bring the thaw, to awaken life within the swamp, to instill it with the vigorous and undeniable impulse toward creation. With spring would come mating season. The rumbling bellow of bull gators would hum through the cypresses and reeds. When one bull met another, they would fight, open-jawed, tooth and claw, the dragons of Bartram's journals.

"Behold him rushing forth from the flags and reeds. His enormous body swells. His plaited tail brandished high, floats upon the lake. The waters like a cataract descend from his opening jaws. Clouds of smoke issue from his dilated nostrils. The earth trembles with his thunder," Bartram wrote. Although the naturalist's writings are a bit much sometimes, and they're often not factual in the literal sense, like the yarns from the backwoods of Florida, these hyperbolic descriptions capture alligators in their essence, as the majestic, ancient swamp rulers they really are. Such alligator duels and the couplings that come after bring forth a new generation to rule the swamp with no less majesty than their progenitors, even as the cold facts of modernity have diminished their magnificence under many an unimaginative gaze.

And so, in place of winter's quietude, summer would follow spring, and with the rising temperatures, the inevitability of new life. The drama and danger of nesting season would seize the swamp once again. With nesting season, Jeff knew, just as inevitable as all that new life, crime would arise again and slink through the shadows of the swamp's hot night.

10

THE BALLAD OF PEG BROWN

If the numbers from the Peg Brown tales were true, then Peg killed upward of ten thousand gators over the span of his career as a poacher. Only counting the time after he returned from World War II up until the Endangered Species Act of 1973, when he allegedly stopped hunting alligators entirely, that's twenty-eight years, or about one gator a day. To put those numbers into perspective, now that alligators are numerous, homeowners can call an FWC hotline to report them—think the "nuisance" gators who take up residence in Nana's Boca Raton pool.

Between 1997 and 2021, Florida trappers caught more than 320,000 nuisance alligators, some of which they released, while others were sold. More than half of those alligators, however, were "harvested," the agency's deceptively bland euphemism for "euthanized." In just those twenty-four years, the state of Florida killed about eighteen times more alligators than Peg ever did by his own estimations, yet those losses have shown little impact on alligator populations overall. In other words, even the most notorious and prolific poacher ever to wreak havoc on the glades would have had very little impact on his own. Peg and his kind, however, made for very convenient scapegoats for the sudden and dramatic decline of the American alligator in the 1950s and 1960s when South Florida's newcomers demanded action, hounding the park service for one escalation after another. The rangers obliged. They bought more planes and stayed out all night to watch for poachers. By the thousands of pages I've read of their barely legible logs, these efforts were successful. They caught dozens of poachers. But Peg, it seemed, always remained just out of their reach. Then they beat him, too. Tired of facing down so much firepower every night, Peg gave up their cat-and-mouse games for good. Or did he?

I went over these numbers in my head as I waited for Jonnie, remembering what Rothchild wrote in *Tropic*: "There is probably no such thing as a truly retired poacher."

When Jonnie Brown pulled up—in a white Ford F-150, just like Jeff's—to where I stood in the breezeway of the Outdoor Resorts of Chokoloskee, I recognized him immediately. I'd never seen a picture of him; it was just that his person very much matched the deep drawl I'd heard on the phone. He was an imposing man with ruddy cheeks from work in the sun and short graying hair. I considered for a moment that, had I been someone else, his stature and blue-collar roughness might have put me on the defensive. Instead, it was those same qualities that made me warm to him even more than I had on the phone. He would have fit right in at a Renner family reunion. I knew that he would take great care on the adventure that he had promised.

We shook hands, and I smiled. "You must be Jonnie Brown."

"That's right," he said. "And you must be Rebecca."

"That's me. It's nice to finally meet you, Jonnie."

I found myself slipping into my river country drawl, a leisurely, broad accent that shies away from hard consonants, an accent not unlike the one spoken in the Everglades. For most of my life, my parents tried to correct that speech away. They would make me repeat after them, *Button. Cot-ton.* By high school, I could speak with the chipper blandness of a newscaster. By the end of college, I wished I could get it back. I wished I could sound like my great-grandmother, who had lived her entire life on the edge of the swamp. Yet that flavor only crawled back into my words when I least expected. It snuck up on me when I stopped trying.

Often when I'd slip back into it while talking with gladesmen, I could see their shoulders relax, their tension uncoiling, as if I had transformed from predaceous outsider to someone who might understand if they spoke their hearts to me.

I didn't see Jonnie having lots of heartache to spill, but I try not to assume. Of course, being a pragmatic man, he launched into planning the day almost immediately. He asked me what I wanted to do, and I said, "You're the boss. It's up to you. Tell me and show me whatever you think I need to see. I have questions, of course, but I don't know what I don't know, you know?"

He laughed. "Right."

What I really wanted were primary sources, documents and the like. My holy grail would be a diary or a journal, and I told him as much.

As we got into his truck, he said, "Don't have anything like that. Don't have much, in all honesty. We lost a lot of pictures. Somebody threw them out."

"Damn," I said.

"Even his war memorabilia," Jonnie said as he pulled in a circle out of the shell-gravel parking lot. "My dad was a war hero. Did you know that? Had a gold star for valor." Jonnie indicated a photograph print on the console between us. It was Peg in his military regalia, spangled with his gold stars. "He was a rifleman in the First Infantry," Jonnie continued. "That much I know. He hardly ever talked about it. In fact, I only heard him mention it once."

They were drinking together at the Oyster Bar, the now-defunct dive bar that the outlaws frequented, and Peg had gotten drunk enough to start reliving long-buried memories: It was December 16, 1944. The pines reached so high in the forest of the Ardennes in Belgium that the whole landscape would have fallen under a false twilight if the thick crust of snow hadn't blanched it. Peg had never seen snow before the war. He was made in the swamp and built for that climate. The cold might have defeated a weaker Floridian, but Peg was tough. He never complained.

The snow deepened as the days went on. The troops were tired. Earlier that month, they had made a drive through the Hürtgen Forest and had withdrawn to rest before pushing forward against an unexpected German offensive.

As the infantrymen fought, Peg and the other riflemen guarded the line. He had learned to shoot in the Everglades, in cypress domes where the junglelike tangle obstructed the view of even the sharpest-eyed hunters. Despite the bitter cold of that foreign blizzard, the air itself seemed clear. Peg let off shot after shot, one hit after another. It was the same as back home, except here there was a man at the other end of your bullet. That wasn't the same as hitting a gator or even a panther. It was best not to think about it. He had to keep firing.

He fired so much that even in that record cold his gun overheated. When the gun got too hot to keep firing, too hot to touch, his assistant rifleman would fill his helmet with snow and dump it on the gunstock. The snow would melt almost instantly, then freeze, forming a layer of frost so thick and stubborn that Peg couldn't fire the gun again until they'd beaten away the ice. They repeated that unending farce, hardly taking breaks to eat and sleep for weeks on end. They pushed the Nazi offensive back, forcing the enemy troops from the wider roads onto barely passable trails. American tanks trundled over waves of rocks and snow.

This long counteroffensive beneath the Ardennes's venerable spruces, a fight that would become immortalized as the Battle of the Bulge, was not a victory of strength over weakness. It was a battle of grit. Plagued by the forbidding elements in a battle that seemed to never end, only soldiers too stubborn to consider quitting held out. On the American line, no matter how weary they became, stubbornness was never in short supply, especially in the boys from Florida, who knew something about hard times. They knew that storms are temporary and that their hardship was nothing compared with whom they were fighting for.

By January 1945, the 1st Infantry had won out. They returned to Germany and crossed the Rhine. The snows of winter were only a memory by the time they reached Flossenbürg concentration camp, where they broke through its fortifications and released thousands of prisoners, many of whom were too starved to walk.

Peg never talked to Jonnie, or anyone as far as Jonnie knew, about the concentration camps or what he saw there. He had hardly talked about the war at all. The sheer amount of liquor it had taken to pry this one story from the recesses of his mind and the tenor of his voice as he recounted it, how he pantomimed the futile gesture of beating the ice from his rifle over and over again, told of a persistent memory more indelible than a photograph. He would never admit that it haunted him, but it was hard to imagine it hadn't. Perhaps it returned to him during his nights in the swamp, the mosquito-thick air suddenly falling chill as the cypresses morphed into spruces and the water and the weeds and the mangroves became snow in the Ardennes, and a hail of gunfire he tried to forget sang out over his head. Or was that the beat of a helicopter blade? The rangers' spotlights through the trees ratcheted Peg's pulse. It's easy to forget where you are, *when* you are, when the past is so alive within you.

As Jonnie drove toward Everglades City, eager to find us a place for lunch, the tableau of the icy gun repeated in my head. It was such a striking image, visceral just like the stories of Peg's poaching, and yet it showed a completely different person from the one I had assumed Peg to be. In the Ardennes, Peg had not been a valiant folk hero, a John Henry–like figure of impossible feats in the swamp. He was just a mortal man faced with the futility of war. With guts and grit, he kept on going, because that's what you did, but not without a significant loss. Something inside of him had broken. He carried that quietly all his life. And it's in the quiet night of the swamp that he was alone with the darkest thoughts he left unspoken.

That complicated inner world of Peg's changed the stories for me. His cat-and-mouse games with the rangers had subtext. After all of that fighting, Peg had come home to find his world changed. Loggers had stripped the land. The Army Corps of Engineers had diverted the water, causing what foliage remained to shift year by year, almost imperceptibly, until people like Peg no longer recognized the Everglades anymore. Alligators, the species that had been his livelihood, took a downturn. Adding insult to injury, rich developers and newcomers blamed Peg and other hunters for that loss even though their impact was small compared to all that new construction. Tricking the rangers made Peg feel less powerless. Perhaps that's when he became the folk hero in his own eyes. Because no matter what else they took, developers couldn't take away the poachers' stories. The wily trickster and his humorous resistance remind the downtrodden the world over that when you're smart you still have power. Some things never change.

Jonnie took us to a little fish house where we ate lunch and then remained in the oversized, shiny booth for our interview. Jonnie was a fisherman, a legal one. In those days, he mainly caught Florida stone crabs. They're so ungodly expensive—with consumer prices for claws ranging from $35 to $95 per pound in 2023—it's almost a crime anyway.

Jonnie reiterated a lot of the stories I'd already heard, adding that Peg had crafted many of them himself, their origin being at the Oyster Bar where many a poacher had spun his yarn.

"The Rod & Gun was for tourists," Jonnie said.

He told me about Peg killing a gator outside the rangers' station, the same one I'd read about in the ranger's report. This particular gator passed his days floating in the estuary in the shade of the mangroves by the station. After seeing the gator every day, the rangers came to think of him as a pet. They even named him and erected a sign by his wallow with that name and a warning not to mess with him. One night, Peg came by, killed the gator, and changed the sign to say the gator was gone, because that dastardly Peg Brown had sent him to heaven. I found that story both grimly funny and sad. I've become attached to many a gator that has shared a habitat with me. I'd be pretty sore if somebody went and killed one of "my" gators. Jonnie told me about Peg getting lost one time and then ending up drinking coffee with the rangers at their station. When his brother showed up to fetch him, the rangers were asking Peg if he knew any poachers, "like that Peg Brown fellow," whom they just couldn't manage to catch.

"Never heard of him," the Browns said before quickly slipping away.

The rangers had initially met Clarence—Peg under his Christian name—because they'd recruited locals to teach them how to navigate the glades. The rangers had come to work at Everglades National Park from all over the country, from the Rocky Mountains to the Ozarks, places they thought made them rugged. They assumed they could surmount any environment—and then they faced the Everglades. Poachers quipped that the rangers were easy to outsmart because they were afraid of the mosquitoes. On hot nights, they'd hunker in their station, unwilling to venture forth into that inhospitable swamp that was both their charge and their foe. The poachers, however, bore the swamp no such ill will. It was their home, their friend, the primary accomplice to their trickery. The locals certainly taught the rangers the ropes, but they left out important details, fudged here and there to stop rangers from stumbling on the hideouts where they poached. It was in their best interest to make the swamp seem unnavigable. This is not the place for the faint of heart. One of Peg's neighbors nailed a sign to a tree that said it all: WHOA YANKEE TURN AROUND.

I had stumbled upon that picture in an archive, and it made me laugh. I asked Jonnie about it, and he said he knew where it was.

"We can go find it later," he said.

I was happy to hear some confirmation of all these tales from Jonnie, but at the same time, I worried that some of them were just folklore. I wanted more than confirmation. I wanted evidence. I wanted firsthand accounts. It was starting to seem like I was out of luck, though, because Peg had gone out so much on his own, and his brother Totch's versions of the tales that made Totch himself the star were the ones recorded in print. If Totch was the famous one, did that make him right by default? I didn't like that. It seemed antithetical to the stories themselves, erasing their element of tenacity. As captivating a storyteller as he was, Totch was no underdog.

So I asked Jonnie, "Do you happen to know anybody who went hunting with Peg who's still alive?"

Jonnie gave me a slow smile. "Well, there's me," he said.

"Really?" I said, alert, my pen poised and ready. "Can you tell me about any of that?"

"Of course," he said. "What do you want to hear?"

In the year 1960, Jonnie turned eleven. By then, great change had already befallen Chokoloskee. In the very early years of Jonnie's life, neither road nor electricity connected the island to the mainland. Jonnie attended a one-room schoolhouse on the island. Some other kids rode in on a boat that acted as their school bus.

The Browns lived on a "house-lighter," their word for what outsiders might call a houseboat. Rather than floating on the water, it stood on stilts overlooking the tide. It was white with blue trim. Jonnie's father had built it himself when he came back from the war.

They had no electricity. Neither did any of their neighbors. Jonnie did his homework by the light of kerosene lamps. Not that he always did it. Jonnie was what he would later call a "real mean" kid. He would shoot cans from their garbage pile with his BB gun and teach innocent neighbor kids how to cuss. He had plenty to be ornery about, but he didn't fully realize it at the time.

In 1956, the state built a bridge that connected Everglades City on the mainland with Chokoloskee. With the bridge came all sorts of outsiders. According to the adults in Jonnie's life, the two worst types of outsiders were the tourists and the environmentalists. Even a journalist had started poking around. Peter Matthiessen was working on a book about endangered species, he said. Yet he kept asking all kinds of questions to anybody who gave him the time of day. He was in love with the mystique of the Everglades, like most of the outsiders were, but he also seemed transfixed by a murder that had happened at the trading post about half a century before. The Brown clan and the Daniels clan, by then united by marriage, had both been involved. Unlike with their other alleged undertakings, they were more than happy to tell the story of how in 1910 they killed Edgar Watson, a violent sugarcane planter who treated his workers like slaves.

"The bastard deserved it," Jonnie said. "Nobody knows who shot him, because near every man in town was there with his gun, and they all shot at once."

Chokoloskee was proud of the Wild West–style justice they had meted out. Uncle Totch had taken it upon himself to become the island's unofficial historian and storyteller (Kent's spiritual predecessor), and so he befriended Matthiessen and showed him around, hoping to catch a little bit of fame along the way.

All this new attention brought newfound trouble. Peg had always made his living fishing and poaching alligators. In those days, the numbers of alligators had shrunk in some parts, while in others, like around Big Fox Lake, they remained plentiful. The outsiders seemed preoccupied with the alligators, even more so than the people whose livelihoods depended on them. They came in seeking to change everything rather than realizing it was the change they had brought that started the problems in the first place. If everyone had just left the Everglades the hell alone, the adults said, the alligators wouldn't be having so much trouble.

Jonnie frequently went hunting with Peg. They would skin the alligators out in the mangroves then take all the hides down the road to the mainland, where they would meet a fellow named Graham, one of the buyers. He would throw the salted hides into the trunk of his car, really load it up until it barely closed, and then he would count out bills from a roll, $5 per foot for hides five feet and over. That was a lot of money back then and well worth the risk.

Everything got more expensive when increasing crowds of tourists came to the Ten Thousand Islands, so the Browns struggled more than ever to put food on the table. Jonnie had two sisters and six living brothers, and he was the second-oldest boy. He and the six younger kids lived with their parents on the house-lighter. The oldest two lived down the road with their grandparents. It was a good thing that fish were free and plentiful. They ate a lot of ibis, too, usually the brown ones. Even though hunting the white ibis was illegal, so many people on the island did it that even folks outside the Ten Thousand Islands started calling them Chokoloskee Chicken.

Come hurricane season of 1960, the gauges on all their barometers plunged, and even before the radios proclaimed the approach of Hurricane Donna, the residents of Chokoloskee knew a major storm was on its way. The adults in Jonnie's life—his parents, his grandparents, and their neighbors—feared losing their belongings. They battened down the hatches as best they could, then evacuated across the island to the Blue Heron Hotel, where the owner allowed them to stay for free. The tourists fled in a panic. As the adults watched and waited, the kids squirmed with that particular excitement that precedes the coming of a hurricane. Regular storms were awesome and wonderful, but hurricanes were something else, mighty and dangerous. Just living through one was an adventure.

Their excitement reached a fever pitch as the wind howled outside. Periodically, they would peek out of the blinds. The big fig tree out front had bent nearly double. The wind gauge on a nearby roof climbed as high as 185 miles per hour. The glass of a car outside flexed with the record low pressure then exploded the way a bubble pops.

During the eye, everything went still. Jonnie couldn't help himself. He ran outside. He had never seen the island so quiet. There were no cars, no people. Not even the birds sang. For a moment, he gazed around in wonder, awed by the stillness wrought by nature's fury. Peg marched out and dragged his dumb ass back inside. Soon the winds picked up again. Torrents of rain pelted the hotel. All kinds of strange sounds enveloped them: the screech of metal, the crack of splintering wood, a long groan that sounded like the song of a whale.

When the skies had cleared, the Browns ventured out into the daylight. Water had risen up to cover the entire island. Peg waded away to get his pitpan. Jonnie followed him through that foreign landscape. On the shore where their house once stood, they only found debris. Their house-lighter was gone. Luckily, Peg spied his boat, or at least a boat that looked enough like his to pass for it. Who knew in all that mess. He and Jonnie went around picking up serviceable wood scraps and piling them in the pitpan. Thousands of fish littered what was left of the dry land, some too far away to have washed ashore on the tide. There were little minnows, puffer fish inflated from fright, even an immense grouper nearly the size of a cow. They ate the fish that night at the hotel, like a Sunday fish fry that they all had together.

Peg built a new house from reclaimed wood. This one was wired with electricity. That wasn't the only change that settled over them after the hurricane. Peg poached less and less. He focused on his fishing guide business, even had a friend paint a sign on the side of their house. NATIVE GUIDE, it said and touted his wares, adventures for sale. He decided to capitalize on the tourists instead of fighting them. Even celebrities sought out Peg, like Christopher Plummer and Gypsy Rose Lee, who came to film *Wind Across the Everglades*, a 1958 film in which Totch Brown played a bit part. They came to Peg not just for guiding services but also for a taste of the exotic life of the glades. As he steered them through the mangroves, sometimes with Jonnie as his assistant, he spun yarns for them, tales that brought the glades to life. Rip Torn came fishing with them, and Peg didn't know who he was. But Rip had heard of Peg. It was always like that.

On the way back to Chokoloskee, Jonnie drove us by the rangers' old houses, two bungalows raised on stilts over their carports. Back in the day, Jonnie would drive by like this to see if the rangers' cars were in their driveways. Then he'd drive past the station and glance over the docks where the rangers kept their boats. If all the boats and trucks were accounted for, the coast was clear to go out hunting. That day, the docks were full with everything from small motorboats to bigger trawlers.

"Looks like the coast is clear," Jonnie joked.

Back on the far side of the island, Jonnie drove down increasingly narrow dirt roads. Near the pebble-strewn beach, a stand of Australian pines, an introduced species, cast cool shadows over the lot. The house was a regular house, not on stilts, not a lighter.

Jonnie mused aloud that he didn't know who lived there anymore. He had moved up the coast decades ago in search of better opportunities as a fisherman, and so he had become disconnected from Chokoloskee. The distance seemed to sadden him, as if he was separated from his past and the person he used to be, and merely visiting did little to bridge that gulf.

He did know the fellow who lived next door, so he drove around and parked next to where a land-bound catamaran waited in the grass. He got out and walked around, and I followed. At the corner of the two fences, there was a clutch of trees. Jonnie gestured at it. "Sign's gone," he said. He meant the WHOA YANKEE TURN AROUND sign we'd gone looking for. It was a marker of a bygone day. Now Chokoloskee's only industry was tourism. WHOA YANKEE COME BACK (AND SPEND YOUR MONEY) would have been more fitting.

Jonnie walked around the house, remembering stories as he studied the changes. He recounted the one time that the rangers ever came close to catching Peg. Peg had been burning prairie grass so he could get his pitpan through to the next waterhole in the slough. Before he knew it, he heard chopper blades overhead. He threw palm fronds over the boat and lay down underneath them. Thus thatched, he hid. The whirlwind from the helicopter drove downward, pressing in on him until he could have touched the landing gear with his oar. He waited, not moving, his heart hammering as the palm blades fluttered. After a while, the chopper seemed to give up, and Peg returned to the hunt.

Planes and helicopters had chased both of them down more times than Jonnie cared to count. Rangers in a plane once locked onto them with a spotlight. It was hair-raising for Jonnie, but not for Peg. Nothing ever ruffled him. At least, it didn't seem to. Who knew what was really going on in that quiet man's head.

Then why did Peg stop poaching? Perhaps it was no longer worth the risk. Perhaps the rangers had won. Perhaps he never stopped. He just stopped spinning yarns about it. Once a poacher, always a poacher, right?

Once when Jonnie had gone out poaching on his own one night, he inadvertently left behind his gun and the salt he used to cure the hides out in the open. Come daylight, a ranger stumbled upon them. Somehow, he knew who they belonged to, and he tracked Jonnie down.

"I was never as crafty as my dad," Jonnie said with a chuckle. "Nobody was."

When the ranger came to arrest Jonnie, Peg told his son to do as the ranger said. "Don't worry," Peg added. "I'll take care of it." These were just the facts of life when you were an alligator poacher. Unruffled, Peg went out to his boat. He never told Jonnie what he did, but when he arrived later to bail him out, he had money that he didn't have before. There was one thing that Peg knew how to do that made good money.

Jonnie had barely finished this story when a car pulled into the driveway. Earlier, we had asked after a man named Mac at the Smallwood Store, which he owned with his wife, a descendant of the original Smallwood. Mac had tracked us down. He was a light-haired, sturdily built fellow with a disarming smile and a carefree attitude that reminded me of the Keys.

"Who's this?" Mac called out from his truck. "She's way too pretty for you."

"Sorry, I'm a journalist," I said in a deadpan, joking tone. "And I'm too pretty for you, too." For a second, they were silent, and I was afraid my joke hadn't landed. There's always that danger when my mouth gets ahead of me. Then Mac and Jonnie roared with laughter, breaking what could have been a tense moment like the popping windshield in Jonnie's hurricane story.

"You got me," Mac said. "I walked right into that one." If he had been closer, he might have slapped me on the back like I was one of the guys. I had proved I could take it as well as dish it out. Once he'd parked and come over, he gave me a firm handshake and a grin, and we exchanged more proper introductions.

My relief came from more than having avoided a tense moment. I've found that many Floridians employ a genre of sarcasm that seems to go over some people's heads. When we're together, we speak in this often-dark repartee, but when outsiders show up, especially when they're extremely serious journalists, they take our remarks out of context, and we go from figuratively misunderstood to literally misunderstood, which would be funny in itself if it didn't happen so often and in such otherwise reputable periodicals.

Mac had become an insider, but he hadn't always been. He lived across the street and knew Jonnie well, but he wasn't from Chokoloskee. He wasn't even from Florida. He proudly called himself a Michigander, yet no one seemed to treat him with the same hostility toward northerners that had once inspired the sign WHOA YANKEE TURN AROUND. Though some of that sentiment still lingered in the Everglades and back where I came from, Mac seemed to exist in a different category. Without having to erase his roots, he had been accepted as one of them; not just allowed or tolerated, he was a pillar of the community. That made me wonder: Why had Mac been accepted while other outsiders remained, well, outside?

I thought back to the celebrities visiting Peg. They took his fishing tours and listened to his stories, but perhaps they didn't really hear him, and by the end, they only saw him as a character, set dressing, part of their experience of the glades, as I had when I first came to Chokoloskee. Then without knowing it, they and other visitors and newcomers, having fallen in love with the Everglades, or only the caricature of it that they were willing to see, rallied for laws and regulations to protect the place from the people who lived there, the very people who had acted as stewards of that land for generations, or, in the cases of the Seminole and Miccosukee Tribes, since before humanity transcribed history into words.

Peg and other guides like him had welcomed tourists, and then those same visitors turned around and begged violence against them from the park service. It's easy to forget that the American alligator became endangered *after* Everglades National Park came in. So what happened, really? Habitat destruction had been the first to take its toll, but no one could drain or build in the park. So it wasn't that. Poachers like Peg did continue hunting, yet the number of alligators they took was statistically insignificant and could not have resulted in their decline. Yet the tourists blamed the poachers, decried history, and didn't bother to look deeper to see their stewardship of the glades. With fewer locals traipsing through that swamp, no one who knew what they were looking at was there to take the pulse of the species.

Given the stories I'd heard, I had a theory. In the 1950s, the Army Corps of Engineers installed a series of floodgates that allowed the Everglades to flow—or so they said. In true 1950s fashion, the corps put out a promotional movie reel, touting their triumph over nature: The corps controlled the Everglades. They told it where to flow, and flow it did in places where it never had before, creating floods made all the worse by Mother Nature's fury. Jonnie's story about Hurricane Donna gave me an aha moment, and it linked, like many things in their stories did, back to Jeff's investigation.

Just like how flooding from hurricanes had ruined a bayou nesting season and prompted Louisiana farmers to call on Floridian egg hunters to replenish their stocks, kicking off the need for Operation Alligator Thief in the first place, after the corps "triumphed" over nature, rainwater from hurricanes, which had once flowed through the Everglades, now pooled and mired and mucked up the place. Then the situation went from bad to worse. Hurricane Donna washed away over half the mangrove trees in the Everglades. This happened in September 1960, a time of year when nesting season becomes hatching season, and vulnerable hatchlings rely on vegetation like mangroves for shelter.

If flooding really did play such a major part in the alligator's downturn, how did the species bounce back? The Army Corps didn't fix their problem. They've been trying to mend that particular blunder to this day. For this answer, too, I can look back at evidence from Peg Brown stories. Although alligators tend to aim for the same nesting grounds that they have used year after year, they are not as unyielding as sea turtles: The alligators moved, many to the southernmost reaches of the glades where Peg continued to hunt and tend the land, such as by burning off excess brush left after storms to prevent blocked flows and pooling water, the very act that alerted the park service choppers to his whereabouts the one and only time the rangers almost caught him.

"You never take more than you need," Jonnie had said to me when he described their family's way of subsistence living. They cared for the world around them, because if they didn't, there would be nothing to sustain them anymore. When outsiders pushed them out of the Everglades, more was at stake than a sense of ownership. The Everglades was everything to them: their home, their past, their future, their culture, their identity.

Championing environmental causes by ignoring the people who live there, or worse, by working against them—wherever that may be—does not work, because to ignore the people is to ignore the land itself. They are the ones who have been listening to the land, many for a long time.

When tourists come down to the glades, or to any culture that has become a destination, it's all too common to partake of that culture like a commodity to be bought and sold. Tourists are so eager to experience what they think that culture should be that they ignore what it actually is. Journalists are guilty of this, too, when they jump in to take down a story without really paying attention, and it's why making fools of those same journalists remains a beloved Chokoloskee tradition. As much as I want to lay the blame elsewhere, we're all guilty of consuming culture like this in one way or another. It's just more apparent, and more hurtful, when it happens in your own backyard.

Although Mac had come from outside, he had done the very opposite: He arrived, he listened, he absorbed. He made it his life's cause not only to protect the place, but to continue its history and retell its stories. Maybe that was why the old-timers had ultimately accepted Peter Matthiessen, and why their descendants let me in, too: No matter what we *didn't* have in common, storytelling bridged the gulf. Matthiessen knew that the most important part of telling a story is, first, to listen.

Jeff had lived like that, watching people, talking to them, trying to understand them. He wanted to see the best in everyone. He wanted to know their story. He knew that no one breaks the law without a reason. He tried to withhold judgment. Because he was a mere mortal, that didn't always work. The same had happened for me on my journey into the Everglades.

I'll admit I'd held a concept of what poachers are like in my mind, and it was not a kind or understanding one, not one prone to listen. *What kind of person hurts a defenseless animal?* I thought, a hypocritical idea to countenance as a meat-eater. I crafted a caricature of the poachers I would meet in my head: rifle-toting, opinionated, camo-clad roughnecks who would have no respect for me or for the environment, who delighted in the pain of the animals they caught. What's worse is that I knew better. I already knew most poachers weren't like that. Yet the stereotype persisted in my thoughts until I had encountered such a shameful amount of evidence to the contrary that any single-celled organism could have understood that I was wrong.

Peg was a soft-spoken man, a listener. It was the creation of the park borders that had defined him as a poacher. Before it came in, he was only a hunter, and there were no Peg Brown stories.

Jonnie had been a poacher, too. He was soft-spoken at times, commanding in others. His livelihood as a fisherman depended on the balance of nature. He and Mac knew that stretch of glades better than I ever would. And instead of keeping me out, they wanted me to know more, because they knew I was ready to take it all in as it was, not as I thought it should be.

Jonnie explained to Mac what I was doing there, and Mac offered to take us out on his boat through the Ten Thousand Islands.

"You game for that?" Mac asked.

"Absolutely," I said. "Let me grab my notepad first."

11

THE HOOK

A tip came to Jeff from his handlers at the agency. They told him to check out a man named Wayne, who it seemed owned an alligator farm and kept half a dozen backwoods side hustles going, including guiding tourists on harrowing alligator hunts at night. So Jeff cooked up a story that he wanted to go into the pet trade. He called Wayne up and asked him if he had any hatchlings to sell that might make good pets.

The fact is that really no alligator makes a good pet. While federal law governs their private ownership because they are considered exotic pets, individual states dictate which animals are legal to own within their borders. It's legal to own a pet alligator in Alaska, but it's a crime in Georgia. In Florida, you have to have a permit and get it renewed once a year. Still, it's inadvisable. Former pet alligators under the care of specialists at rescues and rehabilitation facilities exhibit strange behaviors that range the gamut from excessive aggression to unnatural docility. Some display disrupted circadian rhythms. Others show up at rescues malnourished and missing limbs. Even private owners who believe they're treating their alligator properly are likely depriving it of the basic needs it would be fulfilling in the wild. And just as with any exotic animal that becomes too much for an owner to handle, if the owner releases it into the wild, it's unlikely to survive, as it has adapted to a bathtub and not to a swamp.

"Alligators don't make good pets," Wayne chided Jeff in a buoyant drawl. "I'm more interested in hunting 'em, myself." Wayne told him about his new alligator farm and the hunts he led. The juxtaposition of those two concepts sparked Jeff's interest.

Wonder if he's doing anything illegal, Jeff thought, *like pulling alligators from his farm and planting them to be hunted.* After their conversation ended, Jeff went back to work, all the while thinking about how to get close enough to Wayne to investigate him. He hadn't been at it for long when a dirty-looking truck pulled up the driveway and parked in front of the barn. Jeff peeked outside to see who it was.

"Hey!" A man in a cowboy hat waved, hailing him. "Are you Jeff?"

"Yeah?" Jeff said apprehensively.

"We were just talking on the phone." The young man, Wayne, strode over and gave Jeff a rowdy handshake. "You must be Jeff Blackledge." He seemed like the kind of fellow whose voice you could hear over everyone else's at a party, and yet you didn't mind.

"Nice to put a face to the name," Jeff said. "Come on in."

Jeff invited him into the camper for some beers, and they got talking about everything alligators. Wayne could sure talk. He was a real yarn spinner. A few beers in, the sun had gone down, and Jeff found himself greedily absorbing all the information Wayne had to offer. The time slipped by, and soon he had to abscond home to the missus. Jeff told him to come around anytime, and he meant it. He really did hope that he'd see Wayne soon.

The next morning, Jeff was cleaning the barn when he stumbled on a pair of sunglasses, camouflage-print, expensive ones, the ones Wayne had been wearing the day before. Remembering that he worked in a sporting goods store on the coast, Jeff called him up and offered to deliver them, saying he needed to pick up some hunting equipment anyway. Wayne agreed, sounding grateful, so Jeff made the trek and nosed around the store for a while so he wouldn't look too eager, and then he approached Wayne. To make it look convincing, Jeff bought a T-shirt, and he handed over the sunglasses.

"Tell me again about this hunter you're going to take," Jeff said, referencing a guided hunt Wayne had mentioned the night before.

"You want to help me with it?" Wayne asked.

"Shit, yeah, if you need help," Jeff answered.

"All right," Wayne said with a grin. "Here's what we're gonna do . . ."

A Swedish big-game hunter had come to Florida with the singular purpose of killing an alligator. He contracted Wayne to make that happen.

"This guy wants a ten-footer," Wayne said, talking about the gators at his farm. "I don't believe I've got a ten-footer, but I might have an eight."

So they planned to catch that gator. Setting the plan into action wasn't quite so easy. Two days later, they floundered around Wayne's alligator pond, trying and failing for nearly three whole hours to wrangle the slippery beast. The four other alligators in that watering hole watched that day's entertainment with bored disinterest. When Jeff and Wayne finally dragged their quarry from the water, they wrestled it quiet enough to tape its mouth closed. Then they loaded the gator into Wayne's truck and brought it to an orange grove, where they hooked its mouth as if it had chomped down on some bait, and they staked the hook line next to a canal. Wayne texted the Swede that they had "bait out." No need to mention it was already inside the alligator. Maybe if they couldn't sneak up on one, they could catch a gator that way, he said.

Stepping back, Jeff appraised the gator. *This ain't no ten-footer*, he thought. The Swede had promised to pay Wayne five grand for a ten-foot gator. Jeff didn't know how Wayne was going to figure his way out of this one.

Then they drove back into town, where they met the Swede and his wife in the Walmart parking lot. By the time they reached the grove, Wayne seemed nervous. Jeff had seen him drinking off and on throughout the day, and by then, he didn't trust him behind the wheel. So Jeff took over. *I'll just act like I'm his partner, and this is all part of the plan*, Jeff thought. But he felt embarrassed driving Wayne's truck. It was filthy. Styrofoam cups and other garbage littered the bed. *Blackledge wouldn't care*, he thought. *Now focus. You've got a job to do.*

Jeff acted like a tour guide, giving his hunting party a taste of real Florida adventure as he drove around the orange grove, hoping for the impossible, for an actual ten-foot alligator to show up in answer to his prayers.

They drove around the orange grove, between the rows of trees, crouching and peering through the leaves like fake safari guides at a theme park. For hours, they came up with nothing. Not a surprise. Almost by design, really. The longer the wait, the higher the anticipation. But as the sun began to set, the grove quieting toward dusk, this anticipation began to morph into impatience and dissatisfaction. Wayne decided it was time to turn toward the canal.

"We set a hook out there," Wayne said, his words slurring a bit as he intimated that, surely, they were about to come upon their elusive prey. That was Jeff's cue.

"Look," he said, pointing toward the canal bank. "There's a gator slide." The tourists craned to see it. And there was their alligator, now a bit worse for wear. By then, he had been out there several hours. He had tried to escape, dragging the hook and line along with him into the water, and he'd become tangled there in the weeds and underwater branches. He was hard to see past the sharp lip of the embankment, but Jeff knew he was there. "I think we got something on that line," he said.

Jeff looked to Wayne, who seemed to be downright drunk at this point. Was he playing a character, too? Was this all a part of the ambience? If Jeff had been in his shoes, he would have been nervous. A big-game hunter seems like one of the last people you'd want to dupe.

Jeff grabbed the thick plastic line and gave it a tug. The Swedes piled out after him, gawking and videotaping. *Time to ham it up,* Jeff thought. He wanted to get them excited, so the dullness of their wait would turn back into excited anticipation. "This feels good," Jeff said, laying it on as thick as possible. "Oh boy, this feels like a *big* one." He kept tugging on the line, feigning intense strain. "Oh my God, this guy's heavy!"

They could see the gator now, practically hog-tied by his tangle. He wasn't moving. *Shit,* Jeff thought. *Did we drown this poor fella? What a sorry way to go that would be.*

As if in answer, the gator gave a violent thrash, pulling Jeff off-balance. He let the line slacken, several feet slipping through his hands. If he hadn't, he would have pitched face-first into the canal. The Swede drew his .44 Magnum and let off a round with a resounding crack. They all peered over the embankment. The gator's thrashing had ceased.

"Good shot," Jeff said, clapping him on the shoulder. "Looks like you got him. I'll bring him on up here."

Jeff clambered down into the canal. He reached for the line. A great crash of water and reeds caused him to leap back. Partially freed, the alligator scrabbled toward him. *This joker came back to life!* Jeff thought. He grabbed for tufts of grass, weed stalks, anything to use as a handhold to pull himself up out of the canal to safety. *This damn thing is gonna bite me!* Those jaws snapped too close to his leg.

As Jeff panicked, Wayne watched from the bank, cocking his head at the commotion.

The gator closed in on Jeff, mouth open. Jeff pressed himself against the embankment. He dug into the root-sinewed dirt, desperate to gain purchase and avert the fate playing through his head, of those jaws coming down on his leg and pulling him beneath the water for a death roll.

"Grab your gun!" Jeff hollered. "Shoot him again! Shoot him again!"

"Gimme that," Wayne said, snatching the enormous gun from the Swede's hand and pointing it at the gator. He closed one eye and steadied himself. Jeff yelped and flattened himself against the canal bank. The bang went off over his head.

The alligator tumbled backward, and the splashing ceased. Jeff breathed a sigh of relief. He pulled himself up by a sapling as Wayne reeled the gator in—now thoroughly dead—by the cord. The Swedes snapped picture after picture, posing with their prey.

"Put it on your shoulder," Jeff suggested. They hoisted it up and took more pictures.

Wayne still seemed nervous. How long could they delay measuring that critter? Once they'd loaded the gator into the truck and returned to the Walmart parking lot, Jeff had his answer. He went around to drop the tailgate, and the Swede followed.

"I want to see that it's a ten-footer," the Swede said. "Let's measure it."

"Sure, let me see if we have some measuring tape," Jeff said. On the other side of the truck, he pulled Wayne aside. He told Wayne what the Swede wanted, and Wayne grimaced. Sweat pilled on his brow. "Don't worry," Jeff said. "I have an idea. Let me keep him up here by the head. I'm gonna teach him some more gator anatomy while you stretch the tape on down, and when he's not looking, you holler it's a ten-footer."

Wayne gulped and nodded. Then they set their plan into action. Jeff held the end of the tape on the tip of the snout. "You see this little hole right here," Jeff said. "This is his ear."

The Swede examined the gator intently and nodded.

"Hey, what do you know, he's ten foot two!" Wayne called out. Jeff let go of the tape, and it slithered back with a snap.

The Swedes whooped and clapped, thrilled with their catch. The husband paid Wayne in cash. Then they started for their car.

"Wait, don't you want your—?" Jeff gestured to the alligator.

"No," the Swede said.

"How would we take him on the plane?" his wife added with a laugh.

"We just came from South Africa where I killed a fourteen-foot crocodile," the Swede said. "We left him there, too."

Such nonchalance at the lives and deaths of majestic alligators did not begin and end with big-game hunters. Even within the alligator farming industry, the relative paucity of regulations spoke of either a widespread assumption of the crocodilian's sturdiness or a general disregard for its well-being. Because who could connect with such alien creatures? Who could tell if they were suffering? Jeff thought he could, but sometimes it seemed he was the only one.

There are no certification meetings, no classes to attend. You do not have to prove you can wrangle an alligator. Just about anybody can open a legal alligator farm as long as they have the money and enough know-how to get by. You do not need a veterinarian on staff. You do not really need a staff at all beyond yourself. Maybe that was why the old-school farmers were so reticent to talk. Not only is their world steeped in secrecy, it is also steeped in the trepidation of knowing that the biggest hoop someone has to jump through to do this is to be brave enough to actually see it through. In other words, if you write a check to the state of Florida and manage to pull together an alligator farm of your very own, all you need to do then is file the paperwork and have an inspection, and voilà: You have a legal alligator farm.

But to become one of the Golden 30 is another thing entirely. The Golden 30 is what FWC calls the group of alligator farms that receive eggs from the state with little to no effort on their part. Because the farms don't have to lift a finger, FWC says they are "golden." Of course, as with anything else wildlife-related in Florida, farms have to follow certain guidelines, pay $250, and get a permit. Only the first thirty farms that are accepted to the program get to participate. Theoretically, the farms can take wild-harvested eggs, incubate them, nurture the hatchlings, then raise them into maturity to cultivate a breeding stock. The initial idea was that farms might do this, then after achieving a high enough number of livestock alligators, they should be able to perpetuate their farm through breeding and never have to dip into wild alligator populations again. In this hypothetical eventuality, these farms would be launching entire bloodlines of alligators—thousands upon thousands of individual creatures—who had never seen a swamp before, and never would. To Jeff, it seemed a great loss, but one he couldn't put into words.

Whenever he pictured an alligator, he also conjured up an image of the swamp. In his mind, that vision of a reptile floated almost totally submersed in glassy, dark water, eyes breaking a surface stained nearly black with the tannins of oak leaves, sending out a ring of ripples that warped the reflection of the white-dappled daylight from the canopy above. The alligator's second eyelid might smooth like a meniscus over his green and piercing reptilian eye, itself shining with a vision of the swamp. The association between alligator and swamp was so strong that it was hard to fathom one that had never been there. What were alligators without the swamp? What would they be if their wildness were ever tamed, their status reduced to livestock, seen more like chickens or pigs than the living dinosaurs that they are? If alligators became just another commodity to be bred and bought and sold, even if they weren't gone entirely, even if there were some left in the wild, their mystique would have washed away, and the "dragon" naturalist William Bartram spoke of in his effusive travelogues would have all but disappeared.

It was a good thing and a bad one that that eventuality wasn't on the horizon, as alligators, like most other animals, seldom breed in captivity.

The best farms and zoos, as Jeff was learning, tried to replicate swamp conditions. At Gatorland in Orlando, for example, most of their resident alligators live in a swampy lake environment so large that it seems like the enclosure's only boundaries are the ones that separate the guests from the alligators. There's no outer fence in sight—though surely there is one, right? Jeff's alligators, too, had their own little slices of swamp in his farm's large ponds. Still, at most of these places, including Jeff's, alligators just didn't get frisky, and even if they did, they didn't build nests. While creating his farm, Jeff had talked to biologists about how to make this work. Being the person he is, a problem solver, he wanted to figure out why exactly alligators didn't breed in captivity and fix the problem. Maybe there wasn't enough foliage for nest building, he thought. Was it a privacy issue? Who knew. Come nesting season, he adorned his enclosures with palm fronds and grasses to no avail. Removing gators from the wild had to some extent taken the wild out of them, and with it went their natural imperatives. No need to hunt, as the food came to them. No need to reproduce, because why bother. It was like being a big fish in a tiny bowl. It had no space to grow—and no reason to do so, either. If Jeff couldn't figure it out, it wasn't so surprising that no one else had, and there seemed little need when all the big guys, the larger farms with enough resources and experience to solve this problem, were in the Golden 30 getting wild-harvested eggs practically for free.

Before nesting season called egg hunters into the swamps, FWC called an open meeting for state alligator farmers, so they could discuss the possibility of expanding the Golden 30 into the Golden 35, and what requirements these extra five might have to achieve to become golden. As with all such wildlife-rule meetings, the people who came had strong opinions and pontificated on them like southern lawyers straight out of a John Grisham novel. Jeff always had strong opinions about wildlife law, too, but he wasn't there to sway any minds. He needed to make the connections that'd break open his case.

Jeff used the meeting as a way to schmooze. He shook hands and grinned and gave out business cards. Most people were cordial. That much he'd expected. They were in the part of the world, after all, where even if someone's skinning your name alive behind closed doors, they'll give you a smile in person. Many alligator farm owners either had money or came from money. Farming alligators isn't a lucrative business, so most farms were pet projects for the rich. Which was why Jeff had imagined his character Blackledge to benefit from a trust fund in order to get into the game. Yet, somehow, he still wasn't ready for how politeness greased every conversation, smoothing the way from introduction to goodbye before Jeff knew what happened. After the disorientation of this amiability subsided, he felt like he'd gotten somewhere, even though, deep down, he knew better. These people were playing characters just like he was, their faces veneered with charm. The deeper the pocket, the better the actor, the more entrenched this falsity was within their rung of society. If you went high enough up, people were Russian nesting dolls of façades, motivations inside motivations, deceptions all the way down.

During the meeting, Jeff caught sight of Robert opposite him in the back of the room. He wasn't with his friends from Shady Creek. When the talks ended and the schmoozing began, Shady Creek's main owner, a mega-millionaire whom folks called Brother Parker, made a show of avoiding Robert, and everyone else, it seemed, followed suit. Jeff watched Robert try to network, shake hands, and pass out his business card. Every person he tried to corner managed to slip away.

The last time they'd seen each other, Jeff thought they had a good rapport going. They'd connected over hunting. Robert had promised to call and make plans. That was January. This was May. It was possible Robert had gotten caught up in running his farm. But from the looks of it, more was going on.

As Robert made his exit, he nodded at other folks, but they mostly gave him a wide berth. People treated Robert with even less cordiality than Robert had treated Jeff, and he wondered why. He had a feeling it had something to do with Brother Parker.

I should ask around and find out what happened, Jeff thought.

You dodged a bullet if you ask me," Wayne said. Squinting up his rifle barrel, he swiveled, searching for the doves that had taken flight with the report of his shot. He let off another. *Pop!* "If I were you, I'd stay away from that Robert guy," Wayne went on.

They stood out in front of Jeff's camper, Jeff with a beer in hand and Wayne with his stationed at his feet as he tried to take down the doves. Wayne had gotten into the habit of coming around Sunshine just to hang out with Jeff and drink his beer, libations that Jeff purchased for that specific purpose, but Wayne didn't need to know that. Jeff enjoyed his company. That was what mattered.

"Why?" Jeff asked. "What's wrong with him?"

"Oh, his whole crew is trouble," Wayne said. "I've heard all kinds of stories about him."

"Are we talking about the same Robert?" Jeff said. "He seems so upstanding."

Wayne raised an eyebrow and smiled knowingly. "Really, Jeff," he chided. "You should worry about them the most." He fired a shot into the sky.

Ridiculous, Jeff thought. Wayne's opinion of Robert didn't seem backed up by fact. Sure, Robert may have thought he was too good for Jeff, but Jeff couldn't read the man's mind. He didn't know, and he probably never would. He'd given up on hearing from him ever again. Even if he saw Robert at the hardware store, he probably wouldn't stop to chat. Why bother?

That seemed to be the general consensus others held for Jeff, though: Why bother?

In fact, no one he'd given his card to at the meeting called, and no one called him back, either. But then, on a hot summer afternoon at Sunshine Alligator Farm, Jeff's cell phone started ringing. This was it, finally. The big break he was waiting for, breathing on the other side of the line. He'd known it was coming. He'd put in the work. The only thing that surprised him was the name on his caller ID. It was the last person he would have expected: Robert.

12

THE FIRST EGG HUNT

I want to apologize for missing you at the meeting," Robert said over the phone.

Missing me, huh? Jeff thought. It was the day after the meeting, and Jeff was still smarting from Robert's snub.

"I didn't mean to ignore you," Robert went on. "I had other things on my mind."

Rumor had it that one of those other things was a falling-out with Brother Parker. Left without a job and a steady source of income, Robert had been hustling to get someone else to partner with him—and he had failed.

"Sure, I know how it is," Jeff said, trying to sound magnanimous.

"Hey, what are you doing next week?" Robert asked. "I'd like to come talk to you."

The season was awakening, and the wild things were coming alive from that brief respite that is springtime in Florida. With mating season over, the female gators had already begun to dig their nests and lay their eggs.

Jeff went to Robert's house, where Robert proposed the idea of a business partnership. They would collect alligator eggs from the wild, and Robert would use Jeff's farm facilities for hatching, updating the farm as he saw appropriate. In return, Robert offered to guide and educate Jeff on the alligator industry.

If Jeff had been Jeff Babauta, he might have turned Robert away. As Blackledge, he wanted to chalk their previous missed connections up to misunderstandings. Plus, he needed a way in, desperately—and here it was.

Nonetheless, he sat on it, as if considering the proposal, but really he just didn't want to seem overly eager.

Afterward, Jeff called Lieutenant Wilson at the agency.

"Man, I don't know what this guy's doing," Jeff said, "but I think I just got into an agreement to collect eggs."

"Fantastic," Lieutenant Wilson said. "With who?"

Jeff told him about Robert and the rumors swirling around him. "He seems like a decent enough guy though," Jeff said. "What can it hurt?"

"Let it ride," Lieutenant Wilson said. "See what he offers."

By May 20, Jeff's birthday, Robert had stood Jeff up then called again, and they bartered back and forth for close to a month before it seemed the time had come to lay their deal out on paper. He met with Robert and his wife, Robin, at a gas station on the corner of two desolate country roads.

"So it's all settled," Robert said. "I'll teach you everything you need to know about raising alligators. All you need to do is let us use your facility. We'll even update it for you, make the place state of the art."

"All of that sounds great, but—" Jeff said.

"But?"

"My accountant didn't like what he saw of our agreement," Jeff said. "I am running a business after all. I need to make money. So you can't use the place for free."

"Well, it wouldn't be for free," Robert said. "I would fence in that pond of yours, and I'd transfer in some adult alligators."

"Yeah, that would be great," Jeff said. "You can do that. *And* you also need to pay me." *What I'm asking of you is normal*, Jeff thought. *Don't balk at this.* Jeff was afraid of scaring him away, but at a certain point he risked coming across as a pushover.

"How about $5,000?" Robert asked. "To use your farm for the season."

That's it? Jeff thought. But he nodded. "All right," he said. "That sounds fair." Except it didn't.

"We'll give you half up front and half after the harvest," Robert said.

"It's a deal," Jeff said. They shook hands.

Cars sped by under the live oaks.

Robert took out a set of FWC forms and explained them to Jeff, which made Jeff chuckle in his head. But Robert knew his stuff.

"Can I see your farm license?" Robert asked. "I need to take a picture of it." He did that while Jeff signed the forms. Robert explained how the private lands application would allow him to transfer alligator eggs harvested from the wild to Sunshine Alligator Farm.

"I'll send all this stuff to Florida Fish and Wildlife," Robert said. "Don't you worry. I'll take care of everything."

He further explained that Jeff would only be accepting eggs and not hatchlings or adult alligators. "That's what our permits are for," Robert added. "Eggs only, understand?"

"Eggs only," Jeff said. "I gotcha."

See? Everything to the letter of the law, Jeff thought. *I don't know what the heck Wayne was talking about. These are good people. They got nothing to hide.*

After they both signed the egg-collecting application, with Robin witnessing, they said their farewells and started toward their trucks.

That was when Jeff glanced back and saw Robin had done the same. She was glaring at him.

She's giving me the evil eye, Jeff thought. Once she'd turned around again, Jeff reasoned with himself. *Maybe I'm just imagining things.*

In June, Jeff absconded to the mountains of North Carolina, a brief and much-needed family camping trip that he covered up with the lie of visiting his girlfriend's parents. By the end of the weekend, Jeff knew he had to hurry back to work. Throughout the drive back down to Florida, his phone rang incessantly. The thing gave off every beep and buzz in its arsenal, texts, emails, the whole bit. He glanced at them as he drove. It was Robert sending him paperwork—permits in Curtis Blackledge's name, all ready to go.

I didn't apply for any of this, Jeff thought. *Did Robert just hijack my damn farm?*

It was all happening too fast. That set off an alarm in Jeff's head. Something wasn't right.

Jeff decided to let Robert keep going.

Let's just see how far this gets, Jeff thought.

He hadn't talked to Robert between May and June 7, when Robert asked for his Social Security number to fill out yet another form. After he got back from the mountains, Jeff drove to Robert's house unannounced. Inside, all his planning and paperwork sprawled across the dining room table.

"I've been putting in a lot of work while you've been gone," Robert said.

"I can tell," Jeff said. "I'm impressed.

They discussed when they were going to start collecting eggs, what machines they required, which ones they had that needed to be cleaned or serviced—Robert acting like he wanted Jeff's input when they both knew he was just using Jeff for the farm.

In the coming weeks, Robert threw money around. He bought dozens of large plastic crates for transporting eggs. He purchased equipment large and small, from thermometers and cleaning supplies to an entire airboat.

Where is he getting all of this money? Jeff wondered.

"We got so lucky with this," Lieutenant Wilson said on the phone later. "He took over your farm. He's doing all the work, and now he's buying all this stuff for you? It's a windfall."

Jeff's feelings, however, were more muddled than that. The case finally felt like it was opening up for him. And yet he couldn't help but feel slighted. All the hard work that he'd put into the farm, and here Robert just came in and took over and brushed him aside. It seemed like everything was once again in a whirlwind around him while he was standing still.

Later, Robert and Robin paid a visit to the farm. They pulled up to the barn's back loading door, and, seeing Jeff, Robert announced, "I got some eggs."

"Where'd you get them?" Jeff asked as he helped Robert carry a cooler into the barn.

"We collected them last night from the Seminole Reservation," Robert said.

Jeff lifted the cooler lid to peek inside. Rows of dirty white ovals nestled in a mulch of mud and bark.

"They'll be all right where they are," Robert said, handing him the transfer document. With that, Robin and Robert left, saying they would be back in a few days.

As the investigation progressed, a tragedy was unfolding back at Jeff's home. A few days earlier, Sandy had told Jeff that his K-9, Mack, had been acting lethargic. Sandy had sensed something was wrong. At first, she thought that Mack just had the blues. He missed his patrol partner. Maybe he missed his feeling of purpose, too. He would watch the front door with the other dogs, waiting for Jeff to return. While the others kept up their patient and faithful routine with unflagging earnestness, Mack seemed to fade. Sandy told Jeff she was taking Mack to the vet. Jeff worried, as was his way, but he assumed as Sandy did that the Goldador was only suffering from the kind of homesickness we feel when separated too long from the people we love. Heartache though it was, they believed it one with an easy cure. So with effort, he put the dog out of his mind and continued with his farm work.

Later, under the cover of darkness, Jeff removed his personal phone from its secret compartment. A message from Sandy asked him to call when he got the chance. He did and listened to the ringer with a growing sense of dread.

Sandy told him that she had bad news. Mack had a tumor on his heart, and they had to decide what to do. The vet believed that surgery would do more harm than good. There was only one option, really.

"We have to put him down," Jeff said, a lump forming in his throat. He told Sandy that he wanted to be there. He loved that dog. He didn't want Mack to go through that without him. "I have to get permission to leave, but I'm coming even if they say no."

Sandy agreed that she would wait for him, and after he hung up, Jeff took a moment to breathe. The life he had shared with Mack flashed before his eyes. Their days on patrol stretched out through the pinewoods, hours of quiet punctuated by sudden moments of fear and excitement. "It's time to go to work!" Jeff would say when those moments came. He loved how much Mack would perk up. The eager look in his brown eyes would say, *Yes! I'm ready.* Mack could sniff out anything. Fast on a scent, he would race through the forest, his golden tail alert and rippling like a feather plume. Mack always found his mark. Mack could heel at attention, as poised as a soldier, then at home he would frolic, carefree as any other dog.

The agency had the compassion to let Jeff go. No need to explain to wildlife officers why an animal meant so much to him.

Jeff drove home, tucked his unmarked vehicle away, and went to the vet with Sandy. There, he placed a hand on Mack's soft head. "There's a good boy," Jeff said. "Daddy's here." Mack licked his wrist, but that spark of energy that once propelled him through the woods had faded. Jeff knew that this was the right thing to do. He would save his friend so much pain. That didn't make it hurt any less for him.

Jeff stroked Mack while it happened, reminding him that he was such a very good dog.

He couldn't leave the farm unattended for too long. After it was over, Jeff had to go back. The whole drive, that same lump that caught in his throat remained there, and he tried not to think about how much he was missing by not being at home. The truth was, he'd missed nearly a year in his dog's life. He feared that he was missing more—of his wife, his son, his mother, his siblings, their kids—than he would ever know.

No matter how important this mission was supposed to be, it meant losing time with the people he loved. Jeff could never get this time back. Mack's death reminded him that he had so much more to lose. There was no telling what bad news might come on Sandy's next call, or if someone would call about her. All this worry and heartache had built up over the past year. It made him feel worn thin and old, and so ready for this job to be over. He couldn't wait to go home, his real home.

He pulled into the farm's driveway and shut the gate in the glare of his headlights, those feelings still building up, straining against his will not to let them go. He parked in front of his camper, went inside, and locked the door. He swallowed against the lump in his throat, but it wouldn't give way. This loss of time was so much more of a sacrifice than he ever anticipated making. The heartbreak overtook him.

That was my baby, he thought, and he let the tears flow.

On the last day of June, Jeff and Robert met up with a pilot at the Arcadia Airport, a small municipal airstrip that sat abreast of farmland and trailer parks on the edge of town. The three of them climbed into a helicopter, donned their headsets, and zipped up into the air.

Jeff was no stranger to helicopters. After the Florida Game and Freshwater Fish Commission had merged with Florida Marine Patrol, the new superagency owned more aircraft than any other law enforcement agency in the state. They used them for search-and-rescue missions, flora and fauna counts, spotting covert marijuana growers, and, of course, chasing down poachers. To ignite controlled burns, fire technicians would drop Ping-Pong balls of combustion chemicals from the aircraft. When they made contact with the forest floor, they would burst. A thousand acres of brush could go up in less than a day. On the night detail, they would shine spotlights down through the overgrowth, trying to spy hunters, hideouts, a cache of illicit wares.

Jeff had trained his dog Mack to ride in helicopters, for assignments on barrier islands or other places almost no other vehicle could reach. Mack had enjoyed flying about as much as Jeff did—which was not much.

This helicopter was smaller than the ones Jeff was used to. The smaller the aircraft, the more dramatic its movements feel. It had no doors, so the wind whipped at his hair. It felt like being in a tornado. After a couple of hours, Jeff felt nauseous. He toughed it out. They flew over Avon Park bombing range with its enormous bull's-eyes painted like surreal earthworks over the swamp. The helicopter swooped down close enough to spy the dark mounds of alligator nests. They stood out against the lushness of all that green. Later, they would return on foot to make their harvest.

A few days later, back at the farm, the sound of Jeff's cell phone ringing beside his bed startled him awake. He swore under his breath and swiped at it. He grabbed it and read the screen, its glare washing over his squinting face like he was driving into oncoming traffic. It was about 4 AM. The caller ID said ROBERT. Annoyed and weary, and most of all tired as hell, Jeff answered and mumbled a salutation.

"Hey," Robert said. Then, without much preamble, he launched into his business. "We're going to collect tomorrow," he said.

Collect, Jeff thought, his brain still feeling liquid from sleep. *Collect! He means gator eggs!* He'd been waiting more than a year for this. Sure, Jeff had collected eggs on his own already. But now he was finally getting to learn how a real operation was done. The lightning strike of this opportunity woke Jeff up in an awful hurry.

"I'm interested," Jeff said.

"Get something to eat and head over here to the house," Robert said.

Jeff threw some clothes on, stuffed breakfast in his mouth, and was at Robert's homestead within the hour. The place fluttered with activity, every porchlight aglow, dogs barking, the crew Robert had amassed chatting with excitement. Jeff jumped in to help and found himself in the middle of the fray. Everyone was wired with a purposeful energy. Everyone seemed to have something to do, to be bent on a task and hurtling toward it with conviction; but that's all it was, dramatic energy and forward motion. No one seemed to know what was going on except Robert, who attended to his disarray of papers spread from the head of his dining room table all the way down to its foot.

As Jeff tried to help, he wondered if this uninformed chaos was by design. Keeping people on their toes by denying them necessary information was a well-known manipulation tactic. Jeff paused to study Robert for a moment. It was as if the man stood inside a hurricane's eye, untouched by the tension and nervous energy around him. If this was manipulation, it was good. Well, good for Robert. Effective. Bad for Jeff. Not only did it obscure any possible wrongdoing behind a flurry of activity, but it also meant that he was onto something. Had he sensed something was off about Jeff? *Are you cunning or just disorganized?* Jeff wondered. Robert was more of an enigma to him than ever.

Then he remembered Robin's evil eye.

They didn't arrive in Fort Drum until 11 PM that night, nearly nineteen hours after Robert's call plucked Jeff from sleep. What was left outside Fort Drum's highway oasis amounted to a pioneer graveyard and a scattering of houses under the loblolly pines; it was named after a Seminole War–era battlement that had long since receded into the soil. This was the kind of place where the ground was thick with clay-red pine needles, where the quiet made you think of ghosts and a history long forgotten by all but a few. The town boasted that it was the origin of the St. Johns River, one of the most significant rivers in Florida. That made Fort Drum a kind of belowground juncture, too. Within the cavernous aquifer, living water destined for the glades intermingled with contrarian tides bent on flowing north, a little metaphor for the backwoods attitude if ever there was one.

Millions of years ago, Lake Okeechobee stretched far beyond its current boundaries up the Floridian peninsula, covering the tract that would become Fort Drum and the area that surrounds it with a vast inland sea. While traipsing through the woods here, it's not uncommon to find remaining clues to that sea. Some in the form of animals whose species evolved in isolation upon islands in the sea, like the Florida scrub-jay, a threatened species of corvid with Caribbean-blue feathers and a knowing look in its eyes. Back underground, there lies another such uncanny artifact of Florida's bygone past. The limestone deposits that protect the aquifer have also trapped the chalky shells of prehistoric mollusks. It's not uncommon to stumble upon a trail made chalk white by the pulverized calcium of fossil shells, a sight unusual in the understory's fecund decomposition, like folk magic crafted by the soil itself. This is the oldest kind of magic, where the land speaks even when no one is around to listen. The shells beneath Fort Drum became jagged while still submerged within that primordial sea: Calcite crystals swirled new skeletons around them like sculptures of shimmering finger bones. The land tells its unique story.

Jeff had spent plenty of time in that area as a game warden, but he was seeing it through new eyes on his first trip with Robert's crew.

Their pickup truck caravan trundled along the dirt road that led into Fort Drum Wildlife Management Area, headlights throwing a sallow tunnel forward across the grassland. In the clearing before the tree line, they circled their trucks and parked. Beyond the flat patch where they stood, the world opened up into the darkest night. Without intending it, they had ventured into Jeff's old stomping grounds. The capital of dark sky and the fragile nests of endangered birds. He paused for a moment to look out along the prairie where distant marshland pools reflected the enormity of the cosmos. The result was an optical illusion that made the heavens seem to devour the earth, flooding over its curvature like a dam broken after the rain. It was easy to lose yourself in awe. Not just here, but anywhere in nature that lets you take a breath and notice all the small wonders we usually pass by.

This was why he was here, doing this mission. Any day when things got too grungy, when the job got too hard, when it started to feel like just a job, he would have to remember moments like this. He stored it up in his mental file as a reminder: He was looking for poachers. That much was true. But in that, he was looking to prevent a tipping of the delicate balance. Unlike the story of the sparrows there, who were nearly at the brink of extinction, a place where alligators had been half a decade before, the alligators Jeff was trying to save represented a proactive approach to conservation rather than a reactive one.

There were rumors that, during those trying times for alligators, entire species of plants shifted place in the Everglades. Alligators are ecosystem engineers. But we don't know the entire extent of their influence. If alligators ever faced extirpation or, worse, extinction, there was no telling what would happen to their habitats—and our planet—without them. Jeff's grand-scheme purpose there was to make sure that we would never find out. So he carried this thought with him: He was saving the alligators—along with the sparrows, the panthers, the burrowing owls, the bears—and the constellation of this hopeful act stretched out from that little patch of plain and swamp into everywhere the water flowed, all the people who drank it, all the plants that sucked it up through their roots, all the oxygen that they exhaled—a little thing in the grand scheme could mean the entire world. He was saving the darkness, too, the enormity of the sky only possible because people like Jeff guarded the land from destructive human hands, keeping the channels of possibility open for the primordial wonder we feel, our smallness, our place in the universe, when we look into the stars.

He needed that stolen bit of hope sooner than he expected. They slept in their trucks. The heat of the day had hardly dissipated. It was nearly a hundred degrees out, the sleeping arrangements uncomfortable, the bugs out in their vast array, and even though Jeff always brought his Thermacell, he could still hear them out there in the dark, going *hmmmm hmmmmmm*, lusting for his blood. It was a rough night; a perfect way to launch egg-collecting season.

In the morning, they started about their business. By then, Robert had pulled a suspicious 180, suddenly becoming organized. Or perhaps he had been all along.

They ventured along the trails through the hardwood swamp, toting snake hooks and large plastic containers to store the eggs. Jeff had woken up on the wrong side of the driver's seat, and he remained disgruntled and achy the rest of the day. The sheer weight of the heat didn't help. He kept on guard for nefarious happenings, but he already knew, after a lifetime of experience, that poaching and legal hunting (or egg collecting) looked exactly the same save for two things. The first was that poachers typically did not have the correct paperwork or legitimate hunting tags. The second and more obvious difference was that legitimate hunters seldom ran when you came upon them in the woods. There's an old Irish saying that the guilty man flees while no one makes chase.

The one thing that had stood out to him most was Robert's organization. No matter where they went in field or swamp, Robert always carried an aluminum lockbox, the type used to keep important papers safe. The mystery of what might be inside piqued Jeff's interest. Robert was hiding something. And you don't hide things that aren't incriminating. When no one was looking, Jeff made a note of it on the side of his shoe. Just BOX. He would remember.

Some of them paired off to make more efficient work of the egg hunt. Jeff went with a fellow he'd already met named Tommy. Tommy was in his thirties, perhaps. He wore baggy clothes and small oval glasses, the kind that had been in style when Jeff's son was a teen in the early 2000s. Behind those, he wore a disdainful expression.

As they walked along the trail, carrying the plastic egg tub between them, a tense and uncompanionable silence drew taut between them as well. Jeff grew increasingly uncomfortable, so he made a joke to cut the tension. Tommy acknowledged that Jeff had spoken, but he didn't laugh. His expression remained sour. The longer this went on, the more Tommy's unsociable demeanor got underneath Jeff's skin. Jeff kept cracking one-liners. He got a laugh or two out of Tommy, but he still hadn't drawn the fellow all the way out. He told himself this was more than discomfort. He didn't need Tommy to like him. He needed Tommy to trust him enough to divulge information. He kept pressing.

While this was going on, Jeff and Tommy continued from nest to nest. Jeff tried not to take the lead, just let things flow as they were, because if they were doing something illegal, he had to toe the line between leading the crew into crime and leading them away from it.

They located a nest from the makeshift map they'd made during the helicopter ride. It was a mound of mud and reeds nestled in a copse of water oak saplings and the sharp appendages of saw palms.

"I'm that guy who when Robert says, 'Hey, I need that eleven-footer caught,' I'm the one they call in to go catch him," Tommy boasted as he sifted through the brush to reach the thatched mound of a nest.

"So you're the brave one, huh?" Jeff asked, trying not to laugh.

"Oh yeah," Tommy responded.

Oh, so this is who you are, Jeff thought. He was beginning to miss the terse silence. Half an hour later, Jeff had a feeling that if he was going to blow the operation, it would be on account of Tommy's incessant pontificating, especially in contrast with his results, which were nil. They moved on to the next nest, this time with Jeff glowering silently along the trail as Tommy yakked his ear off.

Good Lord, could Tommy brag. It seemed to be his greatest talent. Worse, he was the king of one-upmanship. If you caught a fish, he caught a bigger one. If you felled five deer that season, he bagged thirty.

They eventually reached the nest. As they approached, a loud hissing noise rose above the rhythmic buzz of the katydids. Jeff paused and cocked his head. He put out his arm to block Tommy from venturing onward.

"What the hell is that?" Jeff asked.

They didn't have much time to ponder before the answer lunged at them. An angry mother alligator darted toward Jeff, putting herself between him and her nest. Her mouth was open, emitting a vitriolic hiss. When people associated alligators with the phrase *Fuck around and find out*, this situation wasn't quite what they had in mind, but it should have been. Jeff and Tommy had grown careless. They'd been too preoccupied by their conflicting personalities. It was just another day at the office. How easily they'd forgotten that, no matter the sense of normalcy Jeff's mind painted over his surroundings, no matter how usual, how tame the swamp had grown in his thoughts, it was the wild, stubborn and unconquerable, both as a reality and as a millennia-old symbol for the forbidding nature of these remote parts of the world, despite human endeavors to bring them to hand.

Jeff and Tommy had fucked around. Now they were going to find out.

They backed off, and the alligator followed at a surprisingly quick gait, undulating her rough-hewn body back and forth, dragging a rapid S-curve across the leaf litter. She closed the gap between them. Jeff was close enough to see the flecks of green and gold reflect from within her piercing reptilian eyes. She stopped. So did they. They paused in a standoff.

While alligators don't usually attack humans, like any animal, humans included, they will attack when they feel threatened or cornered, especially when they perceive the lives of their offspring to be in danger. Many are willing to die for their young. *Will this mother alligator go so far?* Jeff wondered. *Is it worth the risk to find out?*

Tommy must have thought so. As soon as the mother gator began her retreat, he followed. "Cover me," he said. He levered the nest's top thatch open with his snake hook.

"She's already coming back!" Jeff warned, raising his voice.

"Well, swat her with something." Finding a trove of eggs within the stinking refuge of the nest, Tommy straddled their egg box and began picking eggs out and drawing a line on each shell with a permanent marker to indicate which side had faced up. Jeff would later learn why this step is important. If you put an egg in upside down, the hatchling inside will crush its umbilical cord, and it will die.

The nest was open. Now there was no turning back. If they did, they'd waste yet another tally.

Jeff stood over Tommy, putting himself between him and that narrow clearing's scrubby edge. Tommy worked quickly. He plucked an egg, rubbed away the caked bark and mulch, wet with hot rainwater and likely piss, and held it up to the sun. Satisfied that it was fertilized and viable, he put the egg into the box. He wasn't at this for long when the hissing filled Jeff's ears again.

The mother gator crashed through the brush. Before she could jump from the thicket of saw palms, Jeff swatted her on the nose with his snake hook with a dull *whack*. She closed her mouth and recoiled. He hadn't hit her very hard, just enough to startle her. Still, he felt bad. She was defending her babies, after all. He certainly would have squared off against some fucker who was messing with his kid. *Sorry, gal*, he thought. *That's the food chain for you.* Him being there would be better for her—and her future hatchlings—in the long run. Or so he hoped.

He hated having to sacrifice a few animals for the benefit of others, but that's often what conservation comes down to these days. Whether you are hunting animals from an invasive species that have cast their adopted environment into disarray—such as the Burmese python in the Everglades or the lionfish that had spread from a likely introduction point in South Florida up and down the Atlantic and Gulf Coasts of the Western Hemisphere—modern conservation is constantly faced with ecological trolley problems: sacrifice the few to save the many. Populations of species that have gotten out of hand, even endemic ones, threaten to destroy their habitats and decimate the other species around them, whether they are predator or prey.

Alligators have proven so resilient since their earlier struggles that their numbers have skyrocketed into the millions. With an excess of predators, prey species decline. It's impossible to pinpoint just one impact from this. But theoretical dominoes line up to tip into vegetation overgrowth that spurs wildfires, invasive species supplanting native ones, or other species further down the food web either booming or withering. As human influence is usually to blame for such ecological disequilibrium, it's up to us to set things right, or as right as we can. Humans are just as much a part of the grand scheme of ecological balance as are the alligators, or the deer, or the snakes or rabbits.

It's tempting to say the best way for humans to save the ecosystems we've mucked up is to leave. Yes, many parts of the wild are better off without us. But to get really unpoetic here, you can't un-lick that ice cream cone. You can rewild the wilderness, but you can't make it untouched. One is conservation. The other is abdication, and it looks a lot more like abandoning a burning mess than it does leave-only-footprints conservation. Since our human species is just as much a part of this biome as everything else, we need to learn to live within it again. As Indigenous peoples all over the world will tell you, from the Sami of Finland to the Dukha of Mongolia and the Māori of New Zealand, we are in and of the Earth, not apart from it. Indigenous farmers don't clear land, for example. They don't graze grassland till it's bare. The wild is not untouched but listened to. *What do you need? What have we done wrong? How can we make things right?*

As much as Jeff sometimes felt at odds with his mission, he knew that he was already in the thick of things—we all are. To really get something done, you have to break a few eggs, so to speak.

The mother alligator lingered, floating half-submerged in a nearby mire, watching Tommy pick through her nest, but she didn't approach again. Jeff wondered what she was thinking, if she felt defeated.

Sorry about this, Jeff thought toward the mother alligator. *It is what it is.*

Meanwhile, indifferent, Tommy sorted through the nest, launching into a long diatribe-slash-explanation about alligator-egg hunting, and alligators, and hunting, and how he knew better than everyone about everything on this green Earth, and—good God. Jeff regretted ever trying to draw the man out of his shell. How could he stuff him back in?

Tommy claimed to have caught two hundred deer, not just an illegal but a horrifying number. He was one of those guys who seemed to live his life to poach and cheat the system, like the world owed him something, like he was being cheated himself, and, in lieu of an easier target, he was taking his due from nature. If he wasn't bragging, maybe he was just lying to make Jeff feel small, lying to assert dominance. There's a big difference between this and the river country storytelling tradition of embellishment. The former can be a bit underhanded. The latter, when listeners are accustomed to that particular storytelling device, serves for emphasis.

Having ventured too deeply into the weeds of his own lecture, Tommy paused with an egg in his hand above the tub. He furrowed his brow and looked at the egg again. He held it up to the light. The mother alligator continued to hiss but from a safe distance away. With the sun glowing through the shell like a flashlight through a finger, he ascertained the position of the embryo and marked it with a fat permanent marker, then set the egg into the tub with the rest.

13

ALONE IN THE SWAMP

They moved on to Cecil M. Webb Wildlife Management Area, inconveniently located clear across the girth of the state inland of where Punta Gorda projects into Gasparilla Sound. Once again, the crew didn't reach the site until well after nightfall. They set up camp in an area of white sand. From there, Jeff could just make out the ghostly spindles of the pines where they shot up above the flatwoods. To the southwest, the purple of the sky faded into a yellow like a half-healed bruise. The cities lay down that way, Fort Myers and Cape Coral straddling the outlet of the Caloosahatchee River. Except for the light pollution, the night whirred with a peaceful buzz dotted with the percussion of ribbits. The distant sea breeze allayed the heat they'd felt in Fort Drum, so as they set up camp, Jeff thought of how much tonight, unlike the night before, felt like a relaxing camping trip.

With his corner of the camp set up, Jeff wandered over to the group where Tommy sat with CW, another member of the crew. They squatted around a pile of sticks and leaves and criticized one another's bushcraft skills as they tried to start a fire. The crew's numbers had swelled beyond ten. Robert said he anticipated that this location would prove fertile ground for alligator eggs, so they brought every soul they could muster. The guys' wives and kids would join them the next day. It made Jeff wish he could bring his family, but he couldn't, for numerous reasons. For one, he couldn't blow his cover, but even if that wasn't a factor, he didn't want to put them in danger, not that he really thought any of these guys—no matter how annoying or rough one or two of them seemed—posed much of a threat. But getting his family tangled up in this version of his life would put them in unnecessary peril, hypothetical or not. The desire to have them there was moot, though. His superiors would certainly veto the idea. And if all that wasn't enough, Jeff had begun to establish more characters in his backstory, including the girlfriend he claimed to be texting whenever he had to answer a message from his handlers at the agency. When the crew asked why she never came around, Jeff answered, "She's not into this wild stuff." Made a good cover, too, for when he needed to quickly tap out a note or snap a picture for evidence.

"Man, that bitch is obsessed with you," CW had said the last time Jeff made an excuse while he took down a note in plain sight.

Jeff had laughed. "Yeah, but I love her." His reaction wouldn't have been quite so affable had CW called Sandy a bitch. For a fictional girlfriend, that was one thing. For a wife, those were fighting words. He would have broken character.

While Jeff watched CW and Tommy bicker like birds squabbling on a nature documentary, another one of their crew dragged a cooler over and offered Jeff a beer. He took it and thanked the guy, not letting him see his internal hesitation. In every other situation before this, Jeff had faked drinking. He'd used beer as a prop. He tried to act progressively more inebriated, his tongue loosening, divulging fictionalized details about Blackledge's life. *Do I really need to be so on guard tonight?* Jeff asked himself now. *One beer isn't gonna hurt.* He took a swig. That really hit the spot. Jeff always thought cold beer went down smoother when you were out camping. It lifted some of that muggy Florida heat. *It's just beer*, he told himself. *Not like it's whiskey. These guys aren't up to no good. They don't know who I am. And I've been working hard. I deserve to relax.*

Once the fire came to life, they all gathered around it. They shook folded camping chairs open, whipped up dinner, and talked while they ate. Another beer in, Jeff told them more about himself as Blackledge, like why he was getting into farming alligators in the first place.

"My family thinks I'm a fuckup," he said. "I got this inheritance but I don't really got it, you see. I have to prove that I'm doing something with it other than having a party. I wanna prove it to myself, too, though, prove I can do something with my life other than being a waste."

His listeners nodded and let out murmurs of understanding, empathy even. They knew what that was like.

"I'm going to help Brother Parker with something," Robert said, getting up. "I shouldn't be too long." More of the crew gradually peeled away, saying they needed to attend to this and that.

As the conversation went on, Jeff let himself fade back into relaxation. He felt one with his purpose out there. With a sense of calm, he took a swig of the second beer he was nursing and studied the fire. The flames had dwindled so they rippled over the shapes of logs they had reduced to cinders, whitening the bark into scales not dissimilar to an alligator's back. A frill of ash still glowing with a red rim of fire lifted from the bark and wafted skyward. Jeff's gaze followed it up while its glow turned to dust until it disappeared into the murky canvas of the night, a tiny speck indistinguishable among the few rare flickers of the stars. As was his custom, he stilled himself and opened his ears to the night music.

That was all he heard. The night music.

He looked back to the seats around the campfire. Each of them was empty. People had been walking off one by one for a while, but Jeff hadn't noticed *everyone* was gone. A chill ran from the backs of his arms up his neck. Heartbeat rising in his throat, Jeff scanned the tree line. *Where is everybody?* he thought. He considered calling out, but then thought better of it. *Why would they leave me behind like this?* His eyes darted from truck to tent. He looked behind him to the dirt road and followed it into the dark where it faded, then to the woods on the other side. He had let his guard down. Maybe they had wanted him to. Had they found out who he really was? What had tipped them off? Must've been the story he told. He knew he was laying it on too thick, knew he shouldn't have had those beers. It was always like this. You follow regulations to the letter or else—this happens. This was his worst-case scenario. A bunch of fellas, armed hunters all, had suddenly discovered he was the law, an interloper among them. He had deceived them, and now he would pay for that mistake.

What if they're hiding in the woods to ambush me?

Slowly, Jeff rose to his feet. He walked back to his truck, head on a swivel. He wondered if they were in the woods, watching him. As he unlocked his passenger-side door, he scanned the trees. Was that a glint? The eye of a deer? Or the brief flash of a cell phone screen, moonlight catching a watch face. If they were out there, they were armed. They knew how to use their weapons.

Jeff opened the glove box and retrieved his revolver. He didn't like keeping it on him. Even when he hunted, he usually did so with a bow. Some officers toted around their gun like it made them powerful. Jeff knew better. The reality was quite the opposite. His power was in his words, in the way he treated people, in his reputation. He believed that once you had to draw your gun, you'd already lost. You'd already fucked up somewhere. As he had here. Big time. If Blackledge had been found out, then it was time for him to leave. *You guys want to play this game?* he thought. *Then let's play.* He tucked the revolver into the back of his waistband. Watchful of the shadows, he changed into a dark shirt so he could blend in with the night. He exchanged his flip-flops for boots.

I'm Jeff now, he said to himself. *Jeff Babauta. You're in my world. Come and get me.*

For half an hour, Jeff sat alone in the dark, revolver in his hand. What remained of the fire smoldered like crevices of lava beneath the dying coals. Tension gripped him by the shoulders. He didn't want to have that gun in his hand. He was worried for his own safety, but he also felt like a failure. He couldn't believe he'd fucked up like that. He was going to fail just like the guy before him, and now the whole operation would be a bust. If this came to violence, he'd feel doubly guilty. He'd gotten into this to protect the wild, to save what was left of it, not to act like a damn cowboy. He was willing to do anything to prevent that. *You have to defuse this situation*, he thought. *Think!*

A female voice called out in the dark.

The hair on Jeff's arms stood on end. None of the wives had stayed with them overnight.

He looked around. Every shadow of every tree teemed with imagined enemies. Yet none stirred. Perhaps, he considered, he hadn't heard a voice after all. The yowl of a Florida panther sounded eerily like a woman's scream. But those sounded more—banshee-like. This sound had been clear and ringing, the voice of a young woman calling out in question.

There it was again. "Is that a campfire?" she called out. "There are lights there. Stop, stop!"

Jeff turned in the direction of her voice, his heart hammering in his throat. Floodlights made silhouettes of the saw palm fronds. What looked like a truck passed through the trees, first coming toward him, then turning away.

Who was that? Jeff thought. *Biologists? It has to be*, he reassured himself. About twenty years prior, that had been his job. Around this time of year, he would go out at night to conduct the deer census. He and the other biologists would shine their lights through the trees, looking for the reflective orbs of eyes hovering in the darkness. It was both mundane, collecting numbers for statistical analysis, and undeniably spooky.

The logical part of him said that voice belonged to a young biologist. The animal part of him remained alert and on edge.

Just when his pulse was starting to ease, another light swiveled in the pines. A will-o'-the-wisp? No. A flashlight. It bobbed through the scrub, growing brighter, drawing closer. Jeff placed his hand on the grip of his revolver.

A figure emerged from the trees. He followed the path, reached the throw of the camp's light. Tommy.

Recognizing him didn't make Jeff feel better. Then he saw Tommy's face. He was grinning from ear to ear and leading a wheeled cooler like a puppy on a leash. He had some sort of long pole tipped back over one shoulder, and he strode with a buoyant gait, looking like Huckleberry Finn. *That sure doesn't look like a guy who's about to jump anybody*, Jeff thought. He took his hand off the gun.

Seeing Jeff, Tommy called out to him. They met back at the camp, where Jeff saw the implement slung over Tommy's shoulder wasn't just a pole: It was a three-pronged spear capped on one end. Such nasty-looking spears are called gigs, and using them, typically to catch bottom-feeder fish or frogs, is called gigging.

"I caught so many damn fish," Tommy said with a smile. The simple glee on his face really made Jeff want to like him.

Tommy loaded the cooler into the back of his own pickup truck and told Jeff to get in. Jeff, ready to be magnanimous with the fellow on account of his good mood, obliged and climbed into the passenger seat.

Still wanting to impress Robert, Tommy suggested they get a head start spotting some alligator nests before bed. They couldn't open them or pick up eggs then. Their permit dictated a specific time when they could begin, and they had to stick to that. Any egg harvesting outside its strictures would be poaching, but that didn't mean they couldn't look. It was late, but Jeff agreed. He didn't want to stay at the campsite alone any longer.

Tommy started the car and turned down the dirt road that ran through the woodland. *Could he be taking me off somewhere to trap me?* Jeff wondered.

When Tommy slowed the truck to a crawl and leaned out his window to search for nests, Jeff did the same. They pointed high-powered flashlights into the weeds and tall grasses along the marshy roadside, trying to spot nests to revisit in the morning.

He's not crafty enough to trick me like this, Jeff thought. *We really are looking for nests.*

Unidentified bugs hurtled through Jeff's beam like meteors. He wasn't seeing anything, and the tension from twenty minutes prior still nagged at him. Even if Tommy had just been out gigging, that didn't mean the others, Robert especially, weren't out there waiting, plotting. Jeff still had the revolver. It pressed up against his back where he sat. Now even more than before he hoped to God he wouldn't have to use it. He couldn't wait to tuck it back in his glove compartment where it belonged.

When they came to a field, Jeff shone his light across it. It sparked on the glare of a reflector. He darted the light away, but he was sure that had been a vehicle. A white truck. *That's got to be the game warden*, he thought. *Hope he doesn't see us.* If the warden pulled them over and opened the coolers, he'd probably find fish illegally caught out of season. He might charge both of them with poaching. That would mean the end of the operation for Jeff. He looked over at Tommy, about to warn him.

"Shine that light back over there again," Tommy said before he could.

Cautiously, Jeff let the beam flick over the field, arcing over the truck just fast enough to catch the glint of the refractors inside its headlights. Then he drew it back to the roadside.

"Damn, I'll bet you that's the game warden," Tommy said, echoing Jeff's thought.

Jeff imagined the biologists leaving him then, just out of earshot, calling up the agency to report their illegal camping. *I'll guarantee that's him*, Jeff thought. Now a new worry ran alongside the others. Jeff had worked in that exact area for more than a decade. More likely than not, the officer in that vehicle would know him on sight. *He's gonna blow this whole thing wide open.* That would be worse than getting arrested. Because then Tommy would know who he really was, and Jeff would be stuck out there in the wilderness with him, his worst fears coming to life.

The training academy taught all wildlife officers that while on uniformed patrol, they might one day encounter officers working undercover, very likely officers they knew and could recognize even with their disguises. Their training said that if you, the uniformed officer, recognized someone, you were supposed to get out of there as soon as possible. Just cut conversations short and get the hell out. That was what they were *supposed* to do. But regulations were one thing. What happened in the field was something else entirely.

Jeff and Tommy didn't get too far down the road before a set of blue lights flared in the rearview mirror. The closer they came, the harder Jeff gritted his teeth. *Oh God. Here it goes.*

Tommy looked at the rearview mirror, then, as if that might have lied to him, he checked the side view. "Yeah, I knew it was the game warden that you hit the lights on back there," Tommy said. "I guess we need to pull over."

The truck eased to a stop on the shoulder. Jeff's thoughts raced faster and faster. He needed this officer to turn and leave sooner rather than later.

The game warden parked behind them and flicked his lights. By then it was about 10 PM, and wispy streaks of rain darted through the headlights. Tommy glanced back, then got out and walked toward the officer's truck. Jeff stayed where he was, simmering in anxiety. He watched Tommy's reflection in the side-view mirror chat with the officer through his window, then hand over his ID.

"Hey, Jeff!" Tommy hollered. "The officer needs to see your ID!"

"What for?" Jeff yelled back.

"To check if you're wanted," Tommy answered with a laugh.

"Okay." Reluctantly, Jeff climbed out and walked back to the patrol truck. As he handed over his ID, he studied the officer's face. *Who the hell are you?* he thought. Somehow, from that tiny local branch of the agency, there was an officer Jeff had never seen before, much to his relief. He was a brand-new hire just out of the academy, Jeff would learn later.

The officer squeezed the button on the radio receiver attached to his shoulder. "29P," he said. Jeff knew that code. It meant to check and see if this guy was wanted.

Until then, Jeff's undercover license had been just another set piece. He'd never had it run before, not even to check it. He had absolutely no idea if it would work.

A few moments later, their dispatcher's familiar voice called back to him. "Ten–fifty-four," she said. "Ten–twenty-nine P." *10–54. Negative.* That meant, *No, your man isn't wanted.* His ID had worked.

All the tension Jeff had been holding unraveled at once. He found himself smiling. But Blackledge wasn't supposed to know 10-codes. He decided to play it off. He stuck his head in the window. "What does that mean?" he said with mock-worry. "I'm wanted by the FBI?"

"Nope, you're good," the officer said. He handed back Jeff's ID. "All right, guys, you know you're not supposed to be camping out here, right? It's late tonight, so I'll let this slide, but you'll need to find a different campsite after that." He wished them a safe night, and they parted ways.

As the officer's taillights faded, Jeff silently rejoiced. *He didn't recognize me. My driver's license worked. He didn't even check the coolers.*

They sure were lucky that it was raining, and, just like the new Everglades park rangers and the fear of mosquitoes that kept them out of Peg Brown's way, this officer hadn't wanted to get wet.

The next morning, the crew met around the campfire. As they gradually came back to life after that rainy and dismal night, Jeff studied the faces of his compatriots out of the corner of his eye. They drank their coffee, ate their breakfast, grumbled to themselves; the more outgoing among them tried to strike up conversations. None so much as cast Jeff a sidelong glance. No matter how much the rational part of his brain said last night's disappearances had been a coincidence, the other part of his brain said there was no such thing. Even if they hadn't been prowling through the darkness, ready to shoot Jeff and give his body to the swamp, they still didn't trust him enough to apprise him of their plans. This told him two things: One, they sensed something was off about him; two, they had something to hide.

He settled into that uneasiness. *Be cool*, he told himself. *They don't know anything. Acting shifty will just tip them off.* He tried to liven up his posture. He smiled. Nothing had happened to Blackledge. Blackledge had to keep on being his goofy self. He cracked a joke to Tommy. He received a strained smile, a combination of elation from his gigging adventure tempered by the irritation of an early morning. At least Tommy was easy to read. Regardless of how at odds their personalities were, Jeff and Tommy had seemed to reach a kind of equilibrium: Each knew that the other didn't like his particular brand of bullshit, and that was all right as long as they got the job done and didn't end up as Mama Gator's dinner.

As the sun rose beyond the pines and the woolly heads of the cypresses, the sky shifted to a soft yellow and then to a brilliant crosshatch of red, heralding coming storms. Cars and trucks began to arrive, bringing not just the wives and kids of the crew members but also more hands to lighten the work. Robert gathered them around and introduced everyone. He wasn't hiring them. It was more like a fishing trip for most of them, a fun family outing in nature. Jeff had already met Robert's wife, Robin, and their kids. But there were new people, too. Lots of them. Folks from out of state who wanted a taste of the swamp life, friends from the city, anybody who was willing to give them free labor and competent enough not to get in the way.

One fellow whom Jeff didn't know very well yet called himself CW. CW was a caricature of himself. The phrase *blinged out* came to mind. Gold bracelets adorned each of his wrists. Gold necklaces—yes, multiple—were slung around his neck. According to Robert, CW worked as a pesticide sprayer at an orange grove. That made Jeff want to cock his head. *Where are you getting the money to dress this foolishly?* This was just the kind of riddle that made Jeff want to investigate someone. Jeff snuck over to his truck to write down the fellow's name.

The final addition to their crew was David, a retired wildlife biologist in his seventies. With white hair and attire befitting a genteel jungle explorer, David seemed more like a David Attenborough knockoff than a potential criminal. He was supervising the egg hunts to supplement his paltry state pension. Jeff greeted David warmly, and David made a face as though he found Jeff slightly distasteful. That made Jeff want to laugh. As Jeff Babauta, he was even more clean-cut than David. As Blackledge, on the other hand—well, his disguise seemed to be working.

After everyone had been properly introduced, Robert issued his instructions, and the small army of alligator egg hunters split up to commence their search. Robert paired Jeff with Tommy again and assigned them a zone to survey. Before they left, Tommy puffed up his chest and told Robert about the nests they'd spotted last night on their impromptu survey. They'd run into Robert not long after the game warden left, and they'd given the boss a rundown of the night's events—save Jeff's justified paranoia and the heat he had been packing. Robert had seemed concerned about the game warden's presence. The slight change in his facial expression dinged the alarm bell in Jeff's head. Something was off. *He doesn't want the game warden poking around,* Jeff had thought. *Why not?* The expression of concern dissipated as quickly as it had appeared, and Robert said he would take care of the camping situation. He told them not to worry.

Small clues were starting to pile up, and Jeff could no longer write them off as mere coincidences. Something was going on. He had to keep his eyes peeled now to figure out what.

Jeff and Tommy parted from the group and cut down a trail to go deeper into the swamp. Wet earth stuck to Jeff's flip-flop soles. The foliage around them shivered with latent raindrops, a peaceful patter, and the land itself exhaled the scent of petrichor. It wasn't quite enough to cover up the smell of piss exuding from the hot, wet flop of an alligator nest. But Jeff had to take it as it was. As they had before, Jeff and

Tommy set to work. They located a nest. Jeff went to mark its location. But Tommy was already kneeling next to it, opening it up.

"What are you doing?" Jeff asked.

"Checking if there are eggs in here," Tommy said. "What's it look like?" Tommy pried up the top, glanced in, and then, noting the eggs, he closed it back up again. *What the hell are you doing?* Jeff thought. As if in answer, Tommy said, "Robert said we should see if they're full, then wait to open them for when the biologist comes around with us. You know, that way we don't waste any nests for ones that are empty."

That ain't legal, Jeff thought. He wanted to say something, but he bit his tongue. His suspicions had been right. Robert's crew was poaching. Now the question was: How much and for how long? To figure that out, Jeff had to stay the course. *Don't break character. Just keep watching.*

Jeff kept a vigilant eye on the trees for angry mother gators. This time, too, he was wary of the presence of men, of the poachers he may have discovered and what they, in turn, had discovered about him.

They returned to the camp for lunch. Jeff dug out a bottle of antibacterial soap and scrubbed himself down like a surgeon prepping for the operating theater. Only then did he join the others around the unlit fire. With the woods as wet as they were, you'd have to import dry wood from elsewhere if you wanted to get a spark. Nonetheless, the fire circle had become the camp's unofficial center.

The food Jeff brought was part of his character: a can of beans and franks and a packet of saltines. In his regular life, he loved to cook; the food he made ranged from homestyle comfort food to game meat prepared in a way some might consider gourmet. Blackledge, on the other hand, was useless in the kitchen. Being the easygoing fellow that he was, he didn't pay much mind to his diet. He just ate whatever. And since he'd been poor for so long, up until his aunt passed away and left him all that money, he had a taste for the refined in the sense of refined carbohydrates, Cheez Whiz, processed crap.

As he sat down to his beanie weenies, he watched Robert break out a can of Spam, and as if some unheard signal like a dog whistle had issued from it, half the crew lined up to get some. Robert sliced off a hunk thick enough for a sandwich, and Tommy held out his hands. *This is like goddamn Oliver Twist*, Jeff thought. Even though the scene seemed mundane enough, the absurdity of it struck Jeff, and he couldn't let it go. Tommy left the line with his Spam slice and went to the next part of the conveyor belt to grab some Wonder Bread to make a sandwich. The line kept going like that, Robert diligently slicing off Spam hunks and gently placing them in the hands of his hunters; complex and quiet Robert as the schoolmaster, his laborers the wee Victorian children asking for more.

"Want some?" Robert called. He'd seen Jeff staring. Maybe he was calling him out on it, or maybe he genuinely wanted to feed everyone.

"Nah, I'm good," Jeff answered. But he was overwhelmed by the strangeness of all of it. He turned to the person next to him as if they might share a look of understanding. It was David. He sat with his hands folded in his lap. "You a Spam guy?" Jeff asked. David responded with a look that said, *Sir, do I look like a Spam fellow?* That made Jeff grin. "You not eating anything?"

"No, I'm fine," David said.

"You should at least drink some water or something," Jeff said. "'Bout to have a long day in the heat."

"I'm used to it," David said. "I used to be the head wildlife biologist for the Virgin Islands, the American ones."

"Must've been mighty interesting," Jeff said.

David perked up a bit. "Oh, it was." Soon, they got to talking, and David told him about how his research specialty had been mongooses. David smiled, happy to expound to an interested listener. It was clear he realized he had misjudged Blackledge. That quick shift, the ease with which David could overcome his preconceived notions, made Jeff like the guy almost immediately.

It was a good thing they bonded, too, because after the lunch hour ended, the old biologist joined him as his airboat passenger, and together they zipped over the marsh. Intrepid and experienced though he was, David hung on tight, one hand gripping the noise-blocking headset to his ears, the other latched to the underside of his seat. They careened through the spartina grass and the rushes. Snowy egrets lifted up in flocks to escape the startling noise of the airboat's massive propeller.

They met Robert, CW, and Tommy out there on the grass island. By then, the storm clouds augured by the morning's bright sky had begun to gather overhead. Thunder rumbled in the distance.

Robert looked up at the sky. "We may need to make this quick," he said.

The hunters went to the egg nests marked on the map. David followed with his clipboard. Robert, too, kept his notes, the enigmatic aluminum box tucked under his arm, always with him. They'd been to these nests before. Did David know? Jeff hoped he didn't. Lo and behold, there were eggs inside, and the hunters set to digging them out, checking their shells against the light, nestling them in their box for the next leg of their journey. A wet wind blew over the marshes. It smelled like ocean. The storm had traveled far to get to them.

Jeff and Tommy finished their nest. Then they hiked over the marsh island to reach the others, who were doing the same as they just had. David stood, observing.

"What kind of bird is that?" Tommy said, pointing to a great blue heron. Jeff knew it. But Blackledge didn't know squat.

He smiled at Tommy. "Gray one? Definitely a gray one."

"Which bird?" David asked, and Tommy pointed it out. David cleaned his glasses, which the dense humidity had fogged up. He squinted through them. "Ah, that is a great blue heron, *Ardea herodias*, I believe."

"You must know everything there is to know about animals," Jeff said.

"Hardly," David answered.

The sky darkened and they retired to the airboat to wait for the others. From there, they spotted more birds, identified and talked about them, and Jeff forgot himself again. He loved the swamp and the things that lived there. For once, he was in the presence of a kindred spirit. He let his knowledge shine through.

"You know quite a bit about animals yourself," David said.

"Me?" Jeff said, grinning. *Shit, what did I say?* "Nah, I don't know anything about anything."

"Certainly you do," said David. "Frankly, I'm surprised you couldn't identify that heron. Perhaps you need to clean your glasses as well."

How can he be onto me already? Jeff thought. *This fella's too smart for his own good.*

"I guess I just watch too many nature documentaries," Jeff said. "Love to have a beer and turn on National Geographic. Who doesn't?"

"Well, perhaps you've missed your calling," David said. "You've surely retained a great deal of that information."

What are you trying to say? Jeff thought. *You know, don't you. Is my cover blown? No, it can't be. Even if you knew, would you tell somebody? Are you on my side or theirs?*

After a while, their conversation fizzled out, and David, unbothered by his surroundings, clasped his hands over his stomach, leaned back, and went to sleep. Watching David sleep made Jeff wonder if he was being paranoid. David clearly meant him no harm. Their conversations, too, had shown Jeff just how jumbled his identities had become. At that moment, he felt like he was losing both of them, Jeff Babauta and Curtis Blackledge. They had tangled into a new person who was both and neither. Although as Jeff Babauta he had never poached before, through the eyes of Curtis Blackledge, he had seen into the other side. He had witnessed the gamut from casual lawbreaking to perhaps what might turn out to be an elaborately contrived scheme. He would never be the same. Now he knew that even the most clean-cut and religious veneers could hide the sordid, the illegal.

As good a judge of character as he thought himself to be, Jeff reminded himself he couldn't read someone's heart or their mind. *You're not being paranoid*, he thought. Lightning jolted overhead, accompanied by a gut-shaking boom of thunder. Jeff swore. He wasn't usually scared on the job, but sitting in a metal boat during a lightning storm would have that effect on anybody. David shot up, wide-eyed and awake. The others came running down to their airboat as the sky opened up and a veritable deluge flowed over the swamp. *Time to haul ass*, Jeff thought. He cranked up the propeller, and they were out of there.

The crew stayed at Cecil Webb for another couple of days. During that time, it became clear to Jeff that David didn't know he was an undercover officer. He found himself regretting that rather than rejoicing in it, because from the evidence he'd gathered in those same days, Jeff believed David was complicit in the poaching as well. He saw what Robert and Tommy were doing, and he looked the other way. Jeff wanted to set David straight before he could dig himself in too deeply. He just had to figure out how.

When their time in that swamp drew to a close, Jeff, Tommy, and the other central spokes of the crew sat up on the levee with flashlights, counting eggs. It was nighttime, totally black out as the clouds had failed to disperse after the storm. A fog of mosquitoes fell down upon them to feast. While the others broke camp, Jeff, Tommy, and their crew candled the eggs, a process that told them if their eggs were viable, if they could one day hatch into baby alligators. A viable egg would have an opaque white ring around its center. Unviable ones, which Tommy had started calling *light bulbs*, would only show as translucent, a view into a simple yolk and nothing more When they noticed one that wasn't viable, its finder would make note of it, then fling the dud over his shoulder, unceremoniously disposing of it in the marsh below.

"Another light bulb," Tommy said and sent his egg sailing into the dark, where it landed to a rustle of spartina.

All told, their army of hunters had collected 488 viable eggs, many from nests Jeff believed twice or thrice opened, a detail the crew, of course, did not put in the official reports they rendered to FWC.

The crew moved on from one slice of wilderness to another, crisscrossing the state according to whatever permit they had in hand. Many collections happened on public land, but others were on privately held tracts. Jeff soon discovered that the woods harbored strange things, separated from the public and the outside world by just a thick stand of trees, things that even he had no idea existed just out of sight.

Come mid-July, their itinerary took them to Rum Creek Ranch, only a hike from Cecil Webb, but it might as well have been in another world. Past unassuming fields where cowbirds by the dozens stalked like miniature raptors, past the sentinel oaks that stood watch over rain-soaked fields, ten-foot-tall fences cut through the shade of the woods. There, a well-guarded gate opened for the crew, and the caretaker led them inside the secret wildlife sanctuary.

When they stopped at a staging area to collect themselves and prepare to venture into the bush, the caretaker issued a warning. "No photography here," he said. "Not even on your cell phones. What we're doing here isn't illegal, but we don't want anyone to know we're here, got it?"

Got it.

"What *are* they doing here?" Jeff asked once the caretaker was out of earshot.

"They're breeding exotic animals, like endangered ones," Robin said. "It's like Africa in here." She held her camera bag awkwardly. Seems she had hoped to take some pictures, and now she was hesitating about whether or not she would comply with the caretaker's order. Robin and Robert already knew him, so it wasn't like they'd face too much trouble if she snuck a picture or two. The caretaker viewed the others, including Jeff, David, and another of Robert's visitors from out of state, with suspicion.

If people are breeding something in captivity, odds are you can find that something in Florida if you know the right unmarked country road down which to venture. In the Everglades alone, you can find monkeys, camels; everyone already knows about our tigers. Florida is fertile ground for fertility. But Rum Creek wasn't one of those exotic dog and endangered pony shows. Nor was it some rich guy's private menagerie. A billionaire indeed funded Rum Creek, but in the name of conservation and achieving the impossible. As of 2016, the ranch's official report to FWC put its exotic animal population at 1,275 individuals across twenty-four species. "It has, for example, 35 white rhinos, 62 impalas, 338 Javan Bantengs (a species of wild cattle) and about 100 Eastern Bongos, a large forest-dwelling antelope facing extinction in the wild," Mike Vogel wrote for *Florida Trend*.

"I'm sorry, we'll be hunting eggs where with *what*?" Jeff said. He was used to standing guard against alligators, but looking out for rampaging rhinos had never come up in all his wildest dreams and nightmares about this investigation.

The caretaker gestured for Robin and Tommy to follow him. They were going to collect eggs in the rhino preserve. That left Jeff with Robert's out-of-state guest and David. Part of the property was marshland and all but underwater. Avoiding that area, they started collecting eggs along the levee. Every so often, a gazelle would bound by. Jeff would see it, return to his work, then immediately look back up, because *Damn, that was a gazelle!* The peculiarity of it all, and the suddenness of the sightings, cast a surreal hue over their work.

But Jeff couldn't let himself get distracted. Without David going into the rhino preserve with Tommy and Robin, none of the nests they opened there were properly supervised, leaving them all kinds of room to sneak eggs out unaccounted for.

David never said anything when they left him behind. Each time it happened, Jeff felt more certain that the venerable biologist was complicit in their scheme. But a feeling was just a feeling. He needed to know for sure.

After that, Robert's crew split up. Their egg collections took place all over the state, as far south as parts of the Everglades proper, and as far north as Paynes Prairie just south of Gainesville. Robert, Robin, Tommy, and CW drove up there to complete that job. Jeff tried to join them, but their car drove past him going south on the highway, the opposite direction. They had left before he could get there, and they hadn't bothered to tell him, either. *Evidently, they didn't want me to be a part of this operation*, Jeff thought. Jeff called Robert, holding his cell with one hand, on speakerphone. The line rang hollowly. Thankfully, Robert picked up.

"Hey, I'm coming to meet you," Jeff said. "I'm on the highway right now, and I swear I just saw you going the other way."

"We're headed to Gainesville," Robert said. "We got David with us. Go ahead and head back to the farm and start with the hatching."

Something about this made Jeff uneasy. They had kept him out of too many conversations. They were doing this on his farm. It wasn't like he was just some farmhand. He was a business partner. He deserved to know what was going on.

Whoa, Jeff thought. He had slipped into Blackledge without thinking. Those were the kinds of things Blackledge would want. Jeff Babauta needed to be in on their conversations, sure, but for a totally different reason.

Unsettled by them and unsettled by losing himself to the character, Jeff pulled a U-turn and headed for home. *Not home*, he thought. *The farm. The farm is not your home.*

14

SUSPENSION OF DISBELIEF

Mac disappeared and a few minutes later, his boat swung around the bend. It was a broad, long split-hulled boat, a powered catamaran with an excess of seats in the bow for tourists. Mac, among other things, was a tour guide. He wore an affable smile and a Columbia shirt, and he seemed to take great joy in showing off the islands and telling their stories. Mac pulled alongside the dock, and Jonnie, helping out, towed the boat forward until it bumped along the wood. I stepped down onto the deck and chose a seat that faced forward. With Mac at the boat's wheel a few seats behind me, and Jonnie leaning beside him, I knew my position would make interviewing them awkward. I told myself I was there to experience, to witness. I could ask them follow-up questions later. The tableau of nature is often fleeting. Who knew what miracle might unfold before us, a brief glimpse, there and gone.

"Ready?" Mac asked.

As a way of saying yes, I brandished my pen—a waterproof Sharpie.

Mac and Jonnie shared a glance as if they thought me trying to write on a moving boat was crazy. They might watch, amused at my failure, but they weren't about to tell me what to do. I saw echoes of my own culture in the gladesmen. They treated me with kindness. Sometimes I caught them looking at me with admiration, like I was one of theirs who had gotten out and made it, like they were proud of me.

That was something I noticed about the two swamp cultures, the one in the glades and the one a little north in river country: a respect and kindness toward women that is difficult to explain to outsiders. Growing up, my family always had a matriarch. It made sense, as men often died younger, in their sixties or seventies, while the women lived into their nineties or even to a hundred. They had as much as forty more years to accumulate wisdom. Everyone, even the men, treated each woman, no matter her age, like she would be that matriarch someday. This didn't look how you might think. It meant that, in addition to cooking, sewing, and what have you, women were expected to be able to do anything a man could do, as a matter of practicality: gut a fish, fix an engine, run a saw, build, mend, make—you name it. Conversely, the same was expected of the men—not being able to cook, sew, or garden was a deficiency to be corrected, not expected of someone else. The result was that everyone was a complete person, independent and able to subsist in that wild country on their own. That also means that the most rugged men I've ever met—the swamp men, the alligator hunters, the mechanics, the war heroes—didn't waste a single moment of their time worrying about being manly; rather, they endeavored to take care of the people around them. My father is the one who taught me how to sew.

After too many nights alone in the swamp, you realize that rugged individualism is bunk; just because you can subsist on your own doesn't mean that you have to or should. Community and family are much stronger than any misplaced ideas of toughness you've heaved upon yourself, and the best thing a person can be—whatever their gender, whatever their responsibilities or needs—is caring. It takes great strength to care. Looking back at my childhood, the most rugged and determined figures I remember were also the gentlest. That is what I recognized most in Mac and Jonnie. They cared, and it was obvious.

As we motored through the dark water, brackish and murky there at the confluence of the glades and the gulf, Mac told me about the area, the Ten Thousand Islands, a submerged coastal plateau speckled with hundreds of islands before the drop-off of the ocean basin. Even the name Ten Thousand Islands showed a bit of storytelling hyperbole.

"There used to be a lot of oysters here," Jonnie said. "The mangroves have edged them out. None of this used to look like it does now."

What did it look like before? I tried to imagine.

In some places, it looked like jungle, he said. In others, like sandy shoals and beaches. Still more, the grasses of the glades had spread marshy fingers out into the water. To my surprise, Jonnie said that the mangroves were invasive just like Kent had. I was beginning to think that there must be a grain of truth to that. Mangroves weren't invasive in the scientific sense, as they're endemic to Florida; but they had *invaded*, the fast-growing plants moving in over time as settlers cut down trees and others fell prey to sea-level rise, the new salinity in the earth beneath their roots a death blow. Elsewhere, that same process created ghost forests, coastal stands of dead trees that had succumbed to the ingress of salt. But here, there were mangroves, and mangroves were opportunists. They glommed onto whatever soil they could and tangled together to create impassable, forbidding, and ever-changing mazes of life.

Although the landscape was different than it had been, with the mangroves, the Ten Thousand Islands had gotten lucky. Mangroves staved off the death that comes with ghost forests. They gave rise to new habitats. Migratory birds nested in their back bays. Fish from tiny minnows to gargantuan goliath groupers made nurseries in the trees' shade.

Flocks began to light on the trees. Some rookeries sported hundreds, pops of white like bolls of cotton. Moody clouds curled overhead, each lined with the gold of rising noon. The sky cast a glaring gray over the mangrove forests. Birds huddled among the leaves as the wind picked up, scratching whitecaps over the estuary's dark water. A cooler gust carried with it the damp of a coming storm. As if summoned, Mac, Jonnie, and I all looked up in unison.

"Might need to hurry this along if we don't want to get wet," Mac said.

"I won't melt," I said. "My paper might, though."

Mac asked me how I felt about going a little faster.

"Go as fast as you want," I said.

Mac grinned at me as if to say, *If you say so*. He pushed the throttle. As the boat picked up speed, the bow lifted higher and higher out of the water, until we were angled toward the sky, skipping over the whitecaps.

They kept talking, and, much to their amusement, I kept writing.

"Let's see if this brings my friends out," Mac said. "There they are. See 'em?" He nodded toward the boat's wake, and I stood, craning for a glimpse of—dolphins. Two Atlantic bottlenose dolphins leapt in the curls of the waves trailing behind us, gaining height as if they knew we could see them. "Show-offs," Mac said. "But the tourists love 'em."

"Who doesn't?" I said.

"Right?" he answered.

They didn't feed them or anything. The dolphins just seemed to like the attention. This made me think of the dolphins that used to swim near me when I did open-water training back home. They would put themselves between me and the open water, following until I exited up the beach. These same dolphins did this day after day, every time I went out to swim. One time, a fisherman on the shore ran over to me when I walked out of the surf and informed me with alarm about the shark that was in the water.

"Oh, those are dolphins," I said.

"No, past them," he had answered. "A big one." He said that he'd watched the whole thing: The dolphins had protected me from the danger that lurked in the deep water. It seemed implausible, and yet—why would this stranger lie to me?

Of all the animals I've interacted with in the wild, it's dolphins who make me wonder the most. They clearly have memories and motivations. Dolphins are powerful predators. They could have hurt me if they wanted to. Instead, they remained at a distance and observed. Perhaps I filled them with the same sense of wonder as they did me. They have complex and curious inner lives that I will never know.

Ultimately, that may be the thing that captivates me most about nature: Just like any story I have investigated, when I immerse myself in the natural world, I realize that the more I learn, the more there is to discover. Right when I think I know everything, nature strikes me with awe, and I am astonished.

"How are you doing?" Mac asked.

"So far, so good," I said.

That was his cue to really gun the engine. We zipped through the keyholes of the islands. I stopped writing for a while so I could take it all in.

The sky was growing dark and moody, the tail end of that storm front that Kent had warned about. I worried that the sky would open up and drench us. I hoped it would wait so that I might see more of that rugged country.

After a while, shallower waters and no-wake zones demanded slower speeds. We were deep in the wilderness of mud and mangroves. We circled back north and threaded through Sandfly Pass. Mac said we were going to Sandfly Island.

Not a very inviting name, I thought.

Before I had much time to think about it, Mac angled the boat into the mangroves. Startled, I braced for impact. We glided untouched under the canopy, and the hull ran up the shell beach until the bow rested before an outcropping of roots and mud.

"We're here," Mac announced.

Jonnie asked me if I needed help out, but I had already jumped ashore before he finished the sentence. Mac led us up the hill to a bedraggled trail. Some distance away, a national park informational sign indicated that this all had once been kept up. A recent hurricane had battered the islands, knocking down Sandfly's pier and whisking away its porta-potty, among other things. It seemed as though we weren't technically supposed to be there. I only saw the sign that said, DANGER, TRAIL CLOSED, as we were leaving. Mac and Jonnie, had they known, didn't pay it any mind. Those sorts of things were for the tourists, not people like us.

"We won't go around the whole island," Mac said. "I believe half of it's underwater. But we'll go where we can reach."

Sandfly Island was partially artificial, according to Mac. In the Paleolithic era, the Calusa tribe had used shells and earthworking to shape the island into a curve with a bay in the middle that drew fish into their nets. Thousands of years later, when the first European settlers arrived, the Calusa were already gone, but their engineering remained. A fifteen-foot shell mound was the remnant of their civilization. Homesteaders took advantage of the edifice the Calusa left behind. They built a big house, two stories with nine rooms, a veritable mansion in those days. The homesteaders built a cistern, too, and an artesian well that issued fresh water from the aquifer.

We climbed toward it, up the hill under red-barked gumbo-limbo trees. The coming storm and the thickness of the canopy cooled our trek into a mysterious gloom. At the top of the hill, a strangler fig wrapped around a mossy buttonwood tree and reached forth to grasp the archaic concrete walls of the cistern's pool. The water inside was dark, steeped with fallen leaves. On the other side of the path, fresh spring water, its smell verdant and full of life—no salt here—rose up from the lime rock.

"Everybody thought that well had dried up," Mac said. "Then the hurricane came, and it must have knocked something loose. Hadn't flowed in years. Suddenly it came back to life."

The idea seemed both mundane and miraculous: a spring coming back from the dead. I didn't know what to make of it. Hurricanes didn't work like that. It didn't make sense, but here sense was just another made-up rule that reality didn't have to follow. I considered that and the idea of renewal, new growth, hope, as I ventured toward a railless boardwalk like a bridge over a dark pool.

Up ahead, the far length of the walkway disappeared under the water. The boards, sodden from the recent storm, sank with my weight. Over the water, the cool, still air dewed against my skin. Mangrove snappers, schoolmasters, and gar angled and darted beneath my feet. Overhead, the mangroves seemed to weave together to create an intricate and endless knot that blocked out all but the sun's most persistent rays. The canopy was alive with the buzz and whisper of insects. Fish plunked at the water's surface when they swam up for a mouthful of mosquitoes.

Mac and Jonnie followed. We started talking about disappearances. Mac was a relative newcomer to the glades, but Jonnie had known them since the days he went out hunting with his father. He had witnessed the shift, a drawing back of the wild things that had once lived in such abundance. Now there were fewer birds, fewer fish.

"My dad shot a panther in Chatham Bend," Jonnie said. "You might be horrified now. Back then, that wasn't such a big deal. There used to be so much more of them. Now how long has it been since I've seen one? Decades?"

He liked to watch the painted buntings peck at his bird feeder back home. Even they seemed scarce, of late.

"It's the pesticides," Mac said. "All the farms trying to kill their bugs, they end up killing everything else, too."

"Whoa now." Jonnie laughed. "If you aren't careful, talk like that makes people think you're an *environmentalist*." He said it like it was a dirty word.

In another circumstance, I might have been tempted to butt in and defend environmentalism, but here there was no need.

Mac laughed. "Maybe I am," he said with mock confrontation in his voice. "The tourists like to hear that stuff, but—it's no sin to give a damn. You do, too, and you know it."

By then, I had walked so far out on the planks over that little lagoon that I had reached the part that dipped under the water. I could see where it carried on, coming up above the surface again to follow a tunnel through the mangroves before turning out of sight. The walkway sank beneath my feet. The algae-flecked water rose above my ankles and threatened to come higher still. I heard the boards shift. Alligators likely lingered in the shadowy water below, but none gave any sign of movement.

Jonnie called out to me, and I turned around. He was halfway to me on the boardwalk. Mac had remained on the shore. They both looked at me like, *Where the hell are you going?*

"Come on back," Jonnie said.

"We're not going over that," Mac said. "I mean, *you're* welcome to. I'm not going to stop you, but we don't have any towels."

"Fine, let's do the reasonable thing," I said sarcastically, coming back toward them.

Back on solid ground, I looked around at that idyllic place once more, breathing in its surreal beauty. The shade from the canopy did make it look like a dream. Or perhaps it looked like a dream to me because so many of the nocturnal adventures of my subconscious happen in swamps.

The first stray drops of an afternoon shower splashed down on the boat as we crossed the broad sweep of the bay, and the most recognizable building on Chokoloskee Island came into view: the Smallwood

Store. From far away, it seemed much smaller than it actually was. The former trading post rose on pilings above the shell-cracked shore. A storm-worn porch on the upper floor hung over a dock that wrapped around the red building. A single cabbage palm leaned over the tin roof as if posed there on purpose to complete the Old Florida ambience.

Mac ran the boat up the rocky shore beside it.

"I'll meet you inside," Mac said as Jonnie and I hopped out. Then he backed the boat out and returned to open water. We took our sweet time, as one does in those latitudes when touched by a breeze that relieves the oppressive heat, even if that breeze is the presage to a thundershower. As Floridians, we were used to rain. Even though we had made quick work of coming ashore, as small boats tend not to make good shelters from lightning and we hadn't wanted to get fried, the afternoon rains of a Florida summer bring a welcome respite.

The Smallwood Store had started its life as a trading post in 1906 when Ted Smallwood moved down to that last frontier and saw that while the families who had set up there were rugged, they were still in need of produce, supplies, and mail. The store remained more or less unchanged until it closed in 1982. The Smallwoods then locked the doors with the goods inside, a time capsule waiting for Ted Smallwood's granddaughter, Mac's now wife. Recognizing what she had as an intact gem of Florida history, she reopened the Smallwood Store as a museum in 1990, and it has continued on like that ever since. It was open right then, too, and about a dozen visitors perused its aisles.

Venturing inside was like stepping through a time warp—or into my great-grandfather's toolshed. The main long aisle of the store ran from the front door straight to the back door, which remained open to the upper porch and the breeze. Cast-iron skillets, pans, and washtubs hung from the ceiling along with the lazily turning fans. On one side of the main aisle, a counter was piled high with new and old books, worn photographs, hats, canned goods, and endless other memorabilia. The counter itself was slanted inward from the top to accommodate the hoop skirts from back in the day. The next aisle seemed to be a gift shop, but items scattered throughout the store had price tags, making it hard to tell where the true store ended and the museum began. This was especially true of the books, which claimed space on every available surface. When Mac joined us, I asked him, and he said, half in jest, "Anything's for sale if you offer the right amount of money."

"I suppose that's true," I said. I wished it wasn't, that money didn't speak quite so loudly as it did, but it did and always had. Those who had the most gold ruled. People willing to take will keep on taking. That, in part, was the story of the Everglades. I could see that on the small scale in just about everything Mac and Jonnie showed me.

Mac gave me a tour around the store. Jonnie pointed out things donated by his family. There was so much there that I was a bit overwhelmed. They pointed at the upper porch, out the back door, and Jonnie said, "That's where they killed old Watson, the cruel sugarcane planter. If you believe the stories, a Brown fired the killing shot. Then Watson tumbled over the railing, and—*splash*. A bunch of people fired at the same time. He was that kind of hated, and everybody says that his was the bullet that did it."

"Seems they all sort of did the job together," I said. "Bullets work together like that."

"Yep," Jonnie said.

We lingered in thought there, studying the planks, the tide whispering in and out some twenty feet below.

"There used to be a gas pump down there," Jonnie said, the twinkle of nostalgia in his eye. "Smallwood would pay us kids to pump the gas, literally pump it by pushing on this lever to get the pneumatics working and pull it up from the tank."

It seemed the past had lingered longer in this part of the glades. Technology had trickled in more slowly, the things that had come at all. Take away the cell phones, and you would have had an impossible time identifying what decade we were in. I think that might have been part of the place's draw: Life moved at its own pace in Chokoloskee. It reminded me of something my dad used to say: *We'll get there when we get there*. That slow pace made the change that surrounded Chokoloskee seem all that much quicker.

Mac went behind the counter and lifted up a conch shell larger than a basketball, the veneer inside its lips quite pink and alive despite its age, perhaps seventy-five to a hundred years old. "Feel that," he said, handing the conch to me. My hands plummeted under the weight. I barely held the shell above the glass counter. The conch felt like it was made of solid concrete. I turned my head to look inside to see if it was filled with something. It was not.

"Heavy, innit?" he said with a pleased smile. "They all used to be like this. The shells of the conches have been getting thinner."

"Why?" I asked. By that point in the day, I had doffed my journalist hat for one of pure curiosity, as if they were estranged uncles I'd just met that morning, eager to show me around the world that I had missed. I asked why because I genuinely wanted to know. Why would that happen? Why would conch shells be getting thinner? Was it something in the water? Ocean acidification? Was there a reason they would have less calcium to use to fortify their shells?

"Don't know," Mac said. "I think it has something to do with water pollution."

"There you go again," Jonnie said, smiling and shaking his head. "You did, you've turned into an environmentalist."

Mac gave him a look. "Everybody cares about clean water," Mac said. "Especially you. You're a damn fisherman. Look me in the eye and tell me this doesn't worry you. You've seen it, how things have changed. You probably know better than I do."

Jonnie looked thoughtful for a moment. "Fine," he said. He'd noticed the change on other shells, too. It had come slowly, like the movement of the mangroves. He mused that perhaps they were connected. "You know I care. But that doesn't make me an *environmentalist*."

"She's laughing at us." Grinning, Mac pointed at me.

"No," I said, laughing. Jonnie was shaking his head at both of us and laughing himself.

"Well, Miss Writer, do you know why this is happening?" Mac gestured at the shell.

"I could hazard a guess," I said. "But I don't rightfully know, no."

So many things in their world were like that, changing around them as the influx of visitors grew, the tourists never wise to the idea that the

Everglades they saw were not the same as they had been just twenty years before.

"Maybe you could figure it out for us," Mac said, and I thought, *What the hell do I know? I'm just as blindsided as you are to see my world so changed.*

They moved on to other knickknacks, pictures, and displays. We passed a shadow box of shells laid out like rings in a jewelry store. Jonnie pointed to something behind the glass. "I recognize that," Jonnie said. "I found it."

I peered down at it. "What in the heck is it? I've seen a million of those, and I don't know what they are."

"It's a scute," Jonnie said.

A scoot? I thought.

Mac unlocked the case, removed the scute, and handed it to me.

"One of the plates on an alligator's back, under the skin," Jonnie said. "I found that one down in the water, on the beach." I wondered how it had gotten there, and as if reading my mind, Jonnie said, "This one's sort of fossilized. So, long time ago, the gator probably died, and the pieces of him went with the tide."

I examined the porous, bony scale. I had seen those things all my life, and yet I had never thought to ask what they were. The more time I spent in the glades, the more I realized that was true of so many things back in that wild place where I was from: The extraordinary had become ordinary. I had listened to people deride my home for so long that I lost my ability to see its wonders. What else had I missed?

"Those bones are shrinking, too," Mac said, nodding at the scute. I held it out to him to give it back, and he shook his head. "Keep it. That way you'll remember to figure out what's going on."

I nodded, solemn, as if he had bestowed a weighty task upon me.

Later, I would learn that the reason the conches and other shells were thinning was twofold. Over the years, as the pH of the ocean has decreased by what would seem the tiniest of measures, shellfish have become increasingly sensitive to the water's acidity. The acid isn't dissolving their shells. Something more complicated is happening here. The rise of carbon dioxide in the ocean has made calcium more soluble, and so the biological mechanisms that shellfish have used to compose their shells for millions of years no longer function as they once did. The process of converting calcium into shell is now slower. Population dynamics are at play, too. Conches with thicker shells are older ones. If we're only turning up young conches, it means something is happening to the others, likely increased predation or predation by another name, overfishing.

I slipped the scute into my pocket and followed them onward to the far aisle. There, we reached the final display.

A shallow, square-cornered skiff bore the tools of a hunting expedition: a rifle, an ax, jugs, a bedroll. My great-grandfather had one of those boats, I realized. It was a pitpan in the Peg stories, but we'd never called it that. This was yet another revelation that my home was worth having a place in stories after all.

An entire Totch Brown exhibit occupied the far end of the museum, and that pitpan was part of it. A video of Totch telling a story played on a boxy television perched in front of mismatched chairs. Memorabilia piled around that. *Why is this all Totch and not Peg?* I wondered. I felt somewhat slighted by this display, as if Totch had not only lied but also succeeded in stealing someone else's glory and had gone down in history as someone he was not, all because he had befriended Peter Matthiessen, while the real legend of Peg Brown was at risk of being forgotten. I wanted to hate him for this. He was a glory hound and a story thief, and that made him exactly what people expect from Florida, a con artist. I had heard all the Peg Brown stories. I had read Totch's book, which contained some tales that were too close to Peg's but told as if they'd happened to Totch. That seemed to me like a dirty betrayal, made all the worse because they were brothers. I needed to know once and for all: Who was the real poacher, and whom should the stories have been about, Totch or Peg?

"Okay, serious question," I said, and Mac and Jonnie both turned to listen. "I don't know how to put this, so I'll just come out and say it: These aren't really Totch's stories, are they? Is Totch a liar?"

I had expected them to meet that question with either confusion or indignation, but both Mac and Jonnie smiled knowingly.

"Every single one of Totch's stories is true," Mac said.

"They just didn't all happen to him," Jonnie said.

"Well, doesn't that make you mad?" I asked, becoming indignant myself.

"Why would it?" Jonnie asked.

"Because he stole your dad's stories," I said.

"And other people's," Mac said.

"Then why are we celebrating him and not, you know, the truth?" I asked.

A tourist who had been sitting at the exhibit watching Totch weave a yarn gave each of us, in turn, a critical look before getting up and walking out the back door without a word.

"Totch was a storyteller," Mac said. "He collected people's stories and spoke with the real voice of Chokoloskee. Peg knew what he was doing, but he wasn't the fame-seeking type. Sure, he was legendary, and he'd tell a story or two to friends, but he wouldn't have wanted all of this."

"He was a quiet man," Jonnie said. "Not a big talker. Hearing his stories told was glory enough for him."

"Then do you want people to keep believing that all of this was Totch?" I said, feeling disappointed and vaguely defeated in a way I couldn't put into words. "Do you not want me to write this story?"

"Oh, no, no, nothing of the sort," Mac said. "We're tickled that you're interested in all of us."

"We don't need to give old Totch the boot," Jonnie said. "But it's been nice to remember my dad, too."

In other words, I had things backward. Centuries of enmity with humanity had taken their toll on the Everglades, and within their lifetimes, Mac and Jonnie had seen their world diminished in ways they struggled to put into words. The damage was already done, and if nobody cared, it would keep getting worse unseen in those remote reaches of the tropics.

Stories made people care. Stories showed people from outside the Everglades that the place wasn't a wasteland, that there was something down here—myriad things—worth saving. Not just for the animals, not just for the tourists, not just for the people who live here—for all of us.

Curiosity will save the glades. Curiosity will inspire scientists to investigate its mysteries. Curiosity will bring visitors, who themselves will take stories home, igniting more curiosity. My hope is that this curiosity will be the kind that listens. Instead of the destruction we have visited upon the obsessed-over places and cultures of our past, we should come with openness, leave no trace of our presence, imbibe their stories with wonder, and admit when we have been wrong.

I was wrong about Totch.

Perhaps he had been Chokoloskee's original bullshitter. Perhaps also, I could admit, I might not even know about Chokoloskee if it weren't for him. Matthiessen had cared. Totch recognized that. He let Matthiessen in and told him stories. More celebrities took interest, and so on. *River of Grass* had already kicked off Everglades fever, but it was Totch who made sure the stories weren't about an empty place, but one where people already lived. Those people cared before you ever got there.

To Mac and Jonnie, telling stories like this was more important than ever. As the outside world shouted louder and louder, it had become nearly impossible for one voice to rise above the fray—until it did.

To them, the world had room for plenty of stories. Trickster thieves, noble outlaws, curious writers, conflicted lawmen, alligators, and gator poachers—they could all fit. The secret was in the telling. So they had to let the right people in.

15

BACKUP

Late one night after an egg collection, when the rest of the crew had gone home, Jeff stayed to tidy up the barn. While he swept the workroom's concrete floor, his phone rang. The screen said GEORGE, Lieutenant Wilson's first name.

"Evening, sir," Jeff answered.

"How you holding up?" Lieutenant Wilson asked.

"I'm keeping it together," Jeff said. Egg-collecting season had started a week prior, and the work hadn't stopped since. Even sweeping in the draft of the night breeze through the open door felt like a break.

Over the past year, Jeff's relationship with Lieutenant Wilson had shifted. Maybe it was because some days, especially now that he was too busy to go home, it felt like Lieutenant Wilson was his only link to the person he used to be. The tenor of his periodic calls had shifted, too, from all business, checking in on his "asset," to friendliness, until Jeff could read a tone of genuine care in his voice.

Lieutenant Wilson asked about Jeff's progress, and he answered with a tale of his days in the swamp.

"Wait, wait, wait," Lieutenant Wilson said. "What did you say?" He sounded stunned. But why?

The events of his story had blurred together for Jeff. *What could I have said to make him sound so shocked?*

"How many nests did you open?" Lieutenant Wilson asked.

"All of them," Jeff said.

In the brief pause that followed, Jeff imagined Lieutenant Wilson's expression: wide-eyed and taken aback. Such a reaction made Jeff realize how complacent he'd become. He had grown so used to seeing Robert's crew break the law, he hadn't anticipated that the simple facts of his days could elicit shock.

Nobody else is seeing what I'm seeing, Jeff thought.

"You guys aren't skipping any nests?" Lieutenant Wilson's voice grew. His tone was unreadable. Was that anger? Horror? Excitement? Some mutant combination of the three?

"No, George, listen to me," Jeff said emphatically. "We are taking *every* frickin' egg out of *every* frickin' nest that we find."

"*Every* nest?" Lieutenant Wilson repeated quietly. "Robert and them? What the hell happened? I thought these guys were aboveboard!"

"So did I," Jeff said.

It had been a gradual change, the fudging of a few numbers here, opening and closing nests there, whispering out of earshot. And then it was like something happened, something in the background that Jeff couldn't see, and their infractions went from little mistakes and misdemeanors to a deluge of poaching, plain and simple.

Had there been signs? None that Jeff remembered. Except maybe that one time Robin glared at him outside the gas station. Or when Robert kept lying, telling him again and again that, yes, of course he'd call back; they'd make plans. So determined to see the good in people, Jeff had chalked all of that up to coincidence. He still wanted to. There had to be a reason they were doing all the things they did. If he could figure it out, he thought, maybe he could find a way to show them reason, to navigate his maze of identities without revealing them, and save Robert's crew from themselves.

"And that's not even the half of it," Jeff went on. "I give these guys the combination to my gate. Then I'll come back at nine, ten o'clock at night, and there'll be boxes here. Full of eggs. I don't know where the hell they're coming from. So I need a second guy here."

"You know we're running this operation on a shoestring," Lieutenant Wilson said.

This wasn't the first time Jeff had asked the agency to assign another agent to help him. Every other time, he had taken their negative or noncommittal answers. This time, he insisted. His scare in the swamp had pushed him over the line from want to need. And now all of this.

"There are going to be times," Jeff said, "when I just can't be here. Who knows what'll happen then."

"I'll see what I can do," Lieutenant Wilson said.

"Please," Jeff said, "I need this. And the investigation won't wait on him, whoever he is."

Even in his desperation, Jeff worried another agent would blow his cover. Blackledge had been conceived, been born, and lived an entire life in the matter of a year, coming to a crescendo as a fully-fledged human being whose thoughts, feelings, and desires were unlike Jeff's own—initially—but had become increasingly hard to shake. Jeff was Blackledge even when he was alone. Could another person catch up in time?

Besides, the agency had other problems. In addition to scrounging up the money to pay this new undercover's salary, things were happening so fast with Robert and his crew that FWC needed to find an agent in less than a week without blowing the case. So they started looking outside the agency. They couldn't trust the case's veil of secrecy to remain intact, even among the officers of FWC.

Jeff thought back to when he was ferrying fish guts to feed his new gator stock. It was a lifetime ago, and he had needed that lifetime to become one of them. He remembered the guts spilling everywhere. He had been green. Now after every egg hunt, when the crew loaded the egg crates into Jeff's truck bed, he would drive carefully through the darkness, minding the turns and twisting the wheel with a contemplative gentleness of the sort he should have used from the beginning. If he'd been deeper, like he was now, those kinds of clumsy mistakes could have cost him. He and Blackledge had become one and the same. So he as Blackledge, he as himself, would park and one by one heft the tubs of eggs inside into a barn that had become as pristine and precise as Robert's old place. Now he had the skills to care for the eggs like a true alligator farmer, checking the temperature inside the barn, making sure that every single tiny, nascent life had the optimal conditions in which to be born. Could backup do that?

The next day, Jeff opened the door of the camper to find a truck parked outside the barn. He hadn't heard it drive up. It looked familiar, but still—when the hell did it get there? Apprehensive, Jeff crept inside the barn.

"Hey, Jeff!" Tommy called from the end of the barn where the egg tubs were stacked.

"Hey, yourself," Jeff said. "Whatcha doing here so early?"

Tommy gestured to the tubs at his feet. "Got some more," he said.

"Spent all night out there hunting, and I got a big haul. Where should I put 'em?"

"Man, is that even legal?" Jeff said, finally unable to contain the words that had been playing through his thoughts like ticker tape since egg-harvesting season began.

"You worry too much, Jeff," Tommy said.

Jeff glanced at the table beside him. The boom box with the covert recording device sat in the middle, facing Tommy. Jeff couldn't have set it up better if he tried. With one surreptitious move, Jeff turned it on. *Good gracious, Tommy*, he thought. Even though he sometimes found Tommy grating, Jeff felt both victorious and guilty about catching his illicit delivery on video. It seemed too easy, un-sportsmanlike. Yet the voice of Jeff Babauta that remained in his head said, *How you act when you think no one is watching—who you are in the dark—reveals your truest self. I shouldn't feel guilty for turning on the lights.*

"The guys'll get it all taken care of," Tommy went on.

In all the days of this investigation, after having it drag on with nothing for more than a year, Jeff never would have imagined that receiving such blatant evidence as a confession of intent on video would have him reacting this way: irritated, frustrated, conflicted, and wanting to parent this guy, because somebody needed to. He sighed and shook his head. "You can leave 'em here, but don't do any more of that, all right? You're gonna get me in trouble."

"Don't worry so much," Tommy said. He clapped Jeff on the shoulder. "Like I said, nobody's gonna know."

Over the next few nights, Jeff's wariness spiked. Tommy slipping in during the misty hours of morning spooked him. If he had done that so easily, there wasn't much to stop others who might wish him harm.

He texted Lieutenant Wilson and asked him again about backup.

Wilson: I'll tell you when I have something for you.

In the meantime, Jeff beefed up his security, added more cameras, now up to four, one out by the trees near the gator pen, another at the entrance gate, and one outside his camper to protect himself, too. Robert's crew commented on them.

"Watching for coyotes or something?" Tommy said.

"Gator could take a coyote," CW asserted.

"Bet," Tommy said.

"I think they're a good idea," Robert said, joining them around the camera. "We don't want anybody coming in and making off with our hard work."

Rumors of alligator thieves had spread across the state. Because breeders were willing to pay an all-time high for the eggs, they'd become a hot commodity, worth risking life and limb to steal. More willing to face the dangers of the state's most lethal biped than to cross the seldom-armed fury of the prehistoric lizards themselves, alligator thieves had started breaking into alligator farms and egg-napping. Cameras and motion detectors were a decent defense, so even Jeff's slapdash security system had an alibi.

He made use of his false walls, hiding anything at all that might seem incriminating. He had to manually turn the cameras on and download the footage. He downloaded from the game cams every other week and stored the Jumpdrives in hideouts like the one he'd built for his laptop before he could pass them off to Lieutenant Wilson.

One night while Jeff sat at the table in his camper, completing his logs for the day, a noise flicked at his ears. He stopped typing and listened. The low hum of an engine running outside wafted around him. His heart leapt into his throat, and he swore under his breath. He slammed the laptop closed, pried open the secret compartment in the wall, and stuffed his computer inside along with a flurry of papers. Then he peered through the window. His breath fogged up the glass. He could barely make out anything in the dark, just the low glow of idling headlights creating a slim outline of the hood. He couldn't even make out what kind of truck it was.

Somebody rose from the driver's seat and slammed the door. Whoever he was, he was tall, wearing a cowboy hat. The cowboy started toward him. The automatic lights came on, and the cowboy lifted his face to squint through them. *Goddamn it, Wayne.* Jeff opened the door.

"What the hell are you doing here in the middle of the damn night?" Jeff called from the top of his steps. "You scared me half to death."

Wayne guffawed, grinning. He seemed tipsy. The version of Blackledge that Jeff had created in the beginning had spent most of his adult life as a dirtbag partier, the kind of guy who would always have beer, among other things, with his friends. So Jeff kept his fridge stocked. Something that became increasingly difficult as he befriended Wayne, and Wayne helped himself.

"Aw, I scared you," Wayne drawled, his voice sticky with sarcastic glee. "Poor little Jeff. How you feel about really getting scared tonight?"

Turned out, Wayne was on the job as a trapper and wanted a second set of hands to make the work a little more entertaining. Tonight his mission was to catch some delinquent alligators at a camping resort.

"Sure, I'm up for an adventure," Jeff agreed.

Jeff got in the truck cab. Wayne's teenage nephew rode in the bed, whipped by the wind.

Wayne was an entertaining fellow, a real character. Never a dull moment with him. That's why Jeff kept agreeing to tag along, not because he especially thought Wayne would be up to no good. He just enjoyed his company, and living life as Blackledge without a friend ground him down after a while.

When they arrived at the RV resort, Wayne's nephew jumped down.

"We got a nine-footer here two weeks ago," he informed Jeff.

"Did you now?" Jeff said as they trooped toward the camper-surrounded pond. The listening device he kept tucked under his hat picked up their conversation. "What'd you do with it?"

"Put it in my uncle's pond," the kid answered.

Jeff gestured to get Wayne's attention. "Was that the same alligator we used for the hunt?"

A memory of the escapade that had first united them seemed to put a grin on Wayne's face, and he laughed. "Yeah! Sure was."

It struck a different memory into Jeff's head. On the same day all that happened, Wayne had told him he'd gone to this very RV resort with a biologist to conduct the survey he needed for an alligator-harvesting application. Those applications could take a while to process.

For God's sake, Wayne, you don't really have a permit for this, do you? Jeff thought. He wanted to tell Wayne he needed to do better. *Quit breaking the law so much. I don't want to arrest you.* But that would entail divulging his dangerous secret. Spending time with Wayne was like gaining a friend and losing one at the same time. He enjoyed Wayne's company. Yet he knew that the time would soon come that he would have to turn evidence of the growing list of Wayne's crimes over to the uniformed officers who would bang on his door with a warrant.

No more of that sentimental stuff right now, Jeff thought. He breathed out and settled himself back into the persona of Blackledge. And for that rascal, it was time to nab a gator.

They stalked through the camping resort, shining spotlights on the water and in the reeds. Wayne would try to be quiet at first—he didn't want to scare the gators away, because whatever he caught he could sell—but after a while, he just got too giddy to handle the silence, and he'd launch into a story. Wayne was the yin to Tommy's yang. Both bragged and boasted, but where Tommy was trying to be better than others, Wayne was trying to entertain and astound. His stories were half true, half full of shit, and damn, they were good. Adding a little flavor never hurt anybody, he would have said, especially not anybody who was smart enough to tell a storytelling device from a malicious deception.

Unable to sneak up on any gators, Wayne and Jeff strung baited lines across the marshy patches. They waited for a gator to bite before they pounced. They caught one, then another. After a while, they saw a hulking form lift from the water. They shushed each other and craned through the parted weeds to watch.

The venerable alligator closed its great jaws with a chomp. As he pulled away, he dragged the line with him. They scrambled after him, snatching at the rope, but this was a game of tug-of-war they couldn't win. The line whistled through their grips, the friction heating Jeff's palms. He let go, and so did Wayne.

"Did you get a look at the size of that monster?" Wayne crowed. "Must've been fifteen, twenty feet long."

"Twenty feet, my ass," Jeff said. "This ain't Jurassic Park."

That made Wayne bust out laughing.

I like you, man, Jeff thought. *I wish you wouldn't do all the things you do.*

Their night of adventure wound to an end, and they returned with their catch to Wayne's farm.

Wayne threw an alligator carcass into a big utility box right outside his barn. Up close, Jeff couldn't believe the size of the thing. It was evidence of what they'd done that night. The dark around them sang with crickets and frogs. Hardly any of the light from inside reached far enough to illuminate the gator. Jeff had to try to take a picture anyway. While Wayne's back was turned, Jeff held up his phone and took a snapshot. The flash went off, a sudden sharp light that threw stark shadows over the clearing, before they fell into darkness. Wayne turned on him. Jeff could only see his outline.

"What the fuck are you doing?" Wayne yelled. "Are you a fucking undercover?"

"Undercover what?" Jeff said, taken aback by Wayne's anger. "I was trying to find the flashlight on my phone, just so I can see how big this thing is."

Wayne eyed him.

Was this it? Was Jeff done for? They remained in this standoff for a beat. It was a tense moment of reflection for Jeff. *What would I do if I was in Wayne's shoes?* he wondered. *Would I kick the undercover's ass or just kick him out?*

Then Wayne broke his glare and returned to the barn to clean his alligator.

Or, if he was my friend, Jeff thought, *would I pretend nothing had happened?*

He watched Wayne, framed by the harsh light from inside, take off his hat and wipe the sweat from his brow.

Think ahead next time, Jeff told himself. *You've got to be more careful.*

The more days that passed without backup from the agency, the more time Jeff marinated in his anxiety. He began second-guessing himself. He would lie awake, turning through the events of the day, wondering about all the things he might have missed—and all the things he might have seen if he'd been two people.

The next night, convinced something important had happened under his nose, he rewatched the recordings of secret footage taken from the barn.

The egg room appeared on the screen. Towers of egg tubs stacked in the background beside the white of the pegboard made a theatrical tableau into which the voices entered before the characters themselves had shown. Jeff remembered where he was in that situation. He had just turned on the hidden camera, something that had to be done manually before it could record a thing, and he had sat on a cooler, leaning against the wall outside the camera's view, and listened to Robert like he was keen on learning.

"You offered the landowner a certain amount?" Jeff asked.

"I pay the landowner per egg, between $40 and $50 per egg," Robert explained as he and Tommy entered the shot carrying boxes. They set them down and lingered to chat. "Tommy, what are you doing tomorrow?" Robert asked. "Are you taking off, or are you going with me and Chris?"

Chris was a certified biologist who worked for them.

"I'm going—what are you talking about?" Tommy said.

"I kind of do need you there," said Robert. "Now, Chris's going to be a little bit different than what's his name? He's actually going to be a little stiffer than, uh—"

"David?" Tommy offered.

"Than David, believe it or not," Robert said. "Chris will have to visually see every single nest. His interpretation of the laws is a little different than David's. Chris will have to see every nest. He won't have to see it opened. You'll let somebody come behind me and him, and open them."

"So that's what you're gonna do?" Tommy asked.

"What I'll do is I'll bring you all, show you one or two, tell you how to collect it," Robert explained. "And then we will go on to the next. You know what I mean? You all collect it while I'm gone. You'll have to open one, get the eggs, go to the next one. Open it, keep the eggs, but say it was one nest."

Holy shit, Jeff thought, watching. *They're laying out exactly how they're laundering the eggs, their whole poaching plan.*

"Right," Tommy said on the screen.

"See what I mean?" Robert said. "Cover it back like it was never touched, and there's bad eggs in it."

"Leave the bad eggs?" Tommy asked.

"Leave the bad ones, and say it was never opened," Robert said. "The good ones, you can say they went with another clutch. See what I mean?"

"Where y'all going?" Tommy asked.

"We're going to Spanish Trail."

Jeff stopped the video. He unplugged the Jumpdrive and held it in his hand while he paced and called his case agent, his main contact at the agency other than Lieutenant Wilson. When he picked up, Jeff said, "I have something you need to see."

Backup finally arrived. The minute he saw Jeremy Munkelt, Jeff was filled with both relief and worry. Jeremy pulled up to the barn in a black Dodge pickup. Sunglasses on, he swaggered inside. Jeremy had sunburned cheekbones and a scruffy sailboat trash look about him that seemed too real to Jeff to be a costume; that his previous position had been in the Keys didn't help.

Jeff showed Jeremy around, got him acquainted with the farm's setup. As he was going over the minutiae of egg incubation, Jeremy cut him short. "Yeah, I got it." Jeff bristled. Their characters may have been easygoing layabouts, but Jeff and Jeremy were anything but. When Jeff had asked the agency to find the right person, he hadn't considered they would find someone just as stubborn and sharply organized as he was.

"This is a complicated operation," Jeff said. "I've been working it for more than a year. The guy here before me blew his cover and got yanked. This isn't gonna be easy."

"Right. I never said it would be."

Jeff asked him if he had any questions.

"I'll ask 'em when I have 'em," said Jeremy. "We'll tie this operation up soon so we can both go home. Don't you worry."

Jeff pointed a chastising finger at Jeremy's chest. The man was nearly half a foot taller than Jeff, so he felt a little silly looking up at him to make a threat. "I put a lot of work into this operation," he said. "Don't blow it for me." Truthfully, though, Jeff was more worried about blowing it himself.

16

HATCHING SEASON

It was July 23, already time to go out for another egg collection. Jeff set out, leaving all the work he'd put into the farm in Jeremy's care with a great deal of trepidation. The drive wasn't long.

Not far away in Arcadia, rows of orange groves stretched on as far as the eye could see. This was a private collection, the place called Two by Four Ranch. They raised cattle. Within the pastures, small ponds like watering holes attracted every river country denizen that could reach them—egrets, storks, turtles, and alligators, because what was a pond in Florida without the requisite alligator. They stopped at the farmhouse and parked beside Robert's truck.

Robert stood on the porch talking to the caretaker, the owner's daughter. Jeff was about twenty feet away, but he could read lips passably enough to estimate their conversation. Understanding a conversation you couldn't hear was more about body language than the words themselves. The caretaker looked at Robert sternly. She asked for something and held out her hand.

"Let me see your paperwork," she seemed to say.

Robert opened his aluminum lockbox and shuffled through its contents before picking out the right page. He presented it to her, and she looked it over.

"All right," she might have said, reluctantly handing them back. "Just make sure you guys have your shit together. I don't want any problems."

Once Jeff huddled with Robin, Robert, Tommy, and the crew, it became clear what had caused her concern. The permits said they were only allowed to collect 560 eggs. Anything over that would be poaching. Poaching could get the caretaker in trouble, too, as the landowners could be held liable for any known crimes happening on their property. The crew had to be strict today.

Jeff knew almost immediately that this wasn't going to happen. The crew split up, scattered all over the property. Robert's strategy had them all starting on the periphery then closing in on one spot like they were circling prey. They had surveyed the property in a helicopter a while back, and Robert sent Jeff and Tommy in search of a particular nest they'd seen from the air. Robert and Robin split off on their own. Jeff and Tommy climbed into the side-by-side utility terrain vehicle (UTV), which looked like a swamp buggy the size of a go-kart, and got going.

The UTV slogged through nearly two feet of water, a trench of mud that separated grove from pastureland. The black water gurgled under their wheels and threatened to brim over the wheel housings and soak their legs. The UTV rocked and hobbled over the unseen soft bottom of the muck. Out across the wide-open green of the field, cypress domes cropped up like islands of swamp forest in a sea of grass. Jeff looked around, trying to get his bearings. Familiar landmarks began to arrive: a weeded pond area, a stand of pine trees.

"It's gotta be here," Tommy said. He kept one hand on the wheel and held a ruggedized GPS in the other. He looked down at it then scanned the surroundings, down, scan, down, scan. "Gotta be around here somewhere."

"You know what, let's take a right here and go up on the hill," Jeff said—meaning, *Let's stop playing in the mud and get up on dry land*—"and go around the big cypress head. There should be a stand of trees up there."

"How do you know that?" Tommy asked.

"Well, I remember it from the helicopter."

Tommy frowned. He never got invited on any helicopter adventures. Jeff wondered if he resented that, and thinking about the favoritism that showed from Robert, Jeff's chest involuntarily puffed up with pride.

The cypress dome, a wetland characterized by tall trees that grew like an island in a sea of marsh grasses, hid a fantasy world set apart from the mundane by the trees' peculiar protection. Smaller plants grew in the dome's shallow waters. The farther you ventured into the concentric circles of trees that created the dome, the taller the plants grew, because the water flowing through the lime rock below was deepest at a cypress dome's center.

Jeff cut through this wild botanical garden. In the deep swamp, the coolest strata of shade came from pond cypress and swamp tupelo. Deeper still, a subcanopy of sheltered trees with poetic names—sweetbay, slash pine, loblolly bay, coco plum, and dahoon—enveloped Jeff and Tommy. Here within the fold of the cypress shade, fetterbush, wax myrtle, Saint-John's-wort, and willow hung over a grotto of chain ferns and royal ferns, cinnamon ferns and moss. Beneath this smallest canopy, nesting inside all the others up above, cryptic orchids opening their arms to the heavens cascaded in ecstatic shocks of purple, pink, and red. Was it this place that had inspired settlers to dub their wild outpost with such a bucolic name as Arcadia?

Jeff and Tommy traipsed through the fairyland, unaware of the rare and endangered things shrouded in the understory just out of sight. In a narrow shaft of light, Jeff spotted the nest he'd seen from above. They collected thirty eggs from it and found no others. It was the only nest in the entire area.

They went back to the farmhouse, where they met up with CW and his wife.

Tommy and Jeff sat in the UTV, and Tommy leaned over the ledger where he kept track of the eggs, scribbling things down. Jeff glanced at the page. He saw a number 7. Then two other numbers. *We are way over 560*, Jeff thought.

"So," Jeff said, "are we on point?"

Tommy slammed the book shut, like he didn't want Jeff seeing any more of what was inside. Then Tommy looked at him and CW. "No," Tommy said sharply. "We're over."

"Don't tell Mike about this," CW said.

Mike was the landowner, someone Jeff now realized he had met before. The caretaker was his daughter.

Of course we're not going to report it to Mike's daughter, Jeff thought. He felt a tug of guilt at cheating someone he knew, even an acquaintance.

Robin and Robert went to a spot they called the dam area, which everyone had joked about, saying things like, "Which damn area? That damn area." "Well, damn." "I'll be dammed." That is, before the mood of the expedition had turned so sour. The whole crew met up in the dam area later. Robert, Tommy, and CW went off to the side by themselves. Jeff could tell they didn't want him to be a part of that conversation. *They don't want me to hear they've screwed up*, Jeff thought.

Their previous egg collections had been supervised—a biologist (like David) accompanied the egg harvesters and made the call when he thought the crew had taken enough. The collection that day had been unsupervised, which per regulations meant that only a specific maximum number of eggs could be gathered.

"Let's all go back to our staging station," Robert said in a panic, "and try to figure this out."

They hurried back to the property entrance. They hustled, sorting through the boxes of eggs, checking their viability, transferring them from one container to another. Robert stood back with the calculator on his phone, a strained and frantic expression on his face.

"How many eggs you guys have?" Robert hollered at Jeff and Tommy. They answered, and Robert jabbed the numbers into his phone. He asked the same of his wife and punched in her numbers, too. Then he ordered them to load all the boxes into Jeff's truck.

It was then that the caretaker pulled up. She got out of her car. "How'd you guys do?" she asked Robert.

"We collected five hundred fifty-nine eggs," Robert answered, "one shy of the permit."

Jeff watched this conversation from where he stood leaning against his tailgate. He laughed to himself about Robert's howler of a lie. The evidence was right there next to Jeff, nestled in crates in his truck bed.

Back at the farm, he examined it himself.

"Help me unload these eggs," he said to Jeremy.

They brought them inside and counted them together. Altogether, the eggs tallied up to a little more than 700. They were 151 eggs over the mark, and they'd shorted Two by Four Ranch a significant amount of money. Jeff whistled at the magnitude. If he hadn't been sure Robert's crew was poaching before, he was now. And cheating people, to boot. They paid landowners for every egg they harvested. Years before, the sum had been as low as $5 a pop. But after the floods had ruined Louisiana's wild alligator stock, prices were reaching as high as $60 per egg, and that was just what Robert had paid to harvest them. They had just robbed that ranch of thousands of dollars.

Was this the Robin Hood mentality at work or something else?

Jeff felt like the case was cracking open, but he worried his cover was, too. The crew was candling harvested eggs in the barn one day when Robin all of a sudden looked at Jeff and asked him where he was from. Jeff had gotten used to that question, because people of his ethnicity—a Pacific Islander from Guam—are uncommon in Florida. He was also likely the only Guamanian person employed by FWC, so knowing his ethnicity would be a dead giveaway. When he was making up his backstory, he decided to tweak his origins just slightly, but not so much that it was implausible. His story went that his aunt raised him in Florida, and that he was from Saipan, where he'd never been. Saipan is next to Guam.

"My aunt tells me I'm originally from—"

"Guam?" Robin blurted out.

His heart dropped. He collected himself as fast as he could. "Guam?" he said. "I have no clue where that is. I'm from Saipan, but I've never really been there. They tell me it's an island out in the Pacific." He needed to shove the conversation onto a different subject. This was inching precariously close to fearful territory. Did she know he wasn't who he said he was? "So how many eggs are we at now?"

The conversation moved on easily. Still, his racing heart would not subside.

Later, Jeff watched the undercover video of that conversation, studying it to see if he'd missed a tell in her body language that indicated her intent. *I can't believe she said Guam*, he thought. When he told people where he was from, the typical response was, *Where's that?* Robin's assumption had caught him off guard. Yet her body language on the footage didn't suggest much of anything. His own, however, would have been a dead giveaway if Robin had known what she was looking for. He flinched when she said it. His eyes went wide for half a second before he composed himself again.

Had she seen that? Did she know he was lying?

After all these years protecting the wilderness, Jeff had learned to trust his gut. Now, it seemed he was taking any reason he could to doubt it. His gut said that someone had figured him out, that the trap he had set was fixing to turn against him. He had grown to like all of these people. He wanted to be wrong. He had let such softness turn him into a naive optimist, and yet, he wasn't willing to let it go. There had to be a way to keep that empathy without risking his mission. If he couldn't, then Jeff really would lose himself to Blackledge for good.

It was now August, and hatching season was just starting. Jeff had to admit that he was excited, but it meant that Robert and Robin were hanging around the farm far more often, a secretly tense situation after Robin's question had set him on edge. They also brought their daughters to see the baby gators. The little girls marveled at the glossy-eyed hatchlings and asked Jeff questions, and while he answered them, his stomach started to sink. If these girls' parents got arrested, what would happen to them? Where would they go if both parents went to jail? Even temporarily losing two parents seemed like a punishment they didn't deserve. They hadn't done anything wrong.

He had already met many of the others' families out on egg collections. Some had invited him over to their houses. Once, a while back, Wayne brought his wife and daughter to Sunshine Alligator Farm to meet Jeff, and another time, he invited Jeff over for a lobster dinner, a catch he'd brought back fresh from the Keys. Jeff missed his family, and the companionship made some difference, but if anything, spending more time with them made Jeff feel uncomfortable. The state would come arrest them soon on his account. It was becoming increasingly hard to draw the line: He couldn't get too involved in their social lives. That wasn't fair to them. In the evenings, they needed to part ways.

He thought about his own family then, first of his mother, who had feared the worst since his transformation into Curtis Blackledge. She had taught him the Golden Rule: Treat others how you would like to be treated. It went beyond simple reciprocity. It had instilled in Jeff a loud conscience. Some people, it seemed, could ignore the little voice in their head that said, *Thou shalt not*. Jeff's was anything but little. And it was beginning to speak up.

To do what was right, he would have to enforce the law. But his conscience knew that sometimes enforcing the law hurts more than it helps. Arresting these families would tear them apart. Without thinking, he put himself in their shoes. He imagined that he really was a poacher, that his wife and son had come out to help him in the swamp. He imagined his son, Chris, was still a child, and a wildlife officer came to arrest him and Sandy. He imagined the look on his little boy's face as the officer put them in cuffs, on the verge of tears but too shocked to shed them.

There had to be another way. Jeff would have to come up with something fast. He wasn't willing to uphold the law at the expense of his conscience.

For every time that Robert's crew showed up at Sunshine Alligator Farm unannounced, there was another that they should have showed up and didn't. When this happened one day during hatching season, it left Jeff—and luckily now Jeremy, too—running here and there across the barn, helping babies out of their shells and transferring them to their new tanks, the plastic kiddie pools. They set these in an open area on the side of the barn, where all the hatchlings would peep when they walked past. Jeff started calling the pool area Sunshine Daycare.

It was a wonder to see all the tiny alligators climbing over one another. They were anything but calm. They would pick fights for no reason, it seemed, but their inborn feistiness. Once latched onto a brother or sister's tail, the hatchling might commence a death roll, a terrible fate in the jaws of a full-grown alligator made endearing and comical by their minute size and the ferocity of their angry squeaking.

"Quit that," Jeff said, tapping a scaly baby on the head so she would relinquish her enemy's tail. "Break it up." Careful not to hurt them, he pried another pair apart only for them to bite each other's tails again, forming a furious and ridiculous hoop. They would only settle down when he lowered the lid, an inverted kiddy pool cut with air vents, over them and put them to naptime in the cool darkness.

Jeff reached into one of the tubs toward an alligator egg. Bits of mud and bark sullied its white shell, a skin that bulged outward around the hatchling inside eager to break free. Jeff pressed his thumb through the skin at the same time the hatchling tore through it with his egg tooth. The little alligator, wet with amniotic fluid, wrestled himself free.

"Look at him," Jeff said. "Isn't he cute?" Jeff tickled the little alligator's head, and it turned around and chomped down on his finger. Tiny teeth pierced his skin like needles. "Ouch, shit." He gently shook the hatchling off.

The little gator squeaked angrily, and a chorus of hatchlings, newly emerged into the world, joined in.

Cute *and* born mad. Jeff could appreciate the fight in them. Once a swamp creature, always a swamp creature. They were stubborn through and through.

Late one night as Jeff and Jeremy scrubbed out pools, cutting at the scum of alligator poop with bleach, they looked at each other, as if the sheer depth of the drudgery demanded they share a moment. Nothing bonds you to another fellow quite like shared misery. And despite all the times Jeff rallied, telling himself he had a grander mission, that he was there for a reason, to protect the wild, they had plenty of misery, and much of it stank.

"This is something only you and I will ever know," Jeremy said. "How tough this operation was, you know, when it's all over."

Jeff thought back to everything the farm had put him through before Jeremy showed up. The long days that turned into nights. Sometimes a drizzle turned the air to mist, humidity so dense that it collected on glass and pilled into droplets even when it wasn't raining. Those days, it was hard to tell if your shirt was wet from perspiration or ambient dankness, though likely it was both. He'd stand in front of the enormous fan in the barn, its breath turning the sweat to salt crystals across his skin, unmoving enough to practically fall asleep. Having lived in Florida so many years, Jeff was used to the weather, but not doing hard labor in it with no real avenue of escape. He spent those days wet to the bone, wet to the core, wet to his very soul. Other times, he'd dug through nests made of gator feces and leaf litter infested with fire ants, longing for the days when the air felt like bathwater, because at least then he wouldn't feel quite so rank. He cringed just to think about it.

"Yeah, man," Jeff said. "This shit is hard."

Truth was, Jeremy had taken on more than just half of Jeff's burden with the farm. He had alleviated the burden of his loneliness. Jeff came from a big family. Before the investigation, they always got together, had cookouts, and played major parts in one another's lives. They spent hours on the phone, checking in, gossiping. Coming from that to spending most days holed up on the farm like a hermit came as more of a shock than he liked to admit. By the second year of the investigation, Jeff was stir-crazy. He needed to talk to someone about everything that was going on. He needed to talk to someone he wasn't also lying to. Despite their differences, Jeremy's addition to the team came with an immense sense of relief. Finally, Jeff didn't feel quite so alone. And yet it had been a tough adjustment.

Jeremy had arrived thinking he knew everything. He started in with the bad habit of disregarding Jeff's advice, and that always made Jeff bristle.

"You've been an officer for what, five years?" Jeff said one time, confronting him. "We're not gonna do this." He meant their disagreements, going toe to toe. They were allies, and they had to act like it. That didn't change the fact that they were two stubborn people, separated by generation and experience, and so both seemed to know that one would never concede to the other.

Jeremy had his idiosyncrasies, too, ones that didn't quite fit with his character. And ones that Jeff didn't quite agree with. For one, he brought his own refrigerator to the farm and kept it stocked with foods Jeff thought of as fussy.

One morning, Jeff sat down to breakfast with a plate of eggs and bacon, and he looked across the table to Jeremy. He studied the spread the junior officer had laid out before him: six strawberries on a paper towel, a cup of yogurt, and a spoon.

"What the hell are you eating?" Jeff said.

"What's it look like?" Jeremy said.

"You can't be eating like that in front of the guys."

"Why the hell not?" Jeremy bit into a strawberry.

"It doesn't fit with your character," Jeff said.

"Maybe *my character* wants to take care of himself," Jeremy said pointedly. "Maybe *his* body is *his* temple."

"Maybe he oughtta watch what the other guys do and try not to stand out so damn much."

"Nobody's paying that much attention to what I'm eating," Jeremy said.

"You don't know that. Even something little can tip somebody off."

That didn't stop Jeremy. When they went to lunch another day with Wayne, Jeff ordered a hamburger and fries. Whatever Wayne ordered, Jeff tended to copy.

The waitress asked Jeremy what he wanted, and he asked her about the bread. Was it stone-ground rye or pumpernickel?

Jeff shot him a look like, *What the hell are you doing? You might do this in your real life, but you're not playing that life.*

Then Jeremy asked her what type of mustard they had.

"This guy thinks we're at a fancy restaurant," Jeff said to Wayne to cover, but Wayne just grunted. He didn't seem to suspect anything was amiss.

But after a while, Jeremy got the hang of it. He started dressing sloppier, wearing flip-flops, T-shirt untucked. Jeff and Jeremy came to respect each other. Jeff wanted to help him have a good career by sharing his experience. Sometimes, they would drive into town for a bite to eat and have a talk. They would work out together at the bench press they had in the yard, and Jeff even convinced Robert to take Jeremy along for some of his expeditions.

There was always more to someone, Jeff knew, than his first impressions.

Although Robert's crew not showing up left Jeff and Jeremy with more work, their absence also had its advantages.

Early on, when Jeff learned that CW had been poaching an excess of nests and bringing the eggs to the farm, and Tommy had been, too, Jeff knew that simply setting the eggs aside wouldn't be enough to maintain them as evidence, especially as multiple poachers were involved. So he devised a scheme: When the eggs hatched, he needed a way to mark the baby gators that would set them apart from the others. His handlers at the agency gave him an idea.

He mixed glow-in-the-dark paint with waterproof superglue, and on the days when CW's hatchlings finally came out of their shells, Jeff and Jeremy would mark them. They had to do it fast, before the superglue could harden. If the hatchling belonged to CW, Jeff swiped a line of paint along the tail. If it had come from Tommy, Jeremy marked down its leg. If the crew was there, they had to hustle, flicking the paint over the scales before anyone could see. But when no one else was there, they could be more methodical. The little gators squirmed as if the swabs tickled.

Afterward, Jeff hit the lights to see if their sticky scheme had worked.

In the shadows, Jeremy and Jeff stood over the hatchling pools, watching tiny glowing tails and feet flicker and slide among the rest of that black mass like glowworms. Jeff looked down then and found the outline of his hands glowing in the dark.

Despite his initial evasiveness, Robert was also starting to open up to Jeff. Jeff had spent hours at his and Robin's house, getting to know them, building trust—like a real business partner would. He learned that Robert grew up nearby in a fairly prominent family—not that they were rich, but that everybody knew them. In college, he had a scholarship playing golf. He had wanted to work as a medevac transporter. He was smart, learned from everything he did, and advanced, but he remained quiet about it. As a quiet man in a sea of loudmouths and braggarts, his sober reticence came off as lofty and enigmatic. He was organized but didn't want to trouble others with the minutiae of his spreadsheets. He'd even bought a mobile home for his mother when she was about to be evicted.

One afternoon as they sat on the floor of the barn candling alligator eggs, Robert let a name slip that he'd never mentioned before. Benny.

"Who's that?" Jeff asked.

"Oh, Benny Cenac," Robert said. "He's the guy who owns Golden Ranch Farms."

"Who and the what now?"

Robert explained that Golden Ranch Farms, an alligator farm in Louisiana, was where they'd be taking the hatchlings. They'd been paying Robert to find the eggs, hatch them, and get them ready. Cenac also wanted to start an offshoot of Golden Ranch in Florida, and Robert wanted the job of farm manager, an extra motivation to do well besides the money.

Jeff sat thunderstruck, reeling from all this new information. This changed everything. They were poaching, then transporting the ill-gotten goods across state lines. *I might have to get the feds involved*, he thought.

Throughout the operation, Jeff had noted the way Robert threw money around, like when he leased the helicopter to spot the nests from the air. Initially, he thought the money had come from the dissolution of his business with Brother Parker. Then as the legality of their affairs became murky, he'd thought, *Maybe this dude's cleaning all his money*. But now Jeff understood—it wasn't Robert's money. Cenac had employed him to legally harvest Florida alligator eggs, hatch them, and transport the hatchlings to Golden Ranch in Louisiana. Just like all the paperwork he sent to FWC, everything Robert was sending to Golden Ranch made his operation seem aboveboard.

In the past few weeks, Robert had risen in Jeff's estimation from a vague outline of a man to a quiet mastermind. If something truly underhanded was going on, Robert had been covering his tracks so well that Jeff would have to see details—logbooks, ledgers, something concrete, anything—to know on which side of the law he stood. If Jeff had to hazard a guess, Robert was straddling it.

He wasn't going to find out staying in Florida, though. The truth, he knew, would follow Robert to Louisiana, so Jeff had to follow Robert, too.

17

ON THE ROAD

In 1885, when the Everglades was still an untouched wilderness, plume hunter Guy Bradley and his brother ducked among the blooms of muhly grass, searching for the white speck of an egret. Marl prairie spread around the Bradley boys as far as they could see. It took their set of binoculars to glimpse the shifting purple mirage of the pine flatwoods on the horizon. They were scouting the land for French plume hunter Jean Chevalier, who would go on to sell the feathers they'd collected in Key West each for more than the average person could earn in a week.

During that time, a fashion craze was sweeping the globe. Glamorous society ladies wore wide-brimmed hats dolloped with the immense plumes of wild bird feathers. The more fashionable the lady, the larger the plume. Poachers ravaged rookeries from the Everglades to the Carolinas, targeting flamingos, roseate spoonbills, egrets, and other birds with prized "snowy" white feathers.

By 1900, hunters had killed 95 percent of all Florida shorebirds, driving the snowy egret close to extinction and completely wiping out the Carolina parakeet. That wild frontier era had taken its toll on nature. Environmentalists spoke out against plume hunting, and so, the very same year, Congress adopted the Lacey Act, the first wildlife protection law in US history. The original intent of the act was to criminalize poaching, specifically the sale of illegally captured animals and animal products across state lines. The Lacey Act, in other words, essentially outlawed plume hunting in the US, putting Bradley out of a job. Rather than continue poaching, Bradley became one of the country's first game wardens, a short-lived career that would ultimately end in a shootout on a boat and Bradley's untimely demise.

When Jeff heard that Robert was planning to transport the hatchlings to Louisiana, he knew the Lacey Act was about to come into play. As Jeff finagled his way onto Robert's upcoming trip, Lieutenant Wilson got in contact with the US Fish and Wildlife Service (FWS). While FWS runs a variety of programs, including the National Wildlife Refuge System, the US's own endangered species list, and the Migratory Bird Program, the service's law enforcement division investigates wildlife crimes that reach the national and international scale. By crossing state lines with illegally harvested hatchlings, Robert's crew, Jeff and Lieutenant Wilson believed, was in violation of the Lacey Act, and so their actions came under the jurisdiction of FWS. The service frequently partners with other law enforcement agencies, including state agencies like FWC, providing not only the support of additional officers but also the equipment and infrastructure needed to beat the biggest wildlife-trafficking cases. Their arsenal includes the only wildlife-crime-specialized forensics laboratory in the world. Their aid would be invaluable in bringing down this egg-laundering scheme.

Too bad they declined. Lieutenant Wilson's contact at FWS said they couldn't help out, because the federal agency believed they had seen evidence that FWC's operation at Sunshine Alligator Farm was breaking the law by wiretapping.

"Wiretapping?" Jeff shouted. The accusation had brought him from calm to raging in an instant. He thought of himself as mild and even-keeled, so this sudden outburst was uncharacteristic. The feds' denial had come as that much of a blow.

Knowing he was about to undertake a dangerous trip, Jeff had stolen away for a night at home. So what if Jeremy was green. His presence at the farm offered Jeff that small window to take a break. He hadn't been expecting Lieutenant Wilson's dramatic interruption by phone. He paced his sunroom—past his martial arts awards and his trinkets collected from the outdoors, like the rearticulated skeleton of a snake that he had placed on an ant pile for them to clean with their formic acid—trying to expel the anger that had filled him up like a steam valve. He stopped, turned. Terra-cotta tiles paved the floor. He counted them, with each one wishing away the rage. *I've been working so hard*, he thought. *I've been doing things perfectly. Everything to the letter. Always.*

"You still there, Jeff?" Lieutenant Wilson asked.

"Wiretapping?" Jeff asked. "I haven't done any such thing. You know I wouldn't. Where the fuck did they get that?"

"It's that video of Tommy and Robert."

"What?"

"The one in your hatching room."

Jeff thought back. The tableau of Tommy and Robert in front of the pegboard. Robert's detailed instructions.

Leave the bad eggs? Tommy had asked.

Leave the bad ones, and say it was never opened, Robert had answered. *The good ones, you can say they went with another clutch. See what I mean?*

"What do you mean?" Jeff said. "What's that got to do with wire-tapping?"

"The feds think that you got spy equipment rigged up to catch them saying something they wouldn't say in front of you."

"Well, didn't you tell them I was right there? You told them that's not possible, right? That I have to turn the damn camera on manually, and—"

"I did, Jeff," Lieutenant Wilson said. "Of course I did."

"Let me talk to them," Jeff said. "I'll tell them what *really* happened. I'll talk some sense into them."

"I can't let you do that. There's no point. They have their minds made up."

Jeff had thought being discovered by the guys was his worst night-mare. No, his worst nightmare was this.

"That mean we're through?" Jeff asked, feeling stunned. "Just like that? All our work down the drain? This whole thing is over?"

"Hell no," Lieutenant Wilson answered. "We keep going without them."

"What about Lacey?" Jeff asked. They couldn't prosecute for Lacey Act violations without the feds.

"Kelly's smart," Lieutenant Wilson said, speaking then of the district attorney assigned to their case. "She'll think of something."

Night had fallen over the swamp, and Jeff had eased into watching TV, a nature documentary. He was just getting comfortable when his phone rang. Wayne's name appeared across the phone's screen. Jeff listened to it jangle for a moment, contemplating whether he should answer it or not. The last time he had seen Wayne, the hunter had given him a scare. Jeff's heart beat faster just thinking about it.

You a fucking undercover? Wayne had shouted. The light of Jeff's flash had just gone out, leaving behind it a more intense darkness than had been there before, and for a moment Jeff had wondered if he was going to make it out of there alive. Then Jeff played it off. He joked, and Wayne's apprehension seemed to fade. Was Wayne cunning enough to invite him into a trap?

You're being paranoid, Jeff, he told himself.

Jeff answered the phone. "Hey, Wayne, how are ya?"

"Peachy. What are you doing right now?" Wayne asked.

"Watching TV," Jeff said apprehensively. "Why?"

"Well, we just killed a hog and an alligator, and we thought we'd come by and, you know, you can help us out with cleaning them."

Jeff had never skinned an alligator before. This would be the way to catch an undercover who didn't know his way around a hunt. But Jeff had butchered other game animals. Even if this was a trap, it wouldn't catch him, he thought. Plus it would get Wayne off his scent long enough for them to wrap up the operation.

"All right," Jeff said, doing his best to hide the apprehension in his voice. "Head on over."

Wayne and the tourist from that day's hunting crew heaved the gator down on a table in Jeff's barn. As Jeff surveyed it, his confidence fell. *I don't even know where to start*, he thought. A sudden fear rose within him. They were about to realize he wasn't who he said he was. *I can't screw this up*, Jeff thought. By then, he knew a few things about alligator skinning—certain parts of the hide had to stay intact to make boots and wallets, say—but those details fled his mind now. He pictured himself filleting a fish. He cut off the tail. The tourists from Wayne's guided hunt watched, nodding, looking impressed. Confidence renewed, Jeff dove into butchering.

"What the fuck are you doing?" Wayne said.

Jeff's heart leapt in his throat. He froze.

"You're doing it all wrong," Wayne said, marching over.

There was something about the look in Wayne's eyes that said he had caught a glimpse behind Blackledge's mask.

"What? What are you talking about?" Jeff said with a nervous laugh. "This is the way my buddy taught me down in the Everglades."

Wayne studied him warily. "All right," he said. He didn't sound convinced. He took up his knife again and returned to butchering the hog.

He knows, Jeff thought. *Then why isn't he doing anything about it?*

Jeff told himself that this was his paranoia again, that if Wayne knew, he'd at least cuss him out and leave. But perhaps he had misjudged Wayne. It was possible that Wayne was going through the same turmoil as him, the struggle of knowing that he had made a friend on the other side of the law, and of trying to find a way to end all this so neither one of them would get hurt.

Remember, even Peg Brown had coffee with the rangers.

In the middle of August, two weeks before Jeff thought they were set to leave for Louisiana, Robert called. It was early in the morning, so early that the dew mists still hovered over the fields, unfazed by the dawn. Robert's voice sounded breathy, drawn, as if he was in a panic.

"There's been a change of plans," he said. "We've got to leave as soon as possible. I'm on my way right now."

"Why? What happened?" Jeff asked.

"Nothing to be overly concerned about," Robert said. "Just start getting the hatchlings ready, and when they're all packed in the crates, we'll load them up and get going."

Shit, what's going on? Jeff wondered. Robert sounded like a man being chased. Had he, like Wayne, sensed that the law was on his tail? Worse yet, had Wayne said something? *Naw, Wayne doesn't care for Robert. No way he'd stick his neck out for him like that.*

Jeff hurried to get dressed. He woke Jeremy and informed him of the sudden change in plans. Together they removed the hatchlings from the kiddie pools they'd been calling Sunshine Daycare and organized them in plastic crates they stacked in rows inside the barn.

It was August, the hottest month of Florida's summer, so they would keep the little gators in the barn until right before it was time to go so they didn't overheat. In the darkness of their confines, they quieted down, but whenever Jeff lifted the lid to a pool, they would become alert, squirm over one another, chirp and peep. He wished these little gators could live in the wild, that their fate could be different. He wished that the few didn't have to be sacrificed to save the many. In a perfect world, he could save them all. Hell, in a perfect world, they wouldn't need saving in the first place. No use in that line of thinking now, though. There was nothing he could do for them except keep them safe while they were under his charge.

Robert and the others gradually arrived to help out. Then another pickup pulled into the driveway.

"Wayne, what are you doing here so early?" Jeff asked, wiping his hands on a towel as he strode out to greet him.

"Oh, just dropping by to shoot the shit," Wayne said. "By the looks of it, you're pretty busy."

"We're leaving for Louisiana sooner than we planned," Jeff said.

"Need some help?" Wayne asked.

"I'd be grateful for it, actually," Jeff said. Then he explained what Wayne could do.

At noon, they broke for lunch.

"How 'bout some burgers?" Jeff said to Jeremy and Wayne. Jeff and Jeremy returned to the camper to grab supplies, and Jeff went outside and popped open the grill.

"How do you feel about some Chokoloskee Chicken?" Wayne said.

Jeff knew that meant curlew, the common name for *Eudocimus albus*, the endangered white ibis.

Wayne had grabbed the rifle from his truck and headed toward where rainwater had pooled in a nearby field. Jeff followed Wayne's line of sight. Then he saw them—a trio of white birds wading on the other side of his fence.

"I don't think you're allowed to—" Jeff started.

"Watch this," Wayne said.

Wayne sank to the ground and army-crawled through the grass. The door to the camper opened, and Jeremy came down the steps. As Wayne peered through his scope like a big-game hunter, Jeremy pulled out his phone and started filming. He snuck forward and hid behind Jeff's truck to get a better angle on the birds. Jeff started recording, too. Wayne crawled closer. He waited. And waited. Then he popped off a shot, and one of the curlews fell. The other two took wing, circled overhead, and flew away.

Wayne took another shot, but missed. "I didn't have a good angle," he said to Jeremy as they convened on the fallen bird. Jeff watched from a distance as they walked back toward him with the carcass. When it came down to it, Jeff liked Wayne, and watching this left a pang of disappointment in his chest. *Why does he have to go and be so dumb?* Jeff thought. Wayne borrowed Jeff's knife and used it to cut out the breast, which he seasoned and threw on the grill. *No use wasting it*, Jeff thought.

"We need to get rid of this." Wayne indicated the curlew's remains. "I'll drive you out to the gator pen," he added to Jeremy, "and we can dump it there."

They threw the evidence in the pen and waited until turtles and birds, the gators' wild freeloader neighbors, started pulling the carcass away from one another before finally dragging it beneath the water.

Jeremy would later inform Jeff that on the way Wayne's mouth got the best of him. He flat-out confirmed he knew what he'd done was a crime, that shooting curlews was "highly illegal" and punishable by a hefty $3,000 fine per bird. Why had he done it if he'd known? Jeff would never understand the thought process in that. Maybe he was showing off. Maybe drinking had gotten the better of him. Or maybe he was testing them, and he thought $3,000 was a small price to pay to flush the undercover officers out of hiding.

After they all sat down to a less-than-legal lunch, Jeremy surreptitiously slipped his hand over and flicked the power on a camera hidden in the camper wall beside the table. Wayne kept talking and talking, as was his way, his mouth always the thing to get him in trouble.

"I think I know why old Robert's in such a hurry," Wayne said.

By then, they were sitting in the back of Jeff's pickup truck, taking a break for a beer to cut the heat. Jeff cocked his head at Wayne. At the same time, he clicked the button on his key-fob camera and shifted his leg so it was angled in Wayne's direction.

"There's a traitor in our midst," Wayne said.

Jeff's heart skipped a beat. *This is it.*

"I got a call the other day from FWC," Wayne went on, "asking about Sunshine and Robert."

This isn't it! Jeff rejoiced in his head.

"Wow, so you think they're watching Robert?" Jeff said.

"I don't think, I know!" Wayne exclaimed.

"You mean the local game wardens?"

"They ain't local," Wayne said. "Think bigger." He laughed.

"They think Robert's up to no good, and I'm involved?" Jeff asked, keeping his voice even and calm. In actuality, the situation was verging on being too ludicrous to keep a straight face. Good thing Wayne usually made him laugh anyway.

"No, they don't see you as being involved," Wayne said. "They think you're a pawn."

"They must be watching you," Jeff said.

"They weren't watching *me*." Was that a note of smugness in his voice?

"Maybe they got their drones out," Jeff joked.

"Maybe he was sitting in a fucking bush over there," Wayne said. Often, their conversations went like improv sets. One joke spun off into another. *Yes, and?* They laughed. Wayne went on, explaining how the agency had wised up to thousands of eggs disappearing from the swamps. "By the time they get this figured out—and oh, they'll figure it out—it'll be too fucking late, because y'all are fixing to leave. Which may be why Robert called you out of the blue and said, 'We need to leave tonight.' Y'all better go soon and pray you get across the state line."

He doesn't know it's me! Jeff could have laughed out of happiness. But that joy faded nearly as soon as it struck. *Wayne doesn't know, but does Robert?*

Jeff thought ahead to their long drive to Louisiana with a growing sense of dread.

The crew worked all night and into the morning getting ready. In the evening of the next day, with the sunset falling behind the western trees, the crew stacked the crates of hatchlings in Jeff's trailer, about 40 to each crate, making 2,434 little gators in all. Unbeknownst to the rest of the crew, the undercover officers had painted 153 of them with fluorescent forensic dye in the hope that those markings would help them discern the illegally gotten gators from the rest. On top of this, they added three coolers of alligator hides, salted and frozen and ready for sale.

Jeff took his place in the passenger seat, and Robert climbed in the driver's side, where he pulled up map directions on his phone.

"It'll probably take us about eleven-and-a-half hours," Robert said, indicating the line on the screen that led from southwestern Florida, up through the panhandle, and across the Gulf Coast to the bayou of Louisiana. "Stops and fuel will probably make it more like fourteen."

It was about eight thirty in the evening when they set out, crossing through empty flatland pastures, strands of gnarled live oaks with dangling Spanish moss, farms in the scrubland, small bridges over creeks, then back into the coastal sprawl of cloned homes built on swampland, golf courses and advertisements and a thousand indistinguishable street corners of the same gas stations and restaurant chains that now populated the gators' domain.

The modern world had triumphed over the wilderness. The suburb had drained the swamp, bringing with it purgatorial big-box stores and tasteless fast food, country clubs and lawns and grid-drawn streets more deceptive than a swamp maze. They called it "civilization," like it was a good thing that the organized had won out against the untamed.

You, too, can have your own little slice of paradise; all you have to do is destroy that paradise in the process. This kind of banal desire, and the greed that sold it, has been Florida's true destruction. Developers pitted man versus nature, not as it had been before as a struggle for survival out in a harsh and remote wilderness, but as a struggle to uphold a false hierarchy of creation. Humans are more important than animals, they said. The soil is ours to scourge and conquer. Marketing has convinced us that trivial luxuries are more important than the natural world, as if we are not part of the natural world ourselves, as if our consumption is not a bid against our own interests, one in favor of concrete and routine against the unwieldy and awe-inspiring, monotony against biodiversity, pesticides against night music, the greed of a few against life itself on our planet.

Dozens of species go extinct every day, with perhaps a million more under threat of extinction within our lifetime. Corporate greed tells us this doesn't merit our attention. If you feel bad, cut back on your own, because it's certainly not *their* fault. Such PR sleight of hand shifts the blame, feeds our guilt, inflames our anxiety, convinces us to consume more and more, until we give up caring, if we ever cared at all. Without thinking, we have become numb to the quiet collapse going on around us.

Everything is connected. A species dying is a piece of our world dying. If the world dies, we die, too.

After about forty-five minutes, Robert pulled into a parking lot at a massive planned community southeast of Bradenton. It seemed he had just remembered necessary transport paperwork required by FWC, so he filled that out, and they got going again. They followed the curve of Tampa Bay north, past towns with names as varied as Progress Village, Mango, and Thonotosassa. Once they had left the Tampa area behind, Robert said he was exhausted. They stopped to switch places.

You're exhausted? Jeff wanted to say. *You had me running around all night, and now you get to sleep?* At that point, he hadn't slept in about thirty-six hours. He resented Robert for passing the responsibility off on him, but he told himself that, despite the strain, it was for the better. An unconscious Robert would be a Robert he didn't have to worry about. As long as he was asleep, he wasn't going to catch Jeff at anything. That could buy Jeff an opportunity to snoop.

"Drive toward I-10 West until you're exhausted," Robert said. "Then we can switch out." He reclined in his seat, and by the time Jeff was cruising northward on the interstate again, Robert had fallen asleep.

Jeff tried to shake the sleep from his eyes. He was too old to pull an all-nighter, let alone two in a row. *The things I do for my job*, he thought.

As Jeff drove through the dark, the night sky blending with the tree line, a text message illuminated his phone, casting a sudden light through the truck cab. Jeff's pulse quickened. He glanced down and saw that the text was from Lieutenant Wilson. His eyes flicked to Robert. He hadn't stirred. He turned the phone face down so that wouldn't happen again.

The longer time stretched on, the more difficult the drive became. Trees on the roadside loomed to impossible proportions. The ground ahead seemed to well up like a tsunami about to swallow them. The woods writhed with visions, and the oncoming headlights melted and smeared. *You're seeing things, Jeff*, he said to himself. *Just a trick of the eyes. Not enough sleep.* By that point, an insomniac delirium had overtaken him. *I can keep driving*, he thought. He was almost giddy.

He drove up through the land of springs and rivers, of old, untouched pine forests and massive swamps that divided farmland from farmland. They drove through prairies where, unseen in the dark, wild horses and bison slept upright under gray-bearded cypresses that stretched toward the stars, all sharing the world with sawgrass and alligators as the plains flowed into the marsh.

By the time Jeff reached Pensacola, enough of his senses had returned that he had the wherewithal to pull over, cut the engine, and shut his eyes for a moment. In a blink, Robert roused him and asked how he was doing. Jeff held back an exasperated groan.

It was still dark out when they got breakfast, around 5 AM, and Robert took the wheel. Only half an hour down the road, much to Jeff's beleaguered frustration, Robert asked him to take over once again. *He couldn't be fucking with me more if he was doing this on purpose*, Jeff thought. Again, he considered that perhaps Robert was onto him. Maybe Wayne had been, too, even if he hadn't informed Robert. He had gotten too close to these men already. His job was hard enough without letting himself succumb to an overactive sense of guilt. All that aside, Jeff questioned whether Robert would have taken him along if he knew his true identity.

Still, Jeff worried. In the worst-case scenario, a sinister end awaited in Louisiana.

Come daybreak, Robert woke. He sat up and looked around. "Where are we?" he asked.

"Crossing into Alabama," Jeff said. He hoped Robert would tell him to pull over and offer to take the wheel.

"All right," Robert said. "Stay on I-10 West into New Orleans," he instructed. He closed his eyes, leaned back again, and slept.

The bleary, rising light cast a strange pall over the empty roadway. All around them, eerily straight rows of southern yellow pines, tree farms, stretched on without end. A sulfurous stench followed. Paper mills. The interstate narrowed onto a small concrete bridge to cross over the winding Styx River. If Jeff noticed the name, he thought nothing of it. He was too preoccupied with staying alert and on the road.

They crossed over Mobile Bay, a grassy marsh that deepened and widened into a windswept pane nearly the same blue as the sky out into the ocean. The road dipped under the muddy Mobile River and spat them out in a tangle of overpasses, ramps, and causeways, under a scant few skyscrapers, then out among the kudzu.

Robert slept all through Mississippi, then into Louisiana. Through the clatter of the Twin Span Bridge over Lake Pontchartrain. They sliced through the bayou. Then chain restaurants and apartment complexes sprang up around the road again. A high bridge lifted them over a canal, between Gentilly and Desire, and on into that storied city on the Mississippi they call the Big Easy, New Orleans.

Jeff gave Robert a nudge, and he roused. "We're here," Jeff said.

Robert nodded and pulled out his phone. He programmed in their destination out on the bayou, a place called Gheens, and set the GPS to talk Jeff through the directions. At a gas station, they finally switched places. While Robert filled their tank, Jeff reached in to grab his overnight bag, hoping to make himself look more presentable than he felt. Something on the floor caught his eye. It was the transfer document that Robert had filled out at the beginning of their trip, clamped to a silver clipboard. Jeff looked around. Robert wasn't paying him any mind. Jeff slipped his phone out of his pocket, took a covert picture of the document, and sent that to Lieutenant Wilson. He didn't know if there'd be anything on it, but every new piece of evidence was one more than he had before.

On the other side of the Mississippi, suburb once again gave way to swamp. Everything was a lush shade of green. You could almost taste the moisture in the air. The farther out they went, the more the trees dwindled. Claws of dead cypresses withered toward a glaring sky. These were ghost forests. Battered by hurricanes, tarred with oil spills, and inundated with salt water rising through the soil, they made this side of Louisiana teeter on the narrow cusp of a death-haunted future.

In the community of Gheens, too small to be labeled a proper town, stubborn live oaks resisted the salt water's call. They reached out, wide and twisted, some so old and gnarled that their many branches resembled chthonic tentacles. Nonetheless, it was a peaceful-seeming place of farms, houses, and churches. On the other side of that little hamlet, an industrial gate blocked the road. They entered, following the road through fields to the set of industrial buildings that was Golden Ranch Farms. It was a place, like the rest of Louisiana, built on a deep history. If the stories were true, the plot had been the Cenac family homestead some centuries ago. The ancestors of billionaire owner Benny Cenac remained buried beneath its soil.

At the main office, ranch manager Andrew, a young man in his thirties, met them and showed them to the factory-chicken-house-like barn they called the grow-out facility. The entire building was roughly the size of a football field and crisscrossed by echoing, steel-walled corridors and holding tanks. It was darker than Jeff expected. Alligators remained so much more docile in the dark.

Andrew directed his employees to follow them back to Jeff's truck, where he, Robert, Andrew, and four ranch hands began to unload. Before he started, Jeff fumbled at the keys clipped to his belt. With a furtive gesture, he clicked the button on his key-fob camera to turn it on. He had to remember he was two people here: Blackledge delivering the alligators and Officer Babauta, collecting as much information as he could. He needed to know if Golden Ranch realized they were bringing in illegally harvested wildlife. If they did, that would change everything. The case would go from a few small arrests to a high-profile sting, bringing down an interstate wildlife-smuggling operation.

They carried the crates of hatchlings one by one into an industrial tunnel, where they deposited the newborns into tanks through holes cut in the metal wall. Jeff felt a pang of regret as he watched them wiggle around the shallow water inside. He hadn't been foolish enough to name them. But they were still cute little animals. He'd helped them out of their shells the day they were born. Sure, several of them bit him, and who knew if any of them remembered him or not. That didn't matter. He'd always done his job to protect wildlife. Now what he was doing felt like a betrayal not just of his cause but of them as individuals. On an intellectual level, he could reason that it was the sacrifice of the few to protect the many. That didn't turn off the feeling part of him that despised the fate he'd given them—they would live the rest of their lives in a dark metal box, so far removed from the wildness of the swamp that, day by day, the stubborn fury that had lived inside of them from the moment they were born would fade away, until one day in the not-too-distant future, they would docilely go to the slaughtering room, and their hides would become purses, wallets, boots.

They were his babies. He wanted to protect them. But he couldn't. It was so hard to let go.

He pushed the thought out of his mind and turned to walk out into the daylight.

Once they'd deposited the last of the hatchlings, Robert asked Andrew if he was interested in buying the alligator hides they'd brought in the coolers.

"Sure," Andrew said.

They drove to another building, where a short tour showed hatching alligator eggs and farmworkers grading hatchlings by size. Jeff and Robert measured the hides, each with its appropriate CITES tag, and Andrew showed them out to a huge walk-in cooler full of alligator skins to finish their delivery.

They lingered in the other building, talking with Andrew, who would reveal later when questioned that he did not like or trust Robert. Andrew told them a little about the facility: The building where they stood could support forty-five thousand hatchlings. As for the rest of the farm, it covered around fifty thousand acres. It was likely the biggest alligator farm in the US.

He'd first talked to Andrew on the phone—when they'd had questions or problems back at Sunshine, Robert would call Andrew, put him on speaker, and he'd get them sorted out. Andrew had taken over his dad's position. His dad had worked for Cenac for most of his adult life, almost forty years. Then he died suddenly in a helicopter crash out on the bayou. He and Cenac had planned to go out together—some said to look for alligator nests, others to appraise land that Cenac was thinking about buying—but Cenac called to cancel last minute, claiming he felt under the weather. A while into the flight, the helicopter fell from the sky. The NTSB investigated and ruled it an accident. Still, some people thought there were just too many coincidences involved.

Golden Ranch did have a certain moody ambience—it was the old plantation where the Cenacs were buried, steeped in history, sinking into the gulf with the rest of the bayou, isolated from the outside world—like the setting of a southern gothic novel. That didn't mean anything sordid had happened there. Then again, it didn't mean it hadn't. Like an old alligator who had survived so long by not making any trouble, Jeff could recognize when he shouldn't go poking his nose where it didn't belong.

18

THE GOLDEN EGG SHEET

Time was closing in on them. The statute of limitations for any misdemeanors Jeff had witnessed in the early days of the case was fast approaching. Yet he still hadn't gotten what he needed to bring the biggest scheme down. Jeff had to work quickly. If he couldn't find Robert's "dirty" books, the agency would be forced to choose between charging the early misdemeanors or these more substantial crimes.

Of all the possible poachers in their net, Robert's crew represented the biggest catch. Losing them would mean losing the sting. Jeff had considerable evidence against CW and Tommy, both of whom had flagrantly brought in extra eggs beyond their allotted counts. The hatchlings painted with forensic glow would vouch for their crimes. With Robert himself and his wife, Robin, proving their crimes would be much harder. They had also collected beyond their legal counts, but since their hauls had been mixed in with the legal eggs from the beginning, there was no way for Jeff to tally exactly how many eggs the duo had stolen from the wild.

"What you need is documentation," Lieutenant Wilson advised Jeff one night after Jeff had returned from Louisiana. Lieutenant Wilson had come to the farm to retrieve video and audio recordings so his team could comb through them for evidence such as covert discussions of illicit activities. After he'd taken what he needed on a Jumpdrive, he stayed to debrief Jeff and Jeremy in the now much less crowded barn. "You say Robert's fairly organized?"

"Yes, sir," Jeff said. "At least with the paperwork, that is."

Some instances of Robert's disorganization—like the sudden trip to Louisiana nearly two weeks ahead of schedule—might not have been disorganization at all but a clue. Perhaps Robert had hurried them off early for a reason; maybe he had scented FWC on his trail, as Wayne had suggested. Or maybe something else had set off Robert's panic. Jeff tucked this back in his mind to ruminate on later.

"Then he's bound to keep a record of what he's doing," Lieutenant Wilson said. "Look for a ledger or a list of numbers. It might be labeled in a code, but there will be something to differentiate some numbers from the rest."

"Would he really keep something so incriminating?" Jeremy asked.

"You'd be surprised," Lieutenant Wilson said. "You see this with organized crime investigations all the time. There will be a clean book—a ledger that looks aboveboard—and then they'll keep a dirty book that tallies every little detail of what they've done."

Organized crime. *Is that what this is?* Jeff thought. None of the folks he'd tracked in the investigation seemed like hardened mafiosos. But perhaps he should have known by then that people were always more than what they seemed.

"I bet you if Robert's keeping something, it will be in that silver box of his," Jeff said. "Sometimes he leaves it around. I haven't seen inside it yet. But I'll try to take a peek next time his back is turned."

Jeremy agreed to do the same.

The tangible, obvious proof such a ledger would provide was the only thing that stood between Jeff and the Sunshine crew's arrests. It's also what stood between him and the end of the sting. He was ready to go home. He missed his wife. He missed his son. Heck, he even missed the chores his wife would give him on his infrequent visits. What he really missed, though, was being Jeff Babauta.

Robin joined them on their next trip to Louisiana. They set off at night like they did before, this time much more prepared and better rested, and with a third person, the drive was less strained. They traveled up the state at a leisurely pace. Robin kept the conversation flowing, and Jeff welcomed the chatter.

"Look, a Bass Pro Shop," she said, pointing to a billboard. She suggested they stop to shop for a little bit. She and Robert wanted to stock up on gear for hunting season, and since the most Arcadia had was a Tractor Supply, a chance to peruse a Bass Pro Shop was a real treat.

They pulled in and looked around. Jeff ambled by displays of recurve bows. Taxidermied wildlife stared blankly from their perches atop the aisles.

A text message chimed at Jeff's phone. He flinched and looked around to make sure no one was about to sneak up behind him and read his phone. Then he opened the text. It was from Lieutenant Wilson.

Wilson: Your tail has lost visual on you. What is your status?
Jeff: My tail?

Jeff sent a picture of a hatchling coming out of its egg, its comparatively large tail sticking out below a snout that seemed to smile.

Wilson: There is a team tailing you for backup. What is your location?

Jeff could almost sense Lieutenant Wilson's irritation coming through the phone.

Jeff: I'm fine. I didn't realize I had a tail. Everything is still going according to plan. We stopped at Bass Pro Shop.
Wilson: 10–4. Keep us apprised of your movements.

This stop was not a one-time affair. It seemed that every time Robin spotted a billboard for a Bass Pro Shop, they pulled off the highway to go shopping, and every time, Jeff became a little more annoyed.

Wilson: Where the hell are you? Are you at Bass Pro again?
Jeff: Yes.

He confirmed their approximate location.

If we stop at Bass Pro one more time, so help me, Jeff thought. *And I thought I was losing my mind on the first trip.* Somehow this seemed worse.

Wilson: Next time they stop, hang back and look for that silver box.
Jeff: 10–4.

"Oh, Boot Barn," Robin said the next time they were on the road, indicating a sign for a western outfitter. "I need some new boots. Let's see what they have."

Once again, they left the highway. Jeff could feel his anger welling up. Perhaps Robin could sense it.

"Want to come shopping with us?" she asked.

"Do I look like a damn cowboy to you?" Jeff snapped.

She gave him an amused smile. "Or stay out here. We won't be too long."

His irritation smoldered as they walked off, leaving him in the truck. He got out, stretched his legs, and then remembered himself. This wasn't just an annoyance. It was an opportunity. He peered under Robert's seat, and there it was, the silver box. He looked back at the store entrance. No sign of Robin or Robert.

Better make it quick, he thought.

He lifted the box's latch. It wasn't even locked. This was too easy. Maybe there wasn't anything important inside. He riffled through the papers. They didn't look like much, just forms and ledgers. But Jeff took pictures of them anyway. He sent the photos to Lieutenant Wilson. He closed the box just in time to hear someone call his name. He stashed the box under the seat then turned around to greet Robert and Robin, a shopping bag dangling from her arm.

Do you realize what you've found?" Lieutenant Wilson said over the phone.

Jeff had completed the delivery trip with Robin and Robert, once again returning to life on the farm.

"You've hit the jackpot," Lieutenant Wilson continued. "This is the golden egg sheet."

He meant that Jeff had found Robert's dirty books. They had appeared like a revelation in one of the many nondescript snapshots of papers he'd sent to Wilson. The team back at the agency had deciphered Robert's code and realized that he had indeed kept track of every egg his crew had poached.

Jeremy had snapped pictures of his own evidence as well, including forms Robert seemed to have forged in the name of a man who worked for the Seminole Tribe.

They had what they needed to prosecute Robert. Now all that was left was to bring him in.

While Jeff carried on his duties at the farm, his team behind the scenes at the agency started pulling all the clues together.

Cenac flew in himself to collect the last set of hatchlings. Despite Robert's eagerness to impress the billionaire, Cenac seemed keen on avoiding him.

To Jeff, Cenac was an enigma at first. When Jeff looked into him, he turned up mixed results. On the one hand, in 2013, Cenac seemed to have violated campaign finance laws and had pleaded guilty to making false statements to the FEC. On the other hand, he threw his money around for good, too, making donations to things as varied as college culinary programs, the Audubon Nature Institute, and the IUCN Species Survival Commission's Crocodile Specialist Group. Although Jeff planned to check out Cenac and his operation at Golden Ranch more thoroughly, unwilling to leave any stone unturned, the idea that Cenac might be involved in Robert's schemes seemed increasingly unlikely. Not because of his philanthropy, but because of the wealth that allowed it. Cenac was a billionaire. The amount of money to be made poaching alligator eggs was so insignificant in comparison that allowing it was not only pointless, it would threaten the farm's reputation and the conservation initiatives he had funded.

Instead, as the agency deciphered the documents, clues began to surface that Robert was stealing from Cenac as well.

On their first trip to Louisiana, Robert had driven out to Houma in the hope of visiting Cenac. The billionaire shipping magnate kept his offices on a hulking barge on the Mississippi River like a floating fortress.

"It's designed that way so when hurricanes come, instead of his business getting destroyed, tugboats can come drag the entire ship out into the gulf," Robert said. "They anchor out there and let it ride the waves."

They parked and went to the ramp. Security stopped them and asked for their credentials.

Robert explained who he was. "I'd like to see Mr. Cenac if I can," he said. "He knows who I am." The security guard looked skeptical, but he radioed in their presence anyway. After a while, the response came. Cenac didn't want to see them. No further explanation or invitation to come back another time.

It turned out that Robert wasn't just poaching—he was hoodwinking everyone, including Cenac. Cenac had given him an open checkbook, and Robert was using it to buy parts for fanboats to build them for himself, marking those funds as spent on eggs and farm supplies.

He was on salary, so he wasn't even getting paid by the egg. Despite this realization of embezzlement, it didn't make sense that he was poaching so many alligator eggs from the wild. The risk of getting caught didn't seem worth the reward of impressing Cenac, especially while stealing from the man at the same time. In a way, Robert was like Robin Hood after all, poaching and stealing from the rich. He just wasn't giving to the poor, unless he counted himself. The trickster who robs the rich to give to the poor gets called a hero. The trickster who robs the less fortunate, man or beast, to give to himself tends not to win many hearts.

So does the end justify the means like the trickster-hero archetype seems to suggest? As makers and consumers of culture, we're interested in underdogs, Horatio Algers, Davids triumphing over Goliaths, the righteous and deserving getting their rewards. But this coin has another side: The triumph isn't so sweet if those we perceive as undeserving don't lose in the process. As a culture, we're into punishment as much as we are into redemption. The second doesn't taste nearly so sweet without the first.

19

THE MONGOOSE

As counts added up against Robert's crew, Jeff started to let himself speak up more when they were crossing the line of legality. The more frequently he pushed, the more they admitted to their wrongdoing, wearing it like a badge of honor, all except for Robert himself, whose reticence, most times, maintained his plausible deniability.

Of all the people who came on the egg hunts, Jeff had gotten the closest to David. Jeff enjoyed talking to him about wildlife, and in these times, when they were alone, perhaps Jeff would spot a bird and identify it, forgetting who he was supposed to be. It was that easy to exist alongside David, so easy that he found himself slipping back into being Jeff Babauta in a way he thought he couldn't anymore. Such ease, Jeff worried, could be both a relief and a danger, not just of blowing his cover, but of not being able to do his job. With David, he *had* crossed the line. He *had* gotten too close. He didn't want to arrest David. He wanted to protect him.

Lieutenant Wilson and Jeff's agency handlers believed that David was working in collusion with Robert and his gang. Even Robert's own words—especially the ones Jeff had recorded in the hatching room—seem to imply that David was flouting the law, as if closing his eyes to every instance of poaching that he was supposed to be watching out for.

"He could just be making mistakes," Jeff said, advocating for David over the phone to Lieutenant Wilson.

With all the evidence they had amassed over the months, the agency decided it was time for their trap to snap shut, for Jeff to close up the farm, and, as soon as Blackledge had vanished, for teams of uniformed officers to show up at the alligator thieves' homes, arrest warrants in hand, and bring them in.

"I know you like the guy, Jeff," Lieutenant Wilson said. "But that doesn't mean he's innocent."

"Give me one last chance," Jeff pleaded, "to prove he doesn't know what he's doing."

Lieutenant Wilson breathed out. "All right," he said. "One last chance."

So Jeff convinced David to invite him over, a conversational sleight of hand pulled when the subject drifted toward gardening, and David started in on all the fruit trees he kept. Citruses, mangoes—just about any plant that loves the tropics will bear fruit in South Florida.

On October 5, Jeff drove to David's Punta Gorda home, an old-fashioned bungalow with a porch to let in the breeze. Before he set out, Jeff had concealed a Bluetooth recording device under the brim of his baseball cap, and as he drove, he rehearsed the questions he would ask. He needed to unravel David's involvement in the poaching scheme. Was he just making innocent mistakes? Was Robert using him? Or was he the mastermind behind his own actions?

Rain clouds had started to gather by the time Jeff pulled up to David's house, and after they had strolled through David's lush garden, Jeff eagerly listening to a veritable biology lecture on the exotic trees and fruit that David grew, that whisper of an afternoon shower turned into a downpour. Jeff and David ducked into the closest shelter, Jeff's truck. In the sudden cold of his air-conditioning, Jeff remembered why he was there. Now he had to play verbal chess with this smart man, probing to find out how much he knew. If he was guilty of aiding Robert in his scheme to poach and launder alligator eggs, then maybe Jeff could get him to come clean and set him on the path toward redemption, too, all without divulging his own identity behind this mask in the process. Jeff would have to be careful. David was an expert in one of nature's craftiest animals, the mongoose.

The biologist had spent the better part of a lifetime researching mongooses in the Virgin Islands, where farmers had released dozens of the small mammals in an effort to combat pests. The mongooses, however, tenacious and wily—and prone not to listen to instructions, it seems—multiplied and began preying on native species, leading many people to change their minds about the formerly beloved animal: Authorities called the mongooses invasive and crafted plans for their eradication. Quite a long way to fall for an animal that ancient Mesopotamians associated with magic. Stories in classical Sanskrit, though, portray the mongoose as loyal above all, a plucky little hero eager to defy odds and defend its human friends from the mighty cobra. Modern trappers know that mongooses are just as crafty as millennia of stories have portrayed them: Like the tricksters of myth and legend, mongooses have been known to outsmart their ostensibly more intelligent foes, us humans, by unlocking traps and setting themselves free. Perhaps David had learned a thing or two from watching them all those years, whether that be loyalty or—well, Jeff would see.

He chatted with David for a bit until it seemed the rain would not relent, and they would be trapped in the truck together indefinitely unless they wanted to get soaked to the bone. *Now or never*, Jeff thought. *Time to jump in.*

"The reason I was asking you about yesterday," Jeff said. "I don't know what we ended up with." He was referring to the number of eggs they had harvested. Even as hatching season progressed, the crew had continued their hunts whenever they could.

"That's why I didn't want to get in the mix," David said. "Because I actually never counted the eggs."

For real? Jeff thought. *Trying to make it seem like you saw nothing, is that it?*

"You were around in times I wasn't even present," David went on.

"I wasn't sure you were required by the state to keep track of that," Jeff said. "So I don't know what all Robert brought in." Jeff laid on the acting, tweaking his tone into one of anxiousness. After their initial differences, Jeff had tried to give David the impression that he was rough around the edges, but he meant well. By then, he believed that David thought of him as generally good, not a lawbreaker, a fellow looking to start his business up right—one who had stumbled into company who wanted to fool him and use him against his will. That was what was happening to Blackledge, after all. No need to cook up a scheme or backstory here.

"I think there were some other sources," David said, meaning that other eggs were coming in from who knew where. "I'm kind of suspicious of that. You and I both know that CW has brought in lots of additional eggs."

Jeff nodded. He furrowed his brow and tried to look upset. "So my biggest fear was getting—" He took a tense breath. "Robert keeps talking about FWC raiding my place. He has me worried."

"They can't," David said, consoling. "While the number of eggs and the number of hatchlings are justified"—the tallies matched up in Robert's books—"nobody can possibly sort out how many eggs were collected. Now that there's been hatchling gators, and export of gators, there's no way that anybody can verify anything right now."

Jeff tried to seem confused. He needed David to say something, anything, to prove his involvement one way or another. "So I guess what you're saying is if I had those eggs, what's showing up on my clipboard"—where Jeff kept tallies of his own—"does not add up to what we have?"

"I've been aware without actually counting a single egg—I've been aware that's going on," said David. "He knows what he's doing." He meant Robert. "Think if you were a prosecuting attorney. I mean, we both will totally agree that Robert is a sharp number. I've seen him manipulate people. I go along with it, and he tries to manipulate *me*. I think he recognizes he can only manipulate me a little way." He paused and looked out through the cascade of rain over the windshield as if seeing back in time to an instance when Robert tested his wits against him and lost. "Having sat through a lot of law school classes, if I was a prosecuting attorney and wanted to bring a case against Robert, I would look at available evidence and the way we could present things—and I'd never bring a case. It's obvious to me that there were shenanigans done, but that they were done with such finesse that I'm not going to prevail in court. Any defense attorney that's worth his salt is going to be able to get this case thrown out for lack of evidence."

That is where I draw the distinction between Robert and his crew and Peg Brown. Peg wore the title *poacher* like a badge of honor. These wily egg hunters did not. Above all else, it's not how they saw themselves but how they saw other people that separates the Peg Browns of the world from all the others: Peg tricked the rangers so he could get away with poaching, sure. But even as he duped them, he thought of them as men with families, with responsibilities and flaws and consciences, with needs sometimes as desperate as his own. In his empathy, he could read them, and he could give them mercy, and the rangers could do the same. They could chase him down and make his life difficult, build up their firepower until his nightly adventures seemed impossible, but in the end, they had a decision to make. Perhaps that is the real reason why they never caught Peg Brown: They didn't want to. It was better for everyone—for his family, for the island, for an Everglades in need of a hero, and for their consciences—if they let him go.

In many ways, Peg is more like Jeff than he is like Robert and his crew. The "shenanigans" David described at Sunshine seemed to use people, moving them around the swamp like pawns with no regard to their well-being; like the eggs they plucked from the wild, like the hatchlings they passed on to Louisiana, their pawns were a means to meet an end. Such disregard, and the hubris that empowered it, would ultimately prove their downfall, a trap they set for themselves. They thought too little of Curtis Blackledge. Their assumptions took away his depth, and so they didn't see, behind that mask, there was Jeff Babauta, whose unassuming cleverness had been honed not through manipulation but empathy.

As David spoke, Jeff nodded and let his expression soften just a bit, as if relieved by the knowledge of Robert's cunning. David smiled. He hadn't said enough to clear his name or condemn it. Jeff needed to push harder. This was just like the end of the softshell case, when he was questioning Alonso in his backyard as they weighed the turtles. He'd toed right up to the line then, the one that separated curiosity from a suspicious need to know too much. That's how this worked, he realized. When you let yourself go just a little too far, when you risked everything—that's when the most harrowing truths came into the light.

"Let me ask you this, because it's another concern of mine," Jeff said. "Because if I do this next year, I want to make sure I'm following the rules. Robert was supposed to be holding my hand and guiding me." This painful betrayal came bubbling up in his words. It really did hurt that Robert went back on his word. He held Blackledge in such little regard that he'd been willing to use Blackledge's farm to commit crimes for which Blackledge could have taken the blame. He was willing to ruin Blackledge's life, and for what? To impress a billionaire? Laundering eggs didn't earn Robert any more money than he would have gotten if he'd followed the law. So try as he might, Jeff couldn't wrap his mind around why he did it. What was the point?

"You don't necessarily want to do it the way Robert did," David said.

Ah, now we're getting somewhere, Jeff thought.

"Going back to that 50 percent," Jeff said. "Especially like at Webb—we're supposed to go harvest a nest then skip one, technically, under that 50 percent rule, right?"

David nodded. "Yep."

"Then go on to the next one."

"Yep."

I need you to say it! Jeff shouted in his head.

"Harvest that one and skip that one," Jeff said. "We didn't do that."

"We did *not* do that," David said emphatically.

That was it. That was enough. David had confirmed Jeff's suspicions. He hadn't only been supervising the egg collections when he said he wasn't paying attention; he also knew that the crew had been breaking the law, and had just stood by and let them. His job had been to speak up for the state of Florida, for the alligators, and he hadn't. It wasn't a slip. It wasn't a little mistake. He let all of this happen. The revelation came as a blow to Jeff's heart. *Oh, Dave*, he thought. He tried not to let the disappointment play across his face.

"Did we not do 100 percent?" Jeff laughed, hoping that the bittersweetness of that victory did not carry over into his voice. "How is Robert going to justify that?"

"You look at Robert's records, and you'll see." Now David laughed, too. "Robert's records say we only harvested *half* of what we did."

For his whole career, being friendly with the folks who sometimes snatched things from the woods was part of his job, a necessary one. It was part of who he was, too. Jeff Babauta was the kind of person who cared. Try as he might to separate himself, or who he had always believed himself to be, from the man he had to become for his job—he couldn't do it. To defy this part of himself by calling them criminals or bad guys was one part of his identity he couldn't shake when he stepped into Blackledge's skin. He had all but lost himself to the character—except for this. He was told that this was necessary, this loss. He had to forget. He had to be neutral to do this job. But he was starting to embrace that without this compassion he would be missing why he was here in the first place, why he'd become a game warden and dedicated his life to protecting the wild. It was the central tenet of his being. It was the thing holding him up inside on those long nights he spent alone looking after the farm, nights that could have cracked him open and left him in the dark valley of his soul. Without compassion, there was no point to him being here, doing this, not any of it. Without compassion, he would lose Jeff Babauta for good.

Even though he was about to bring charges against so many people he had gotten to know, Jeff still saw room in there for a little much-needed compassion.

"I don't think we should arrest Robin, or any of the wives, for that matter," he told Lieutenant Wilson over the phone.

The agency was working with the DA to put together charges, and while that was building up, Jeff's time as Blackledge was winding down. It was December, with Christmas around the corner, and Jeff was eager to get back to being himself again, whoever that was now.

"Why not?" Lieutenant Wilson asked. "Robin was as involved as anyone else there, maybe even more so."

"If we arrest both of them, who's going to take care of their kids?" Jeff asked. "They have three kids, George. Do you want to leave them without a dad *and* a mom? I don't."

If they had to choose one of them to prosecute, Jeff said, it should be Robert, whom several of their crew had called the mastermind behind their schemes, on camera no less. Though Robin was no less intelligent—and perhaps even more perceptive—than her husband, she had not orchestrated any plans to defraud the wild. She had only been accessory to them.

Most of the poachers had brought their families along for egg harvesting. Husbands and wives had worked as poaching teams. Most of the wives knew what was going on. But if both husband and wife were arrested, what would happen to the kids? Jeff thought about his own family. He imagined a world where both he and Sandy were suddenly taken away, leaving their son when he was young. That's a loss he never would have recovered from. Hurting those kids would have been wrong. All of Jeff's career, he had tried to treat poachers as he would want to be treated. Now this was his final test. If he wanted his career to go out with a bang, he'd have rounded them all up and brought them all in, and the number of arrests would be glorious. But if he wanted the operation to reflect his career, to reflect who he was as an officer and an environmental protector, he would have to trade glory for redemption.

Jeff thought of himself as the kind of person who always did the right thing, even when it hurt. This hurt now, for sure. But he would be able to sleep at night knowing that he'd done his best for both the animals and the people. He had vowed to protect the wild. That meant protecting the people who lived there, too.

Lieutenant Wilson breathed out, and Jeff was afraid he'd veto that plan for compassion before they could discuss it. Maybe Lieutenant Wilson would say Jeff had gotten attached to the poachers and their families, and if he was being honest with himself, Jeff would agree. Maybe Lieutenant Wilson would argue that this sting was the crowning achievement of both of their careers; lowering their arrest numbers would be selling themselves short of their full glory. Things like that didn't matter to Jeff. He didn't need glory. He just needed to do the right thing.

"Just the men?" Lieutenant Wilson said. "I'll run it up the chain, but—I think we can do that."

"Yeah?"

"Yeah. I'll see what I can do."

As Blackledge, he made excuses to all the new people in his life, both Robert and Robin, Tommy and CW, and the harder goodbyes to Wayne and David. Lieutenant Wilson and Jeff's team at the agency had decided that it would be too dangerous to leave Jeff in place at the alligator farm while the arrest warrants went out. So Jeff had to disappear as cleanly as he'd arrived. He needed to dismantle the farm, spirit away the spy equipment in the dead of night, sell all the alligators, and take his personal effects home, always keeping watch in his rearview mirror as he drove for cars that seemed to follow just a little too long.

"What, you dying?" Wayne had asked. He had showed up once again to drink Jeff's beer, and they stood, looking out over the alligator pond.

"No, no, nothing like that," Jeff answered. "I'm just—I'm done with this game."

"I hear ya," Wayne said knowingly.

How much does he really know? Jeff wondered. *If he knows, wouldn't he have said something by now? Then again, wouldn't I?*

With Wayne, Jeff felt caught between loyalty to his mission and loyalty to their—was this friendship? On the surface, it felt like friendship, but below that, Jeff knew you couldn't really be friends with someone who didn't know who you were. He liked Wayne. In another life, he and Blackledge could have continued their harebrained adventures. But this was reality. In this life, Jeff reminded himself, he had come here with a mission to protect the wild. Wayne had violated that wild, even though Jeff knew he loved it. He'd flouted the laws put in place to protect nature. Why? Some could have been simple mistakes. Others seemed to hover close to the same mentality of the gladesmen that had begotten Peg Brown, a dogged defiance spun from injustice and woven into myth. Problem was these were no longer the days of Peg Brown, nor was it the age of Robin Hood. Since then, the way we see animals has changed.

In the poacher-as-hero narrative, animals often amount to little more than props. That's largely because this narrative hails from a time and a place, medieval Britain, when the common sentiment toward animals denied them agency. Some writers have blamed the prevalence and dominance of Christianity in that time; however, it more likely came about as a part of rejecting pagan beliefs in their entirety instead of as a wholly formed belief itself. Either way, medieval stories mark animals as beasts of burden, food, foe, or ready symbolism—though sometimes they're pleasant scenery if they're lucky enough. However, the further away we've gotten from those so-called Dark Ages, the more the general attitude toward animals has returned a selfhood to them, especially when we tell stories about them.

That is why the poacher-as-hero has seen his downfall. When his adversary is an animal, we no longer see him as David: He's Goliath, so we want him to lose. And with loss, in this narrative scheme, comes punishment. Because that's what we want as consumers of story. Loss isn't enough unless we get revenge; we want that fulfillment, because revenge isn't something most of us get (or thankfully even strive for) in our lives off the page. So poacher-as-hero narratives have gone the way of the dodo, and, unless the writer and readers gloss over his poaching acts, he is replaced generally by the poacher-as-villain.

Perhaps, in this way, the most satisfying end to a poacher-versus-billionaire story would be one in which everyone loses. But reality is never so simple and clean as it appears in stories, and the machinations of time certainly aren't looking to create the most satisfying narrative end. People aren't archetypes. Poachers, like the rest of us, contain multitudes, like how Peg Brown was a dedicated war hero, a good dad, a pillar of his community, and a damn good storyteller. It's easy to forget that everyone is the hero of their own story. Most of us are just doing our best to get by however we can. Sometimes that means making difficult choices in order to survive.

The people who insist that every act is morally unambiguous are the ones who are suspect, because they fail to see the conflicts others face: A poacher may hunt to feed his family. A thief may steal because he feels powerless—from not being able to make ends meet, from the grind and hustle modern life has forced upon us—so he's stepping out of bounds, transgressing, freeing himself for at least one act, but everything we do has a consequence. The people who think they've never hurt anyone or anything in their lives are the ones most oblivious to the trail of pain they've left behind. If you're living—really living—there will be consequences. Even if you're always following the law, the law isn't always right.

Jeff, a wildlife officer, seems an unlikely person to have this realization. He spent his whole career upholding the law. Yet, through all those years, he saw that even laws that protect the innocent, the wild creatures who depend on us to be stewards of this planet, can have profound consequences for the people who break them. Jeff had watched all his career. He'd listened. By then he knew that guilt did not mean someone was beyond redemption. No one is. They were all just real people trying to survive, forced to make some of life's most difficult choices. The small act of trying to feed your family can shatter your life. Jeff didn't want that to happen with the poachers caught in Operation Alligator Thief. If he could, he wanted to do his job by causing the least damage. And if he admitted it, he'd come to really like the people. They had trusted him, brought him into their homes. He felt guilty, too, because of this. He was the traitor in their midst. He'd betrayed all of their trust.

"So what are you going to do with the gators?" Wayne asked.

"Sell 'em, I guess," Jeff said. He took a swig of beer, a real one this time. "Why, you want 'em?"

"Hell yeah," Wayne said.

They bartered a dirt-cheap price, and later, they set out on their last escapade, to wrangle the remaining alligators and put an end to Sunshine Alligator Farm.

So, this is it," Robert said.

"This is it," said Jeff. They stood outside what had been Sunshine but was now a shell, their decals peeled off the walls, the alligators gone. Jeff was more than ready to be gone, too, and he was definitely done with Robert. As he gave Robert a stiff handshake, he looked him in the eyes for a brief moment. *You think you're such a mastermind, like you're so much smarter than everyone else,* Jeff thought. *You think you've played all of us, don't you?* Jeff wondered how Robert would feel when he realized he was the one being duped all along.

Robert signed the check for $2,500, the remaining fee for using the farm. "Sure I can't interest you in another season?" Robert asked. "Next year? We could really use you."

I bet you'd like to, Jeff thought.

"No, I think I've had my fill of alligators," Jeff said. "This is it for me. I'm moving on to something else. But I have to thank you. I really learned a lot."

After Robert left, Jeff took out his phone. He opened David's contact page. His finger hovered over the call symbol. *No.* Jeff shut the app and put the phone in his pocket. He couldn't face the man knowing what he was about to do.

December came and went, and in the new year, the state built a case against the alligator thieves. Without the possibility of bringing Lacey Act violation charges, the DA had to come up with something else. In a twist, she decided on racketeering charges, ironic because big corporations often wield the RICO (Racketeer Influenced and Corrupt Organizations) statute against environmental activists, journalists, and public figures who have gotten in their way or otherwise spoken out against them. (This practice is so common that activists and journalists have a name for it: SLAPP, or strategic lawsuits against public participation.)

The warrant for Robert's arrest charged him with racketeering, conspiracy to commit racketeering, scheming to defraud, and fourteen counts of unlawful possession of alligator eggs, a number of eggs that reached into the thousands. Tommy's list of charges was a little bit thinner, with conspiracy to commit racketeering and six counts of unlawful possession of alligator eggs. Although CW had harvested over a thousand illicit eggs himself—earning $58,000 in only three months—his charges included only four counts of unlawful possession, and also, of course, conspiracy to commit racketeering. The charges against David said he was in on their scheme. His arrest warrant accused him of conspiracy to commit racketeering, one count of unlawful possession of alligator eggs, and uttering a forged instrument, a special law in Florida that criminalizes lies and counterfeited or forged records made with an attempt to defraud. Last, there was Wayne, who received the least of the charges. The accusations against him included three counts of unlawful possession of alligators, take (poaching) of white ibis, and attempted take of white ibis. In all, the state of Florida brought charges against eleven people in Operation Alligator Thief, including six suspects not mentioned in this book.

Before long, May arrived, and it was time for the trap to snap shut.

The day before the arrests were scheduled to take place, the agency along with the DA held a meeting to brief all the officers. Jeff sat at the side of the room, taking it all in. He was so moved that he had to record. He took out his phone and scanned it slowly over the crowd as the DA presented the case. Over sixty officers from five counties were listening to her speak. They were there because of the work Jeff had done, all of them, uniformed officers, plainclothesmen, protecting these prehistoric beasts that Jeff had come to love.

He could barely sleep that night. That morning, he told his wife that if anything happened, if anyone came after her or Chris, she should call him immediately. They reassured each other that everything would be fine. He left the house while it was still dark and drove to the command center, the secret location from which he, Lieutenant Wilson, and their team would direct the arrests. He met Lieutenant Wilson inside.

Lieutenant Wilson clapped him on the shoulder the way a coach might rouse his star player before the big game. "How you feeling?"

Nervous. Excited. Worried. "Feeling good, George," Jeff said.

"Good," Lieutenant Wilson said. "It's showtime."

The takedown clock began ticking at 6 AM. The longer it took for the field officers to make the arrests, the more likely it became that the suspects would catch wind of the sting and flee. The electric pulse of worry thrummed inside Jeff. He was safe there, surrounded by his fellow officers, but what about his wife and son? What if that car he'd seen had been following him? What if the poachers knew where he lived? What if they heard about the sting? What if they slipped away before the officers arrived? What if—

All across the state, the officers banged on doors. They shouted the suspects' names. "Open up," they demanded. "We have a warrant."

One by one, the doors opened.

One by one, the suspects presented themselves to the officers.

One by one, the officers read them their rights and cuffed their wrists.

The only one who protested was David. He insisted then and kept insisting he didn't know what he'd done.

EPILOGUE

As I explored the stories of *Gator Country*, a phrase in Latin kept returning to my mind: *Et in Arcadia ego*, roughly translated as, "And I am in Paradise." The most famous use of the phrase appears as the title of a painting by French baroque artist Nicolas Poussin in which toga-clad shepherds and a woman examine an epitaph inscribed on a tomb, possibly *Et in Arcadia ego*. This instance isn't the first use of the phrase, and it's far from the last, with others ranging from mentions in novels such as *The Sound and the Fury* and *Brideshead Revisited* to more recent appearances such as the title of two episodes of *Star Trek: Picard*. With much of this book occurring in a town called Arcadia, every time I heard the name, I thought, *Et in Arcadia ego*, turning the phrase over like a stone worn smooth by the current of a river.

Beyond its literal translation, *Et in Arcadia ego* has come to mean that even in paradise, death awaits us all. Memento mori and all that. That phrase and *Et in Arcadia ego* were, excuse the pun, done to death by the invention of the movable-type printing press. And like every popular trope, they deserve to be subverted. Death waits for us. Sure, okay. But so does new life.

Nature's most deathly places are where it's most full of life, not despite that death but because of it. Dead things decay and enrich the soil. Endangered salamanders in electric hues scamper under fallen pine trunks half consumed by time and worms. Bogs mix life with life, congealing it together into its most fertile essence. Rare orchids unfurl over the mire. Death comes for all things, but so does a kind of resurrection. Death is inevitable, as those phrases remind us, but as millions of years on this planet have shown, so is the triumph of life. Life blooms from death. Life is not the victor. Death is not the enemy. Life and death are not at odds but in inseparable agreement.

Even people who don't believe in a literal afterlife can still look forward to a reincarnation back into soil, back into life, because the elements that make up our bones and flesh also make mother-of-pearl, birds' wings, lilies, and stardust. We are a part of everything, quite literally. To make an enemy of swamps is to make an enemy of yourself. On the grand scale, swamps are massive carbon sinks, swallowing up the gasses that endanger our planet. On the smaller scale—an infinitesimally smaller one—microorganisms in healthy soil may boost the human body's microbiome, one possible reason why people who spend time outdoors live longer. Our bodies benefit from nature, likely in more ways than we can even imagine or have yet discovered. Our relationship with nature is symbiotic. When nature thrives, our bodies thrive, our species thrives. The antithesis is also true: When the wild faces ruin, so do we. We don't just lose a metaphor. We don't just lose a playground. We lose ourselves.

Just as we are connected with nature, so is every other animal. The loss of a single species poses a threat to all the rest, including us. That is why Jeff and FWC put such an effort toward protecting alligators.

All told, the crew from Sunshine Alligator Farm took more than thirteen thousand eggs from the swamp in a single year, far more than the numbers allowed on their permits, far more than even Peg Brown, whom Chokoloskee storytellers called the most "notorious" alligator poacher to ever live, took from the Everglades over the span of three decades. It's true that alligators are far more plentiful now than they were then. That is, at least in part, because of regulations that limit egg harvests. As Jeff told me during one interview at his house, the population of any species will have a tipping point, and if we're not careful, it can go from plentiful to in decline before we know what's happening. Harvesting all the eggs in an area, for example, puts alligators there in danger of extirpation, the word for a localized extinction. If alligators disappear, their prey animals get out of control, and the domino effect goes on to other species, to vegetation, to the earth itself, and it could ripple outward from that spot to others. When nature tips out of balance, it's impossible to know just how far the damage will spread. That is why FWC and the state of Florida wanted to punish the poachers to the fullest extent of the law.

They hoped to protect more species than alligators by showing that the risks of poaching far outweigh its rewards.

But did it work? Well, yes and also no. Operation Alligator Thief sparked a conversation about alligator conservation—and about preventative instead of reactive conservation in general—which eventually reached me. Before I listened to the yarns of my student, though, the operation had already borne fruit, as evidenced by the way I heard about it in the first place.

A good yarn well spun takes on a life of its own. Just like how the Peg Brown stories became Everglades legends, the strongest yarns keep traveling until everyone knows a version of the tale. The wild story of Sunshine Alligator Farm and the chameleon wildlife officer who had brought it to life had spread through what seems like every backwoods outpost in the state before any writer even dreamed of putting it to paper. That did something more than entertain: The young man who told me the story swore off poaching. Likely, others did, too. To Jeff, that is a success. Though he never met my student and probably never will, Jeff's efforts set him straight. As my student retold the story, perhaps it had the same effect on others. Some of his listeners likely retold it as I am now. You never know who's watching, was the moral of his tale. Don't do anything you aren't willing to defend later. Ultimately, I realized the story of Operation Alligator Thief came full circle back to the reason I started telling stories in the first place. It had the same moral as the stories my family told on our dock all those years ago: Who you are in the dark is your truest self.

The guys accused in Operation Alligator Thief would agree, as most of them fought their charges. At the time of their arrests, however, they didn't know what was happening. After the officers served their warrants and booked each one of them into a holding cell, they had time to wonder. Wayne, in a bittersweet way, must've felt affirmed: *I was right*, I can imagine him thinking. *There* was *a traitor in our midst.* But who was that traitor? The crew wouldn't know for sure until he appeared in his uniform in court.

When they saw him, they kept their irritation, anger, and feelings of betrayal to themselves. They couldn't do anything that would jeopardize the arguments against their charges. As Jeff took the stand, he looked out at their faces. Sometimes, they avoided looking him in the eye. Most of the time, when their glances landed on him, their expressions read of cold indifference as if they were looking at a stranger. And he was one, wasn't he? They didn't know him, not really, he would tell himself. Likewise, he didn't really know them. Yet the times he had spent with some of them—like joking with Wayne and chatting with Robin—had been genuine. Maybe in another life, they would have been friends. They weren't so different from the people he knew already.

The wives whom Jeff opted not to prosecute, however, showed less stoicism than their husbands. When Jeff walked by Wayne's wife, where she sat next to the courtroom aisle, she hissed a single word at him. "Asshole."

It could have been worse, and Jeff didn't begrudge her the anger. There were so many things he could have said in return. What good would that have done either of them? Were the tables turned, maybe his wife would have said the same thing. No, he kept on walking. It was best for everyone if he pretended he hadn't heard.

As the trials rolled on, the tension increased. The crew really seemed to believe they hadn't done anything wrong. Yet, one by one, their arguments failed, and the court found each one of them guilty of their crimes. The judge slapped Wayne and David with fines and probation. Tommy and CW, tried in tandem, received sentences of almost a year of jail time each. The crew that had convened at Sunshine was also sentenced to pay restitution to the State of Florida to the tune of more than $80,000. Adding insult to injury, the state tacked on reimbursement costs for the investigation as well.

In 2019, while the trials were still going on, Jeff, Lieutenant Wilson, and the DA left the courtroom. They waited together in the hall for the elevator. They were done for the day, on the way out, and they chatted about their plans. When the elevator opened, they turned toward it. Then they stopped. The three people already in the elevator likewise stood frozen: Robert, Robin, and their lawyer. Robert was on his way to plead out in hopes of a lesser sentence, Jeff would learn later. The judge would sentence him to three years in prison, a small fraction of the maximum possible penalty, an egregious 160 years. Right then, Robin pulled Jeff's attention. The anger, no, fury, in her eyes stabbed at him. None of them moved. Then the elevator dinged, and the doors slid shut, gradually eclipsing the burning hatred on Robin's face until all Jeff could see was his own blurry reflection.

Over the course of my writing this book, Wayne, Tommy, and CW all appealed their sentences.

After he was arrested, Wayne would swear up and down to anyone who would listen that he suspected Jeff was an undercover officer from the beginning. When I first started looking into the story, I thought that didn't sound right, but the further I dug, the more my previously held belief came into question. I realized that the stereotype I had believed about poachers had informed my doubt. *If Wayne had known*, I thought initially, *then he would have jumped Jeff out in the woods*. He had ample opportunity. Yet he didn't. As the months went by and I got to know more poachers—and their legends—I began to consider that Wayne could have been going through similar inner turmoil to Jeff.

Should I tell him that I know? Wayne might have thought. *Naw, I'll just play it as it goes.*

If that's true, then the betrayal of his arrest would have stung all the deeper.

After he learned I was writing this story, David sent me frantic emails affirming his innocence in the hope that I could help, but what could I do? He was afraid that this black mark on his record would overwrite his lifetime of research and conservation work, and I don't think it should. My hope is that it's clear no one is a villain, that we are all flawed. Personally, I don't trust stories about perfect people. Perfection means that something's missing.

In the absence of perfection, though, sometimes we have peculiarity.

In their appeals, Tommy and CW argued that the RICO statute did not apply to their case, and so their sentences should be overturned. Their harvest of eggs, they claimed, was a victimless crime. CW's lawyer argued that poaching alligator eggs was not theft in a legal sense, because the Florida statute states that theft is taking "property of another," and therefore their acts did not fall under the umbrella of the RICO law.

At CW's new hearing, his lawyer took that argument a step further. "The only entity that owns wildlife is a higher power," he stated, "not the State of Florida." In other words, theirs was a crime against God.

"While remaining duly agnostic on the counsel's theological premise," Judge J. Andrew Atkinson of the Florida Second District Court of Appeal wrote in his November 2021 mandate, "this court finds the gist of the argument persuasive and dispositive." No one owned the eggs the crew had allegedly stolen, he said. "Perhaps more importantly," Atkinson wrote, "the State's attempt to shoehorn the violation of a regulatory statute into the enumerated RICO offense of 'theft' illuminates a damning deficiency in its case: the legislature did not include violation of alligator egg harvesting regulations among its list of predicate acts that can form the basis for a racketeering conviction." In other words, whether or not it was a crime against God, conspiring to take alligator eggs could not be a violation of RICO. Although taking eggs without a valid permit was a crime, the judge wrote, "it did not constitute theft sufficient to support conspiracy to commit racketeering," because no individual person owned the alligator eggs while they were in the nests—neither the private landowners nor the state.

The Florida legislature added wildlife crimes to its definition of racketeering activity in 2021, about five years after the commission of the acts in this book. Therefore, the court mandate states, the trial should have acquitted CW. His original sentence was upheld in part and reversed in part.

"We vacate the conviction for conspiracy to commit racketeering but affirm the remaining convictions and sentences," Judge Atkinson wrote.

Tommy, however, didn't get so lucky. The same court of appeals upheld the original decision in his case. Both Tommy and CW received downward departure sentences, punishments below the typical minimum sentence for such crimes.

As for Wayne, he pleaded guilty to the counts of poaching and attempted poaching of a protected species (the white ibis), but he appealed the charges of alligator poaching. Since Florida law bars people found guilty of alligator poaching from making money through the alligator industry for a set number of years after their sentencing, a guilty verdict on these counts put Wayne's livelihood on the line. Initially, it seemed like luck was on his side. In early 2021, the court reversed its decisions on Wayne's three counts of alligator poaching and remanded the case for a new trial. That trial took place only a few months later, and Wayne's luck finally ran out. The court once again rendered a guilty verdict on all three counts and sentenced Wayne to pay fines and complete four years of probation.

Neither David nor Robert have appealed their sentences.

While Robert was still serving his sentence in prison, he passed a message to me through his correctional officer. "I just want to put all of this behind me," he said.

W*ho owns the wilderness?* The true answer is both an existential one and a legal one, and according to the law, who owns the wilderness depends on where the wilderness is. In American courts, most of the time, animals, especially wild ones, do not have legal agency. An alligator, obviously, cannot sue on its own behalf. Although I believe that wildlife crimes, first and foremost, are crimes committed against wildlife itself, such crimes committed on public land like Everglades National Park are crimes against the nation and anyone else who would come to enjoy nature's majesty.

Still, there are places in the world where nature itself has more rights than simply to be owned. The Everglades Headwaters is one of them.

In the 2020 election, the majority of residents in Orange County, Florida, "voted yes on the Right to Clean Water Charter Amendment," as I wrote for *Sierra* magazine in 2021, "making this seemingly esoteric legislation, which passed by a landslide margin of 89 to 11 percent, the most popular item on the ballot." According to the charter amendment, the county's rivers and lakes, including Shingle Creek, from which the Everglades springs, have the "right to exist, flow, to be protected against Pollution, and to maintain a healthy ecosystem."

Inspired by the *Citizens United* verdict of 2010, which said more or less that corporations can be legal persons, the Florida lawyer who spearheaded the charter amendment thought that rivers could be people, too. They already are considered as such in many parts of the world. Judges in India and New Zealand, among other places, have granted the rights of personhood to natural features in their countries. Now Florida has joined their ranks.

It doesn't seem like such a stretch to say that a crime against nature is still a crime. And when nature loses, we all lose. Orange County citizens can sue on their rivers' behalf. What does this mean, if anything, for poachers? Only time will tell. However, the charter amendment's landslide passage does make one thing clear: Most people, regardless of their political leaning, do care about the welfare of nature as an end in itself. That gives me hope.

Jonnie Brown, the most infamous alligator poacher's son, cares. It seems his father did, too. They had intimate knowledge of the Everglades, that wild place they called home. If the newcomers had respected that and listened, and if developers and the Army Corps of Engineers had never carved up the glades' flow, maybe alligators as a species never would have gotten in trouble in the first place.

In fact, conservationists have already been on the long road toward learning how to listen for decades now. Down in the Everglades, one result was Big Cypress National Preserve, the creation of which took in the voices of native tribes and other long-time residents, making a protected area where it is legal to hunt (with restrictions, of course) and play while still respecting the splendid gifts of the many-faceted wild that is gator country.

After finishing my trip to Chokoloskee, I reversed course and returned north, back through the Everglades, going opposite to their flow, through sawgrass plains and wild strands of jungle, through dry savanna to the land of lakes and rivers where those same glades spring forth—that is to say, I went home to Orlando, the state's epicenter of tourism and perpetual road construction.

Back home, having spent so much time out in the wilderness, I couldn't seem to stay inside. On a whim, I drove east to the coast, where Merritt Island National Wildlife Refuge sits under the rocket launches of Cape Kennedy. To the uninitiated, the sprawling barrier island and the lagoon it protects look like the Everglades. The two places are indistinguishable in pictures unless you really know what you're looking for. The refuge is a place of wild boars and endangered birds, carnivorous flowers, orchids, turtles, and, of course, alligators.

Armed with my camera and a thorough coating of bug spray, I ventured off the boardwalk and into the thick of the hardwood forest. As I walked, I listened to the birdcalls, the rustling in the brush, the shift as shadows fell over the narrow path from the whirring insects of the day to the croaking, chirping chorus of the night. The air smelled verdant and damp, rich with petrichor and sweet with woody decomposition. I squinted to see. I hadn't brought a flashlight. I hadn't planned to stay so long, really, but the farther I followed the path, the more I felt compelled to continue forward. I didn't know what waited in front of me. It was the excitement of venturing into the unknown that had captured my attention.

The same sensation had hit me when I was in Chokoloskee. After Mac had dropped us off below the trading post, I had looked out over the water, thinking it was like something in a movie. It also reminded me of my home. *If this place is paradise*, I thought, *how much of my own world have I missed?*

I had grown up about thirty miles north of the wildlife refuge in land that looked much the same, a woven backcountry of swamp and marsh. For years, I had seen my home as little more than a backwater. I had let people convince me that the clichés about Florida were true. I found myself wishing that I was from someplace interesting, someplace that mattered. Then, as I researched Jeff's story, I started learning to see the world as he saw it. I learned the names of birds and flowers, of trees and fish, and it shocked me how I'd failed to notice the many extraordinary and wonderful things that had made the backdrop of my young life. I was struck to discover that the little purple flowers that peek their heads over the mud, making the swamp a riot of color in the right season, were orchids. They were rare and beautiful, yet I had let them grow mundane to me. *How many orchids have I stepped over without a second look?* I wondered. Hundreds.

Venturing into that darkening wild, I was stunned to see it new. In the process of discovering gator country, I had rediscovered the majesty of my home. I sloughed off the opinions that had been cast upon it. I learned to see again.

Wonder, I believe, is a necessary component of hope. Without hope, even our greatest efforts will fail. Writing this in the darkest of times, I have been reminded to see the world like Jeff, not only with a sense of wonder but with a sense of compassion as well. If the past few years have taught me anything, it's that finding a scapegoat is easy. Working to fix problems, like the economic issues that push most people into poaching in the first place, is hard. With hope, we can do the hard thing.

The first hard thing is challenging our own expectations. I did. I got to know some poachers. And you know what? I liked them. I didn't agree with them or what they'd done, but I understood why they did it. I cared about them. I realized I could care about both humanity and the wild. It isn't cowardly to stop seeing the world as black-and-white. It doesn't make you complicit. The gray is where compassion lives. You can care about people who are doing things you think are wrong. Jeff did, too.

I got to know Jeff pretty well in the course of writing this story, to the point where, when a hurricane smashed through Central Florida, I predicted exactly what he would do after the fact: load up his truck with tools and see who needed help. Still, sometimes he would surprise me.

Midway through my research, I drove down toward the Everglades, this time stopping in Arcadia. Jeff had asked me to meet him in the parking lot of the Walmart where he had once bought alligators to stock his farm. He gave me an external hard drive of photos and files, and he drove me around town, showing me the farm and other locations he had mentioned in his stories. Back in the parking lot again, I went into the store to grab a snack, and when I got back outside, I couldn't find Jeff. I hesitated to open the door to his truck while he wasn't there. Then I saw movement inside. I squinted through the window. Jeff had bent double to hide under the steering wheel.

What the hell is he doing? I thought. I opened the door. "What's going on?"

"Shh," he hissed. "Get in and shut the door."

Confused and a little bit paranoid, I glanced around then did as he said. He put a mask over his mouth and nose and, thus disguised, rose to peek out of his window.

Are we being watched? I thought. I sank down in my seat.

Jeff examined a truck and trailer that had parked next to us, watching its driver as he got out. The closer the driver came into view, the more Jeff sat up. I scooted up to do the same.

"I thought that was Wayne," he explained, taking off the mask.

"If it had been, would there have been a problem?" I asked.

Jeff studied the look on my face—perhaps one of concern and confusion, likely one eyebrow raised. Then he looked down at where he'd been hiding. He sat up tall and laughed at himself. "No," he said, "probably not."

It was clear to me, though, that while I had been inside, he'd thought danger had come to call. Though Operation Alligator Thief had ended about five years prior, the anxiety that it carried had lingered with him. On paper, the sting was over. But for Jeff, it would always be there.

Ever the journalist and not one for small talk, I swooped in with a pointed question. "Do you think the operation changed you?" I asked.

"No," he said. Then he thought about it. "Well—"

When he returned to being Jeff Babauta, the first thing he did was cut his hair. After spending a little time with his wife and son, he drove to his mother's house. Over the course of the operation, she had watched him change, her once polished and together son seeming to fall apart. He couldn't tell her anything, and when she called, asking where he was, his wife would have to lie. Her heartbreak at the unexplained change in him made him feel so guilty. It was one of the worst losses that had come with the sting.

When she opened the door and saw her son polished and together once again, hair buzzed short, shirt tucked in, a grin spread across her face.

"There's my boy," she said, immense relief apparent in her voice.

They embraced, and then he said, "Have I got a story to tell you."

And yet, Blackledge came back when Jeff least expected him.

He would jump whenever he heard the ringtone he had assigned Robert on his undercover phone. He no longer had that phone. So it would happen in public. He'd flinch, his heart racing, as if expecting new orders from the man who had planned it all. He would remember himself bit by bit and then go about his business, but in the back of his mind, Operation Alligator Thief would always be there.

Some days he would forget to be himself. He might catch a glimpse of his reflection while running errands and realize he'd left the house in flip-flops and a paint-flecked shirt. He'd quickly tuck that shirt in and shake his head.

You're not Blackledge anymore, he would think, scolding himself for the uncharacteristic sloppiness. *You're Jeff Babauta.* That thought would cause another memory of the sting to spring forth: Driving home from the farm, he had waved his hand over his face like an actor collecting himself for a scene, saying, *Jeff Babauta. Jeff Babauta. Jeff Babauta.*

In that parking lot, Jeff admitted to me again that the alligators never really scared him, but the fear of reprisal refused to fade. So, too, it seemed that Blackledge would always be with him.

After our final interview of the day, I had stepped out of his truck and was heading toward my new Jeep when he stopped me. I was afraid he'd ask me not to write about something he'd said.

"A little bit ago you asked me if I was afraid of anything during the operation," he said, leaning through the truck cab from the driver's seat.

I held the door open, wary. "Yeah," I said.

"I don't think this is what you were looking for," he said. "It's silly, but it is what it is. My biggest fear in the whole operation wasn't about getting hurt or anything like that. It was that nobody would care."

He recalled hatching time, helping the baby alligators out of their shells. For many of them, he was the first thing they would ever see. The hatchlings' feisty personalities endeared them to him. Even though their fate ended at a factory farm, thousands more of their brothers and sisters remained in the wild, where Jeff hoped they would survive and flourish.

I remembered how he told me about the other wildlife officer who had dismissed the sting as unnecessary. *Alligators?* the officer had said. *Why bother?*

By then, I had already ventured through the Ten Thousand Islands. I had become immersed in the legend of Peg Brown. I had learned how sometimes the most outlandish and impossible things are true; I had befriended poachers who had become environmentalists; I had heard stories about fish falling from the sky, of nature defying man, of man defying expectations. I understood now how stories tell us who we are and who we're supposed to be. The best stories do more than show us that underdogs can triumph: they ignite hope within us and inspire us to do the same.

Before I started writing this book, I might have agreed with that officer. But then all of these people came into my life. Jeff, Jonnie, Kent, Mac—and voices from the past, Peg and Totch Brown, too—challenged my expectations about the Everglades, its people, and the alligators that call it home.

"I care," I reassured Jeff. "And a lot of other people will, too. I promise."

ACKNOWLEDGMENTS

So many people helped get this story onto these pages and onto the shelves that I could write an entire book just to thank them. Instead, I have to squeeze it all into just a few pages, so here it goes, in no particular order:

I would like to thank my dad, Ken Renner, who raised me in a house full of books with a head full of stories. While the parents of other would-be writers tried to dissuade them from pursuing their dreams, my dad always believed in me and encouraged me, even when I had all but lost hope myself.

Then I need to thank my high school English teacher Mrs. Mularkey (great name, right?) for developing my love of stories into a love of literature. She read the terrible fantasy pirate novel that I wrote at fifteen, and she encouraged me to keep writing even though it was objectively not very good. She deserves a gold star for that.

Later, in college, my professor Mark Powell helped me find my voice. As he guided me through southern literature and fiction writing, he became the first person outside my family to treat the stories I told about the place I'm from as if they mattered. When he reads this book—and I know he will—I'm sure he'll recognize the parts of it that grew from ideas I had just started to contemplate while in his class. Thanks, Mark. You helped me become the best version of me.

There were so many other professors who inspired and helped me along the way: Dr. Farrell, Dr. Davis, Lori Snook, Dr. Terri Witek, Juan Carlos Reyes, Veronica Gonzales, Laurie Foos, Chantel Acevedo, and many others.

I also need to thank the many magazine editors who kept me afloat after I quit my day job—Corinne, Libby, Marcy, Nsikan, and too many more to list, thank you all for taking a chance on me. I couldn't have gotten this far without you. At the same time, I found a community of journalists who welcomed me into their fold. Their camaraderie and commiseration helped me remember that I am not alone. I am especially indebted to my adamantly encouraging peers like Wudan Yan and the mentorship of veteran journalists, including Murray Carpenter and Craig Pittman, who answered even my stupidest questions with a magnanimity I hope to pass on one day.

Thank you to my friend Molly Beckwith, who introduced me to my agent and who has been there for me through all the trials and tribulations of finishing this book. And thank you to my agent, Julia Eagleton, for seeing something in me even before I had anything major published. When lecturers at writing conferences describe the perfect agent, they must have no idea that Julia exists, because she is so much better than that. Julia, I am grateful for everything you do.

Then there is Bryn, who edited this book. She is the most tireless, patient, and compassionate editor I've ever worked with, and that is really saying something, because I've worked with so many wonderful people. This book isn't exactly what I pitched her. It is so much better. Like I did while investigating the story, she put aside her expectations and let herself see the astonishing, even when I didn't. That takes a lot of talent and a lot of hard work. Thanks, Bryn.

Circling back to my family, I have to thank them for their excitement and encouragement. Most of all, I have to thank my aunt Kate, who nagged me absolutely to death, making sure that I wrote this book. Even after losing so many people, I'm grateful to know there is still somebody who loves me so fiercely. Love you back, Aunt Kate.

Next, I have to thank Alex and Melissa, my first beta readers when we were in high school. Now you finally get to read something of mine that's good. Thanks for reading all the crap along the way.

Thank you to everyone I talked to in Chokoloskee. You made me feel welcome. It was like being back home, and I won't forget it.

And finally, I have to thank Jeff Babauta for his lifetime of protecting nature and the people who live there, too. Thanks for trusting me with your story, Jeff. I hope I did it justice.

ABOUT THE AUTHOR

Rebecca Renner is a contributor to *National Geographic*, and her writing has appeared in the *New York Times*, *Outside*, *Tin House*, the *Paris Review*, the *Guardian*, the *Washington Post*, the *Atlantic*, and other publications. She holds an MFA from Stetson University and is the recipient of the Florida Book Awards' Gerald Ensley Developing Writer Award. *Gator Country* is her first book.